SPIRIT AND THE MIND

Samuel H. Sandweiss, M.D.
Birth Day Publishing Company
San Diego, California, USA

Library of Congress Catalog Number: 85-61734

ISBN 0-9600958-9-6

Printing rights for the use of quotations and passages from Sathya Sai Baba's discourses granted by the Sri Sathya Sai Education Foundation, Brindavan, Bangalore, India. I wish to thank Sai Baba and the Foundation for this privilege.

COVER

Japanese photographer Shiro Shirahata spent eighteen months in the Nepal Himalaya mountain range on a photographic project which resulted in his magnificent book *Nepal Himalaya*. His photograph from that book of Mount Sharpu (in Tibetan, "Shar" means "east" and "phu" means "high spot in a valley"), estimated height 7200 meters, appears on the front and back cover of this book. The power and glory of this rugged and wild scene of rock, ice and gusty winds swirling around peaks at dazzling heights, seems a fitting abode for divinity, and a dramatic expression of His omnipotence. And in fact Lord *Shiva*, the Hindu God who destroys obstacles to God realizations, is said to dwell and dance among the high peaks of the Himalaya mountains. Here, where the elements meet the sky in such natural glory and delight, where mind moves from stark solid snow and stone to soar into swirling space, can we sense the relationship of spirit and mind. I am grateful to Shiro Shirahata and Yama-kei (Publishers) Company for use of this fine photograph. (© Shiro Shirahata *Nepal Himalaya* published by Yama-kei Publisher Co., Ltd.).

Published by Birth Day Publishing Company
P.O. Box 7722, San Diego, California 92107, USA

To Sathya Sai Baba

Acknowledgments

Los Angeles writer and filmmaker Dick Croy was indispensable as editor and adviser. As with my first book, I continually relied on his organizing and writing skills and his sensible treatment of the material. His contribution was invaluable and most deeply appreciated. Also my warm appreciation to Lila Youngs whose clear and close attention to detail during the final stages of editing and proofreading assured a happy completion.

My heartfelt thanks goes to Larry Smith, San Diego artist and designer, for helping design inside and cover. I'm also grateful for the use of photos offered by Richard Kaplowitz, Peter Keyser, Peter Rae and David Lenhoff. And a special thanks to Mr. R.K. Karanjia, Senior Editor of *Blitz* news magazine for permission to reprint in its entirety his revealing and exciting interview with Sathya Sai Baba.

I am grateful to the following publishing houses for permission to use extended quotes: To Sage Publications for the use of Ken Wilber's material which appeared in the *Journal of Humanistic Psychology*, Vol. 22, No. 1, Winter 1982, pp. 57-90; Harper & Row Publishers, Inc. for the Erich Fromm quote which appeared in *Zen Buddhism and Psychoanalysis*; Vedanta Press, for the quotes from the *Bhagavid-Gita* translated by Swami Prabhavananda and Christopher Isherwood; Free Press, a division of Macmillan Publishing, Inc., for the quotes from Ernest Becker's book *The Denial of Death*; the medical journal *M.D.* for the quotes from Stanley R. Dean's article "Psychiatry and Psychosocial Futurology"; and to writer W.H. Macintosh for the use of a portion of his article which appeared in the London newspaper *Psychic News*, December 1977.

Extra-special thanks to members of my family, who have been a constant source of strength and support—to my father and mother, who painstakingly edited my life through crucial developmental years—to my children Ruth, Rachel, Beth and Judy, for understanding why their dad was locked in his study for long periods and may have been inaccessible when they would have liked otherwise, for helping with the typing and editing and for asking innocent and crucial questions which influenced the thinking in this book.

And eternal love and gratitude to my dear and dedicated wife Sharon, who has been my closest companion, confidant and critic for over a quarter century.

Translations

All Sanskrit and Telugu words are *italicized* and defined in the Glossary beginning on page 315.

Contents

Introduction

These are historic times. A major transformation is taking place in the mind of man. Old ideas are dying and new are being born. We are beginning to realize that our basic identity is not mind or body, bound by birth and death, time and space—but, more fundamentally, it is spirit: an infinite consciousness which is universal and eternal. Dawning is the awareness that consciousness is not a function of the mind, centered in the physical brain. No, quite the opposite; infinite consciousness, our real self, *created* mind and the cosmos as well. Consciousness is beyond time and is unaffected by death.

Today there is growing scientific confirmation that consciousness is fundamentally infinite and eternal and that our minds deceive us into believing otherwise. Findings from such diverse sources as Jungian psychology and dream analysis, experimental ESP phenomena in the field of parapsychology, age and past-life regression during hypnosis, reports of out-of-the-body and near-death experiences as well as particle physics[1] have done much to show the thinking world that consciousness is not limited by time or space.

Generally accepted now are the phenomena of clairvoyance and telepathy, of prophetic dreams and unusual knowing at a distance such as described in the life of Edgar Cayce. He, for instance, could diagnose and successfully treat a person's illness often at a distance, sometimes by phone, sometimes by just holding an object once worn by the individual. And Carl Jung showed through his work that people in intensive analytic therapy could retrieve information through their dreams and intuitions of a dimension beyond their own personal life experience—could be in touch with what he called the *collective unconscious*, a dimension in which all of mankind's experience from the beginning of our species' time on earth and covering the entire breadth and width of our existence since, is recorded.

Add to this the very convincing evidence of people's vivid recollections of past lives, their detailing of specific events, names, dates and places with uncanny accuracy—material they would seemingly have no way of knowing other than having been there and lived through that time themselves—and we have a growing body of experience which can no longer be discounted as mere fancies of imagination.

Even the hard sciences like physics are drawing closer to realizing the fundamental laws of spirituality. The leading edge of physics[1] is discovering that the planet is not a separate piece of dead mineral in an indifferent, unloving, unconscious universe. The cosmos and all in it are coming to be recognized as one entity: inseparable, whole and alive with consciousness, a manifestation of the one, Universal Consciousness—permeated with love. The oneness of the universe is being recognized as the material expression of the oneness of consciousness—which is experienced in the heart as love.

In his book *The Tao of Physics* research physicist Fritjof Capra explores the parallels between modern physics and Eastern mysticism. He relates the world-view emerging from the theories of subatomic physics, relativity and astrophysics, to the mystical traditions of Hinduism, Buddhism, Taoism, Zen and the *I Ching*. What emerges is a picture of the universe of the modern physicist likened to that of the Eastern mystic, or as the book's dust jacket says so well: "a universe engaged in a continuous cosmic dance—a system of inseparable, interrelating and ever-moving components of which the observer is, himself, an integral part." More and more scientists, like Einstein, are awed by the grandeur of creation and are coming to realize an underlying unity and wholeness—which they recognize as *holy*.[2]

As duality—seeing reality as composed of separate and distinct entities as opposed to one unified whole—crumbles, so do the differences between peoples and religions. A nondenominational science of consciousness is developing which is defining universal laws and principles governing the expansion of consciousness, thereby bringing science closer to spirituality and the great spiritual systems closer to one another. We are coming to recognize that all the great world religions emerge from a common universal reality, and although they use different symbols, ceremonies and forms, they all express the nature and dynamics of the one universal and eternal consciousness, or God, from which all matter and energy arise.

If all this is indeed true, if all religions are fundamentally one, if the entire cosmos is a manifestation of Universal Consciousness—and if in fact we ourselves are Universal Consciousness beyond any limit; if our real self is, in fact, infinite and eternal—why are we not aware of this?

Science is beginning to look to spirituality for answers to this timeless question—to the great world religions which have from the start declared that the material world is a manifestation of spirit or infinite consciousness. The ancient wisdom of sages and saints tells us that the crux of the problem lies in the mind, which deceives man into believing himself separate and limited.

Although the eternal ocean of spirit is oneness without a second, infinite consciousness wills a mysterious spell upon itself by creating the mind. So attracted by the mind's powerful forces, by the dual world of pleasures and pains, desires and impulses, ego and the senses, infinite consciousness mistakenly perceives differences and limitations—separate names and forms—the appearance that it is separate from itself—duality. Why the limitless willed this delusion upon itself is creation's greatest mystery. I will offer an explanation at the end of Chapter 4.

The great spiritual systems describe the mind as a bubble in magnitude, compared to the vastness of the ocean of spirit or pure consciousness. Infinite consciousness attaches itself to the filmy wall of the bubble-mind, erroneously identifying itself with the finite and limited content within. But the bubble can burst! The deluding film that prevents our personal consciousness from realizing its universal nature can dissolve, freeing the personal to merge back into the universal—to realize boundless, eternal awareness, pure unlimited being, unconditional love and bliss. Spirituality has much to teach psychology about this path to transcendence.

Western psychology has penetrated deep into the mystery of

man's mind, defining its nature, the principle of duality upon which it rests, different levels of evolution of mental development and its various strengths and fears. The outer boundary of this young science is now approaching the realms of wisdom of the great ancient spiritual systems. It is as if—as in Michaelangelo's famous image on the ceiling of the Sistine Chapel—we are reaching that electrifying moment in time when God, beckoning from heaven for dormant mankind to awaken, actually touches us, moving us to arise and become aware of our own divine nature. This book is intended to focus attention on the nature of that awakening touch and the stirrings in man that follow.

In the course of this book I will tell you about an Indian holy man, or *Avatar*,[3] named Sathya Sai Baba, as well as something about his mission and message, because I am convinced that the life and teachings of Sathya Sai Baba represent the most compelling living proof of the existence of Universal Consciousness, or God—and that becoming aware of his meaning will help us bridge the gap between God and man and help us understand the relationship of spirit to mind, spirituality to science and Universal Consciousness to man's personal consciousness.

From the start, because people are skeptical and wary about preaching and proselytizing, I'd like to make it clear that I am not interested in promoting Sai Baba. My intention is not to add yet another name to the growing list of competing spiritual figureheads and messages—nor to try to influence readers toward one path and away from another. My intention, rather, is to remind us that as science and spirituality converge, and as different religions come together, it is quite understandable that new insights and advances in thinking will come from a "scientist of consciousness" or a spiritually evolved teacher, who is able to speak in a universally understood language.

And I must tell you that I feel Sai Baba's importance to our age cannot be overemphasized in this regard. I am convinced that he not only talks about Universal Consciousness but that he *is* Universal Consciousness. The wonderous and inexplicable happenings and miracles that are part of his life are concrete and convincing evidence of the supramental, transcendental, spiritual dimension and signs of a consciousness without boundary.

If this is true, what a unique opportunity to see into the very center of our innermost reality—a chance afforded humanity perhaps two or three times in all of recorded history, and never before to this extent. Never before has such striking evidence of Universal Consciousness in the form of astounding miracles accompanying profound acts of compassion and selfless love been witnessed in such vast numbers and variety and by so many people.

And yet the extent of our resistance to such material—our self-defeating avoidance of inquiry into the possibility of our immortality—is immense. When we grasp the meaning and significance of our real identity actually being Universal Consciousness, the impact on our lives will be literally transforming. But in the meantime, this resistance is enormous. There is nothing like religion or politics to inflame the emotions and create conflict. It's been my continuing observation in the course of my professional work with clients, as well as observing myself and many seekers along the spiritual path, that our hesitancy and avoidance have to do with powerful underlying fears. And there is a reason for this.

Part of our skepticism and reluctance may be the result of having been fooled many times before and learning not to be so naive and idealistic. Our age has idealized so many, only to find feet of clay upon closer inspection, treading paths which eventually turn out to lead nowhere new. In addition, many of us have put our faith in psychology, hoping to find new insights into the meaning of life. And psychology by and large has been skeptical of spirituality, perhaps generalizing and overreacting because of the psychological damage occasionally observed as a result of overly punitive spiritual approaches.

Then, too, many of us have our own strong religious beliefs which, when clung to rigidly, block openness and receptivity to worthwhile but unfamiliar information. Because these personal beliefs purport to answer the most basic questions about our existence, protect us from the unknown, and give us a sense of belonging and safety in a world which might otherwise seem too mysterious and unfathomable, it's understandable that we would cherish and protect them. But when this is done in too narrow and rigid a manner, at the expense of our openness, sensitivity and respect for others, it may entail blocking out a large segment of reality.

Serious students of the scriptures know that warnings have been voiced by tried and true spiritual masters about being spiritually deceived. They rightfully warn us to avoid being gullible and overly accepting where such an important dimension of life is concerned, without serious inquiry and study. But then why do we resist this inquiry and study when we learn of the extraordinary evidence already becoming common knowledge—much of which will be presented in this book?

Because, above all, I feel that most of our resistance arises from a profound, pervasive, irrational and fundamental fear that the mind has towards spirit. For the mind to seriously consider the possibility of man's immortality, his existence beyond any boundaries including those of life and death, it must be open to seriously confronting our apparent mortality—death and the possibility of our non-existence. We must be able to stand face to face in front of death and peer unswervingly into its very depths. This in itself is frightening enough. And the mind's intuition that to merge with the other entails the surrender of one's own cherished ego, one's sense of self-identity and self-worth, offers an even more trying and challenging threat.

What a task! For to become one with Universal Consciousness means to transcend duality—to transcend all limitations—to be unaffected by pleasure or pain, desires or threats to the ego, the pull of the senses to the tantalizing outer world of separate names and forms. Naturally, the thought of renouncing all that we hold as real makes us recoil in fear.

In the last analysis, even a man as perceptive and intuitive as Jung, a man who presented psychology with the idea of the collective unconscious, even he did not think mankind had the capacity to fully transcend the mind and move beyond the sense of a separate ego. No wonder that a mind which grasps the full extent of this challenge would reel, avoid and resist the path to self-transcendence.

This book, then, is my attempt to investigate spiritual reality and to put it into a language which is relevant to psychiatry. It is divided into four section. Part I investigates the growing need to integrate spiritual and mystical insights about the dynamics of consciousness into Western psychology. We will also explore the nature and depth of our resistance to spirituality.

We'll move beyond the theoretical to investigate the relevance of spiritual insight in the crucible of daily psychiatric practice. I will report the everyday appearance of subtle, and some not so subtle, spiritual phenomena, as well as some dramatic "miraculous" events which require a broadening of our concepts to be comprehended.

We'll examine clinical evidence which supports the hypothesis that all fears—those of patients and those which prompt our own resistance to spirituality—arise from the *mortal* fear of facing the delusion of duality. I'll interview a prominent psychiatrist who exemplifies—and fully admits—such resistance.

We'll take one more step as well. I will show, through my experience with Sathya Sai Baba, that abstract concepts about consciousness, duality, love and the primacy of the spirit have meaning even to those hardcore behavioral scientists who believe that the final solution to suffering will be found in brain chemistry and psychopharmacology. For them there may be no sense of a connection between biology on the one hand and morality, devotion and higher levels of consciousness on the other. But if Sai Baba's apparent materializations of matter from "will"—which he calls expressions of love—are found to be real, then we are seeing concrete evidence that matter is a function of consciousness, and not vice versa. If higher levels of consciousness are fundamental to biology, then one day we may ultimately rely on the achievement of these states of consciousness for the treatment of all earthly ills.

In Part II, I will offer suggestions on the type of education and training necessary for the development of the New-Age therapist of consciousness. Drawing upon my experiences with Sai Baba, I will attempt to describe how spiritual insight relates to a psychotherapist's personal growth, his way of conceptualizing psychological problems, his therapeutic approaches and thus, ultimately, his capability as a therapist. And finally I will relate some of the humorous and moving experiences I've had in trying to introduce psychiatric colleagues to spirituality.

In Part III, I will look at the possibility of Sathya Sai Baba's being an authentic world teacher who will have global influence in the years to come. I'll present a discourse, in his words, explaining the meaning of his "miracles"; describe an international conference on *Service to Mankind*, held at his *ashram* in November, 1980, and attended by 200,000 people from almost every country in the world;

and present a particularly revealing interview that he gave to a prominent editor of the largest national Indian newspaper, the *Blitz*, in which he describes his world mission.

Part IV consists of four Appendices, and is directed especially, although by no means exclusively, to therapists. Appendix I is a glossary of terms related to consciousness, and I suggest that you refer to it from the start to avoid confusion. Appendix II summarizes some of the current spiritually-oriented trends in psychology, neurosciences and physics. Appendices III and IV compare Western scientific concepts about mind and consciousness to Eastern spiritual concepts, and provide a conceptual framework which shows the relationship of higher levels of consciousness to those with which we are already familiar. This working model of a hierarchy of consciousness goes even further. It also prompts us to consider a new way of understanding disease: possible causes of illness other than those already accepted; a wider range of therapeutic interventions; and the possibility of levels of functioning and "health" that have yet to be identified by psychiatry.

And now let's begin with an incident that occurred in December, 1978, which was centrally important in my life and deeply affected my thinking about the nature and relationship of spirit and mind.

Notes

1. See Appendix II, p. 276.

2. ". . . Every one who is seriously involved in the pursuit of science becomes convinced that a spirit is manifest in the laws of the Universe—a spirit vastly superior to that of man, and one in the face of which we with our modest powers must feel humble." (Albert Einstein)

   Helen Dukas and Banesh Hoffman, eds., *Albert Einstein The Human Side*: New Glimpses from His Archives, (Princeton, New Jersey: Princeton University Press, 1979), p. 33.

3. *Avatar* is a Sanskrit word derived from the verb-root tri—to cross, and the preposition ava—down. Defined by the Concise Oxford Dictionary as, "A descent of diety in incarnate form," an *Avatar* comes down, decends, to reveal the true nature of man, to demonstrate and perform holy works, and with His divine love and power to draw man closer to God.

   According to Hindu scriptural tradition, a true *Avatar* manifests 16 special qualities. The most profound, and those which clearly distinguish him from mortal men, are his complete mastery and transcendence of the physical world— including the ability to materialize objects at will; qualities of omniscience, omnipotence and omnipresence; the capacity to manifest a flow of pure and inexhausti-

PART I Universal Consciousness

The most beautiful and most profound emotion we can experience is the sensation of the mystical. It is the sower of all true art and science. He to whom this emotion is a stranger, who can no longer wonder and stand rapt in awe, is as good as dead. To know that what is impenetrable to us really exists, manifesting itself as the highest wisdom and the most radiant beauty which our dull faculties can comprehend only in their most primitive forms— this knowledge, this feeling is at the center of true religiousness.

(Albert Einstein)

The Bubble
and the Ocean

CHAPTER ONE

PROFESSOR PREBEN Plum is chairman of the Department of Pediatrics at the University Hospital in Copenhagan, Denmark. A prominent and respected figure in his medical community, he has spent his entire professional career treating and caring for crippled children. He was chairman of the Danish Medical Research Council and influential in the direction medical research has taken in his country. Now, 72, and facing retirement, he was turning his attention to spiritual matters when he read my first book *Sai Baba: The Holy Man and the Psychiatrist*. He contacted me from Denmark. "I would like to see Sai Baba and wonder if I might join you there one day."

We met on the *ashram* grounds one drizzly December day in 1978. Plum was accompanied by his friend Hagen Hasselbach, who had been making Danish professional films for some forty years. Plum excused himself for being a bother, hoped that he didn't take up too much space in our small 12 ft. square austere cement-floored cubicle,

3

and in a sweetly humble manner blew up his flimsy air mattress and made himself comfortable on the floor.

Two psychiatrists had joined me on this trip. But Baba hadn't paid much attention to us until Plum's arrival. Then he invited Plum, myself and Hagen in for an interview.

Sai Baba sat on a footstool in front of us while I sat on the floor to his left, the professor directly in front of him and the film-maker in back and to the left of the professor. About ten others were in the room but farther back and sitting against the walls.

Dr. S. Bhagavantam, a well-known Indian physicist, past chief scientific advisor to the government of India and now Sai Baba's main interpreter, came to the doorway. Baba said, *"No need for you here. Sandweiss will translate."* That was startling news to me. Even though stunned I had to chuckle, as I hardly know English let alone Telugu or Danish. Luckily Baba chose to speak in English and let me elaborate on some points—pausing when he knew I might be able to add something—and in a sweet and loving way giving me something to do so I could feel as if I were really helping.

Baba looked gently at Professor Plum. What a sight—this old professor, now at the end of his career, sitting humbly before the Master.

Everybody was quiet with proper respect, and then Baba began to speak to Plum: *"What is science? What is a scientist?"* Professor Plum hesitated and Baba continued with the following discourse and exchange:

> *"Science is a way of looking at the outer world through the mind. The mind's nature is duality; it divides reality into different names and forms—it dissects, compares, contrasts, separates, categorizes—tries to define and bind reality in terms of words and concepts.*
>
> *"All of this cosmos—the entire material universe, as vast an expanse as it seems—is just a flake of froth, a bubble, on the ocean of reality. And the mind which views it through its senses and tries to grasp and comprehend it—this mind is even bigger than the cosmos; it can eventually encompass and understand it. But even this vast mind is like a little wavelet on the ocean of reality. You are the ocean. You're not the flake of froth and you're not the wavelet—you are beyond separation. You are everything—you are the ocean.*

"The mind sees separateness, duality; but there is another way of experiencing reality—as unity. It is through the heart, by the process of love. Love reaches out to merge with the other; two become one. Love sees unity. For the limited little wavelet self to know that it is the ocean, it must merge back into the ocean—through love.

"The scientist says, 'What is this'—this which lies in the outer world and is seen through the senses. The spiritual aspirant says, 'What is that'—that which lies beyond the outer world and the senses, beyond duality and the mind as well. 'That' is the ocean from which all 'this' arises."

Baba asked, *"Why is it that everybody says 'I'?"* And then pointing to some of us in the room for emphasis, he continued, *"She says 'I', he says 'I', I say 'I', you say 'I'; we all look different but there is this common sense of 'I'-ness. What is the meaning behind this? We have to look beyond this constantly changing world of different names and forms in order to see the underlying, unchanging and immutable reality: the reality that always was and always will be, the underlying unity which gives rise to all this diversity. How can the scientist with his mind try to grasp unity. The mind sees separateness; love sees unity. The only way that the wavelet can know the ocean is to merge back into it—to become one with it. Love is the way; merge with love, through your devotion to God."*

Baba paused a moment and then became more animated. *"My name is Sathya, truth. I represent that which is beyond mind. I have come to show you who you are—the reality that lies beyond mind. How can a scientist comprehend me? I am all places at all times—everything that ever was or will be. I can transmute the earth into sky and the sky into earth."* He paused a moment with a playful twinkle in his eye. *"But I don't do it often because it causes inconvenience to some people."*

We all laughed and Baba was immensely joyful with our happiness. He continued, *"How can the scientist understand my reality? See, how can you understand this?"* And with that Baba became even more animated and began to move his hand in a large circle in the air. In a startling, electrifying instant he was holding a beautiful silver ring. It had come as if in a flash of light—and at such a moving point in the spiritual discourse that we were left stunned and gasping. I almost fell over. The mind simply becomes humbled and lost in the face of this magnificent mystery.[1] It is as if one is sitting in front of the creative force that gave birth to all matter.

At that moment, Baba beamed with happiness. He showed the beautiful ring to everyone and then, looking at the professor, said, *"How can you understand this?"* He took the professor's hand in his own, and Plum turned into a little child. It is something to see, this instant unmaking of a person, this transformation of even the strongest and most reluctant into an innocent, giggling child.

Baba slipped the ring on Plum's right ring finger and it was a perfect fit.

Then, quite unexpectedly, Baba reached over to me and brought me to his side. He took my hand and looked at the ring he had materialized for me about four years before.[2] Taking it off my finger, he examined it carefully. It was made of a silver-like material with his image, which seemed to be an enamel painting on copper, on the surface. Wanting to protect it, I had put about twenty coats of fingernail lacquer over it.

Pointing to the large glob of lacquer rising about an eighth of an inch above the surface, he asked, *"What is that?"*

"*Swami*, I was trying to protect the ring from being nicked and hurt," I answered.

Looking at me playfully, he said, *"You brought it back to the repair station—I'll fix it."* Holding the ring between thumb and index finger of his right hand and in plain view, he slowly blew on it three times. I watched carefully with the utmost attention and, suddenly, the ring instantaneously and completely changed before my eyes.[3]

It was completely changed: a different border, different picture—a completely different ring, yet exactly the same size. Baba gently replaced it on the same finger and it fit perfectly.

We left the interview elated. The ring Baba had made for Plum was larger than mine, a perfect fit for his larger finger, but similar to mine in appearance. The creation of the rings brought a feeling of awe and wonder, a new appreciation of the infinite consciousness that has created all matter. The perfect sizes implied a sense of intimate relationship, of his knowing us better than we knew ourselves: a profound personal connection with a transcendental, loving being. The holy atmosphere awakened reverence and devotion. And Baba's gentle compassion and patient, protective, knowing love—a love beyond words—prompted the kind of joy and bliss which inspires one to turn godward. A simple act—but one with profound impact.

We walked quietly for some distance, allowing the experience to settle. I finally said, "You know, Praben, I'll bet this is a sign that Baba has been with you throughout your entire life—understanding you when you thought you were alone, giving strength when you thought no one was there. How wonderful to sense his omnipresence —how fulfilling to know that he saw, understood and was satisfied with your selfless offering to the crippled children in Denmark and your struggle with problems and pains. All that time he must have been very happy with the sacrifice and love you gave to his needy children. Now he has brought you to him to give you the holiest of gifts—his omnipresent love. I know that the ring he gave is a sign of his intimate closeness, a wedding of you to him."

I looked up, and the old professor was weeping.

*   *   *

During this brief drama with Professor Plum, Sai Baba had given me the small part of "interpreter," even though we both knew I would fall far short without his help. Was he showing me through this moving discourse and touching exchange the kind of innocent love which dissolves ego, turns into devotion and merges the wavelet back into the ocean? And could I have witnessed in this intimate personal experience the hint of a more general major wedding between science and spirituality which is to occur in the near future? In answer to these questions and with the encouragement and strength from that experience, I am attempting this book, and with his help will try to "interpret" his message about *Spirit and the Mind* to fellow behavioral scientists.

Notes

1. For a brief description of the extraordinary powers attributed to Sai Baba, including the materialization of objects from the thin air, see Note 3, of the Introduction.

2. Photo of first ring is on p. 264.

3. Photo of second ring is on p. 264.

.

Our time is distinguished by wonderful achievements in the fields of scientific understanding and the technical application of those insights. Who would not be cheered by this? But let us not forget that knowledge and skills alone cannot lead humanity to a happy and dignified life. Humanity has every reason to place the proclaimers of high moral standards and values above the discoverers of objective truth. What humanity owes to personalities like Buddha, Moses, and Jesus ranks for me higher than all the achievements of the inquiring and constructive mind.

(Albert Einstein)

Basic
Assumptions

CHAPTER TWO

THE BEHAVIORAL sciences[1] are undergoing great change. As mentioned in the introduction, information from diverse sources in both the hard sciences like physics and the soft sciences like psychology—to say nothing of the view held by virtually all religions, that man's soul extends beyond the life of his body—challenges our most basic assumptions about human consciousness. It is time for a new vision and a broader conceptual framework, which can consolidate the multiplicity of new hypotheses and concepts in the behavioral sciences and link them to the hard sciences.

Beyond this, many in the behavioral sciences believe we are facing an even more critical *moral* crisis concerning the fundamental values and priorities in our field. I think the two issues are related. The purpose of this book is to point out some of the limitations which I perceive in our basic assumptions concerning human consciousness and to propose changes leading not only to a more unifying and comprehensive science, but one which is more spiritually based as well. For it seems clear to me that the great scientific discovery of our time—taking shape now in the behavioral sciences—is that consciousness is far more than a function or product of the individual human mind centered in the physical brain. It is nothing less than the creative force of the universe. I believe we are drawing closer to scientific confirmation of the intuitive insights of the great spiritual systems, which see mind, as well as the material cosmos itself, as creations of a Universal Consciousness—the divine. If so, then morality may be a major force directing the unfolding of man's individual consciousness as it evolves, through mind, toward eventual awareness of its own divinity.

In the course of my work I have been struck by a remarkable lack of appreciation in our field for the wealth of information from spiritual systems. One may speculate that the spiritual dimension is so subtle as to defy scientific exploration. Or perhaps this lack of appreciation represents our criticism and skepticism toward a system which, in many cases, has given rise to overly punitive practices damaging to psychological health. Or we ourselves may hold strong spiritual beliefs (some say that psychology itself is a spiritual system for many in the West) which protect us from uncertainty and the unknown.

Because such beliefs provide safety and protection in an otherwise frighteningly mysterious and unfathomable world, we may cling to them so rigidly and dogmatically that they may enforce a narrowness of vision. Then again, some of us may intuitively grasp that the spiritual dimension is important, yet not know how to integrate it into our everyday lives.

But even taking all these factors into consideration, I have found that this avoidance, this marked resistance observed in psychotherapists from all theoretical persuasions, represents something even more fundamental: a basic, inherent problem the mind has in dealing with the spirit—a hidden conflict which cries out for illumination. Therefore, I wish to investigate not only the dynamics of man's unfolding and expanding consciousness, but our resistance to this opening process as well, our resistance to conceiving ourselves as linked in some way to the timeless and eternal: to the possibility, in other words, of our own immortality.

I'll start by investigating this resistance—a technique with which all therapists are familiar and which will lead us more quickly and deeply to the heart of the matter. In the next chapter I'll define a *mortal* fear which prompts this resistance, and the kind of transcendental insight—or, again in spiritual terms, love—which resolves it, and which is thus the basis for a whole new psychological approach. But now let's turn our attention to the resistance itself, and its point of origin in the human mind.

MIND

Modern Western psychiatry (the word "psychiatry" derives from "psyche," the mind[2]) and ancient Hindu tradition[3] agree on the major components of mind—that it is comprised of thoughts, has reasoning ability, is aware of itself (self-image), relates to the outer world through the senses, operates according to the pleasure/pain principle and has both conscious and unconscious needs, impulses and desires which influence, motivate and direct it toward gratification in the outer world.

As an outgrowth of his clinical observations, Sigmund Freud, the father of psychoanalysis, discovered for modern psychiatry the importance of biologically determined primitive impulses and drives—needs and desires which press for gratification and for avoidance of pain, according to the pleasure/pain principle. He thought that these needs and desires are the primary forces determining the focus of our thoughts, feelings and behavior, and directing the way our mind works. If these drives are blocked from expression and gratification, such as by family or societal censure, then conflict will arise with the resultant possibility of symptom formation.

Freud's therapeutic aim was to bring to consciousness these hidden unconscious needs so that the conflict could be resolved and the individual would have a better chance of achieving gratification of them within the constraints of society. Freud felt that this was the goal of therapy and one of man's highest accomplishments.

Freud's concepts were limited by his particular orientation and objectives. They grew from his study of abnormal mental states and his interest in how the individual adjusts and adapts successfully to the outer world, and were developed in part to provide a framework from which to practice therapy. He was mostly interested in how the mind accomplishes the complex task of gratification of drives while adjusting to society. He did not study higher states of consciousness nor did he seriously question the nature of consciousness.

Yoga (an ancient and continuing system of empirically scientific spiritual thought and practice within the Hindu tradition), on the other hand, has always been interested in achieving higher states of consciousness. Viewing the mind from this angle, it sees mind as a potential obstacle to higher consciousness. *Yoga* agrees that mind is an invaluable tool—essential not only for operating in the outer world, but for spiritual growth as well, up to a point—and agrees that desire is the very fabric of man's mind, like the threads of a cloth. But it differs from psychiatry in declaring that the purpose of life, after a certain point in the evolution of consciousness, is the *removal* of desire rather than its gratification, so that the mind will disappear—thus leading to awareness of the real self, Universal Consciousness.

BROADENING PSYCHOLOGICAL CONCEPTS

In the Appendices, I'll elaborate on the extensive work already accomplished toward establishing a workable synthesis of psychology and spirituality—work which broadens our concept of mind and sets the stage for a serious reappraisal of the nature of consciousness, but which hasn't yet been seriously integrated into mainstream thinking. Ernest Becker, in his brilliant Pulitzer Prize-winning book *The Denial of Death*, argues that psychology and spirituality have been inextricably connected since the beginning of existentialism, with the famous Danish philosopher whom he calls "the psychoanalyst" Kierkegaard. Becker notes, "that at the very furthest reaches of scientific description, psychology has to give way to 'theology' . . . ."

> The further one pushes his study of Rank the more his writings blur into those of Kierkegaard—all the more remarkably, as we now fully appreciate, because of the far greater sophistication of clinical psychoanalysis. By now it should be clear that this blurring of Rank and Kierkegaard is not a weak surrender to ideology but an actual scientific working-through of the problem of human character. Both men reached the same conclusion after the most exhaustive psychological quest: that at the very furthest reaches of scientific descripton, psychology has to give way to 'theology'—that is, to a world-view that absorbs the individual's conflicts and guilt and offers him the possibility for some kind of heroic apotheosis. Man cannot endure his own littleness unless he can translate it into meaningfulness on the largest possible level. Here Rank and Kierkegaard meet in one of those astonishing historical mergers of

thought: that sin and neurosis are two ways of talking about the same thing—the complete isolation of the individual, his disharmony with the rest of nature, his hyperindividualism, his attempt to create his own world from within himself.[4]

Thus Becker draws attention to the agreement between psychology and theology, that man's suffering—his neurosis and sin, which are one and the same—result from his sense of separation and littleness—in other words, from duality. We must not be misled into thinking that Becker, Kierkegaard and Rank are talking only about the psychological dimension. For here there is a recognition of a level of consciousness beyond the psychological—beyond duality.

The theological point of view and that of this book is that there is a unitive dimension of consciousness beyond the mind and duality, and that the "heroic apotheosis" of which Becker speaks—the theology to which psychology has to give way—refers to the possibility of transcending duality, of actually *being* omniscient, omnipotent and omnipresent.

Becker also sheds light on the reasons for psychology's resistance to spirituality, as we shall see in Chapter 4. William James' *Varieties of Religious Experience*, written in 1908, was an early recognition of the psychological significance of spiritual beliefs and phenomena. And of course Carl Jung's concept of the collective unconscious postulated the existence of a level of consciousness extending beyond time and space and shared by all of humanity.

Awareness of the importance of spiritual and mystical insight is a significant part of humanistic psychology. Humanists feel that behavioristic formulas and overattentiveness to Freudian unconscious determinants of personality are offensive to human dignity. A more complete picture of the total human being can be gained from the study not only of pathology, but of the normal and exceptional as well. Yes, there are lower animal drives, housed in man's unconscious; yes, conflicts can be buried deep in the unconscious; yes, man's behaviour and thoughts can be determined and "conditioned" by past events—but man is more than this.

Abraham Maslow, considered the father of humanistic psychology, showed that man had higher human drives and needs—such as the need for meaningful work, for being fair and just and for morality—along with the more primitive drives defined by

Freud. From his studies of highly developed and creative people, he defined a transcendental level of human experience which he called the "peak experience." This was a powerful transcendental state of consciousness in which the individual experienced a sense of heightened clarity and understanding, intense euphoria, and an appreciation of the holistic, unitive, and integrated nature of the universe and one's unity with it. It was his hope that studies of peak experiences would ultimately help to bridge the gap between the relative and the absolute and establish a truly scientific basis for experiences of unity and eternity. He believed that the human being could live fairly consistently at this higher level of awareness, could "live casually in heaven and be on easy terms with the eternal and the infinite." (1971).

Although psychology was becoming aware, then, of higher states of consciousness and that our essential identity lies beyond the limited Freudian view,[5] the relationship between mind and consciousness remained unclear in the literature until the recent (late 1960's) emergence of transpersonal psychology. Suddenly the stages of development staked out by psychology were defined as lower levels of consciousness, and their relationship to higher mental states—including the psychic dimension relating to "psi" phenomena, the *siddhi* powers of *yogis*, and the supramental and highest spiritual states of *samadhi* (Hinduism's mergence with the undifferentiated) and *nirvana* (Buddhism's egoless state)—was clearly shown. In elucidating a hierarchy of consciousness, transpersonal psychology also clarified what's at stake for man to move from his predominantly mental stage to a spiritually-oriented state of consciousness which includes and transcends the mental.

However, mainstream psychology still doesn't recognize this work and fails to understand the relationship of these higher states of consciousness to the "normal" and "abnormal" mental states with which it most frequently deals. It has difficulty integrating the information and techniques it is slowly learning from such diverse fields as acupuncture and *hatha yoga*, which deal with a subtle energy, relatively unexplored by Western science but understood by *yogis* to be very much related to the evolution of higher states of consciousness.

Our concepts aren't fundamental enough, for instance, to allow for a clear understanding of the interrelationships between the subtle energy flow of acupuncture and that of Western bioenergetics; or between the breath control exercises, body postures and moral and devotional practices of Eastern *yoga*, and the mentally-oriented talk therapies of psychiatry. A deeper appreciation of spirituality would bring valuable understanding here.[6]

Why isn't spiritual insight being more seriously integrated into Western psychology? Why isn't its wealth of ideas being translated into treatment strategies and approaches? Spirituality has been treated as taboo by psychology for far too long. Not even the subject of childhood sexuality presented by Freud at the turn of the century met with such resistance. Charles T. Tart, Ph.D., professor of psychology at the University of California, Davis, and well-known author in the field of transpersonal psychology and altered states of consciousness, recognized this resistance when he wrote:

> Orthodox, Western psychology has dealt very poorly with the spiritual side of man's nature, choosing to ignore its existence or to label it pathological. Yet much of the agony of our time stems from a spiritual vacuum. Our culture, our psychology, has ruled out man's spiritual nature, but the cost of this attempted suppression is enormous. If we want to find ourselves, our spiritual side, it is imperative for us to look at the psychologies that have dealt with it . . .[7]

CONSCIOUSNESS

Most spiritual systems teach that Universal Consciousness and love, or spirit—most commonly called God—is the most fundamental reality, beyond any kind of boundary or limitation, including space and time. *Yoga* says that by some sort of "divine play" (which I will discuss in Chapter 4), Universal Consciousness created not only the delusion of being limited (this substratal delusion is called *maya* by the Hindus), but the vehicle which perceives, promotes, protects and sustains this delusion as well—mind.

Universal Consciousness created mind with the unique power to deceive itself into believing it is limited. By virtue of the mind's senses, which focus attention to the outer world and perceive things as separate and distinct entities . . . by virtue of the strength of the mind's desires, which trick consciousness into believing that one thing is better than another, and that meaningful gratification and happiness are found in the fleeting and momentary pleasures of the outer material world and that pleasure is preferable to pain . . . by virtue of mind's thoughts, which capture and isolate a segment of reality in a symbol or concept so that imagination and fantasy can work their magic distortion—including the creation of a false self-image called ego, an image which perpetuates the delusion that I am separate from other . . . by virtue of the brief periods of its apparent success and mastery over the outer world . . . by virtue of all this, the mind seduces consciousness, luring it into its domain of duality, intoxicating it and obstructing it from realizing its boundless nature.

But there is a special higher aspect of mind, wisdom consciousness,[8] which intuitively grasps the nature of pure Universal Consciousness—a divinely inspired spark of mental activity which is aware that its most fundamental objective is to merge back into the source from which it was born.

In the preceding e-merging-into-duality process, consciousness moves successively through many stages of mind—first through primitive stages centered mostly in body awareness and concrete survival-oriented thinking; then through lower psychological stages (lower mental consciousness)[8] and on to awareness of subtler feelings and more abstract thinking—including an awareness of Maslow's higher aspirations and yearnings (higher mental consciousness)[8]—allowing for a greater range of conscious activity and freedom, but also binding man by a more highly developed sense of separate self.

Psychiatry has contributed much to our understanding of the different developmental stages of the *lower* mental consciousness of mind, such as Freud's psychosexual stages, including the oral, anal, phallic and genital stages. With each new stage, man develops a characteristic self-image with which he identifies—unaware of the true *boundless* nature of pure Universal Consciousness because of: (1) *ignorance*—the mind isn't evolved enough to grasp the possibility or hasn't been exposed to it; (2) *bondage*—the mind intellectually knows but hinders direct experience by trapping consciousness in it's (mind's) senses, desires, pleasures, pains and ego so that consciousness is not free to expand; and/or (3) *fear*—the mind intuitively knows that in the process of transcendence from ego-directed to Universal Consciousness it must relinquish control, even sacrifice itself, and recoils in fear.

Yoga clearly describes the dynamics and mechanisms by which consciousness moves from stage to stage within the mental dimension in a series of transitions and transformations, expanding and evolving in an ever-widening and broadening sphere, as it wends its way back to the ocean, to finally escape the mind and merge back into the universal whence it came. (In Appendices III and IV, I describe this view of psychological development and compare it with our Western orientation.)

The most critical and difficult of these transformations (of which mainstream Western psychology remains almost totally unaware and with which this book is primarily concerned) is that in which consciousness frees itself from its imprisonment in mind (lower and higher mental consciousness) and expands to appreciate itself as spirit (Universal Consciousness).

This monumental victory over duality marks man's most heroic triumph. For before this transition can be made, the individual is faced with a challenge demanding herculean effort. First the mind must be mastered. There is no way to avoid the work necessary for the acquisition of mental strength and skill and the development of a good, just and moral character. The character must be purified through the acquisition of a superior morality which, by confronting selfish desires, leads to selflessness, thus weakening the delusion of duality. Only then is the mind ready for the final challenge.

Final transcendence of duality then requires detachment from and renunciation of the mind itself, as well as of the outer world—a hard-won subtle spiritual attitude and approach not to be mistaken for the psychological defense mechanisms of denial or repression. This includes the transcendence of (being unaffected by) pleasures and pains and all the cares, worries, anxieties and failures—as well as all the joys and triumphs—of the outer world. It means giving up attachment to, and need for wine, women, wealth, personal status, reputation and the fruits of our labor as being essential for our sense of self worth and personal identity.

And although this may sound like a *desirable* state (and is),it means renouncing all that the mind holds as real, including that heightened awareness of our mental self—the ego. The mind sees this as nothing less than a death and recoils from it in terror. So difficult is this transcendence that the final steps can be carried out only through the grace of a divine, infinite, unconditional love.

Notes

1. The *Psychiatric Dictionary* (fifth edition, Oxford University Press, 1981) defines the behavioral sciences as "a multi-disciplinary pursuit of knowledge about behavior in its roots and manifestations in man and animals, in individuals, groups and cultures and in all conditions normal, exceptional and pathological. Among the many disciplines contributing to the behavioral sciences are all those ordinarily subsumed under the grouping of natural sciences, which explore the inanimate and animate universe in which man finds himself; the social sciences, concerned with the political, social, legal and economic structure he has given to the world around him; and the humanities: the study of man's lasting intellectual and artistic creations."

2. Ibid.: "The most comprehensive schematization of the mind is that drawn by Freud, consisting in general of the conscious and unconscious divisions, each of which is made up of a great number of components"—the three major components being ego, superego and id. In psychoanalytic psychology, the ego is defined as the mediator between the individual and reality. Its prime function is the perception of reality and adaptation to it. It is reality-oriented and ruled by rational, logical thinking.

   By means of its facilities of judgment and intelligence, by the application of logic and reality-testing, the ego blocks the tendency of the instincts toward immediate discharge—determining if and when it is safe to satisfy them. The ego is concerned with self-preservation, the acquiring of pleasure and the avoidance of pain. The id is ruled by the pleasure principle and the tendency to want immediate discharge of drive energy, or gratification. The superego is the representative of society within the mind—prompting one to behave according to what parents and society think is right and wrong.

3. This ancient wisdom is broad enough to embrace countless varieties and ways of worship—and so deep and penetrating in its inquiry into the nature of spiritual practice in general as to be considered a science of consciousness; describing the process of consciousness-raising found in all world religions, as well as the place and meaning of religious symbols, rituals and ceremonies in this process.

4. Ernest Becker, *The Denial of Death* (New York: The Free Press, 1973), p. 196.

5. See Appendix IV for more discussion about the differences between ego psychology and humanistic psychology.

6. See Appendices III and IV.

7. Charles T. Tart, Ed., *Transpersonal Psychologies* (New York: Harper and Row 1975), Introduction, p. 5.

8. See Appendix I for definition.

Mortal Fear

CHAPTER THREE

TRANSCENDENCE REQUIRES overcoming fears. In psychology we observe how people defend against reexperiencing the fears associated with early childhood traumas. In the course of a treatment we see how difficult it is to overcome these defenses so the fears can be resolved and transcended. Confronting what Becker and others have called our most basic and pervasive fear, the fear of our own mortality, the fear that blocks full transcendence, may prove an even more complex and difficult matter. But it is time to try.

Man shares fears with the lower animals—fear of bodily pain, of hunger, of any threat to body-self preservation. And by virtue of his more highly developed mind he holds some exclusively human fears as well. Most fundamental, pervasive and frightening of these is the fear of mind-ego dissolution, or what I will call *mortal* fear.

The ego referred to here is what spiritual systems regard as not only an inflated sense of self-importance but, more fundamentally, an aspect of the delusion of duality: the sense of one's being separate, different and, usually, special and important. A uniquely and distinctly human attribute, it is an outgrowth of man's higher-order level of awareness—characterized by his awareness of *being* aware, his higher intellect and abstract thinking ability, his expanded appreciation of himself as a mental being, and his insight into his mortality and finiteness. Partly fashioned by our lower animal desires and needs, the sense of ego-identity includes an awareness of our higher mental needs as well, such as social needs and the higher-order, more selfless needs (such as the need to be moral) described by Maslow.

Fear of mind-ego dissolution is more profound and of a different nature than the fear of body death. Suicide reveals that fear of mind—ego dissolution is more fundamental than the fear of physical death alone. It is the fear of no mind, of being lost in an overwhelming mystery without meaning— the possibility of non-being, of nothingness. We protect ego integration with every means available, including deluding ourselves about the nature of reality if it threatens ego safety.

This fear has been referred to by the existentialists as *angst*, or death-terror (see the quote by Ken Wilber in Chapter 4). I chose to call it *mortal* fear because that word meets all the various dictionary definitions for this quintessential fear: being uniquely human, a fear *about* death, a fear which even *causes* death in its devastating impact, and which keeps us mortal, bound to death, by frightening us from reaching for our immortality.

It has two aspects. First is the fear of our inherent separateness and aloneness in the face of ultimate physical extinction. More awesome still is the fear of losing even this brief hold on any sense of identity at all.

I'd like to emphasize from the start, you see, that this is no ordinary fear. And although we will talk about it in theoretical, philosophical and psychological terms, let's not be mistaken into thinking that it is limited to these dimensions only. *Mortal* fear prevents us from achieving higher levels of consciousness and enslaves us to the bondage of duality. It stands like a grotesque mythological dragon guarding the entrance to a vast kingdom (Universal Consciousness) which holds treasures beyond imagination. If we have the courage to challange this dragon and slay it, if we can face the force of this fear and remain unaffected by the possibility of non-being and egolessness, the rewards are greater than any psychological state so far described by the behavioral sciences.

We're talking about breaking the bondage of all mortal shackles—the ineffable treasure of attaining a higher consciousness which merges into the timeless and eternal to become one with the creative force of the universe. We're talking about the possibility of realizing our own divinity. To understand this, let's look more deeply into the nature of ego.

BIRTH OF EGO

Sai Baba, voicing the insight of many of the world's religions, has said that all of creation is based upon the delusion that there are a multiplicity of separate and discrete entities in the universe, when there is actually only one. This is the delusion of duality—referred to as *maya* in Hindu scriptures. According to Sai Baba, this is such a necessary part of the drama we perceive as reality that it was actually the first principle God created. Ego, our mental construct of being distinct and special, is an aspect of this delusion, manifesting through the mind. The sense of a separate identity is the very basis of the ego's existence. To conceive of anything else, of no-mind, threatens its integrity. We are faced with the threat of dissolution of all that we trust in for our sense of safety, security and certainty.

The ego is a grand mystery. Although spiritual systems see it as an obstacle to transcendence after a certain stage of psychological development, on close examination one must, at the same time, appreciate it as one of evolution's greatest achievements. We may gain greater respect for this powerful delusion, and the strength with which we hold to it, by appreciating its origin and the nature of the struggle in which it was born. For the power that created the ego and which maintains its integrity in the face of all obstacles is the same awesome power which created the cosmos.

Scriptures tell of a monumental moment when divine will created duality. In an instant, birth and death, right and wrong, pleasure and pain, separate shape and form manifested. Out of this primordial eruption was born the powerful process of differentiation and individuation—a process fired with an intensity great enough to prevail against the awesome destructive forces of the cosmos.

The ego's relentless drive to evolve, differentiate and master is an outgrowth of the fundamental process of life itself—life screaming and struggling to separate itself from the primordial slime. How desperately ego has worked, how long and intense its struggle to gain mastery and meaning in this mysterious world! The power of this process is seen no less in the patient, persevering evolution of species than in the convulsive throes of the infant separating at birth.

In Appendix IV, I discuss the evolution required for limited consciousness to arrive at the stage of human ego. It involves passage through inorganic, organic, plant and animal forms to finally manifest in man's distinctive mind, with all the marvelous capabilities and qualities that we humbly attribute to ourselves.

But man's powerful mind is a two-edged sword. By virtue of its heightened self-awareness man acquires and sustains a personal identity, an ego, unlike that of any lower creature. A stronghold in the mighty flux of forces that surge eternally around him, it is considered by many mankind's most courageous achievement. Yet because of it he is caught in a terrible bind: the transition between the possibility of a glorious transcendental leap in consciousness . . . or devastating annihilation.

DEATH OF THE EGO

This book is an attempt to define more clearly and in depth the dynamics of this major turning point. In the last analysis, the triumph of ego identity is short-lived. Differentiation and separateness ultimately lead to the suffering of isolation and loneliness, the first aspect of *mortal* fear. It is then that the deepest innate yearning to transcend all boundaries and merge again with the universe awakens. The mind, which has led man into this trap, must now be used to escape it, through transcendence. *"The thorn that is the splinter is the same thorn that removes the splinter,"* says Sai Baba. Realizing the nature of the trap by virtue of its heightened self-awareness, the mind must now will itself to detach not only from its own sense of importance, but more basically, any sense of being a separate entity at all—so that consciousness can be freed from its subtle yet profound bondage.

It should be emphasized that the spiritual yearning for egolessness is not the suicidal wish of a troubled mind unable to cope with the outer world, nor the desire to avoid the effort and responsibility necessary for proper psychological development. For one to stand at this brink of transcendence, the mind must have been mastered and stilled; one must have gained the mental strength and skill to operate successfully in the outer world—but also the deeper insight that true peace and happiness lie beyond it.

The aware individual knows what's at stake in this cosmic gamble. In order for union, one has to be willing to chance the loss of the hard-won sense of a separate self. No thinking person would simply throw this away, even when driven by the dream of celestial union. The threat of relinquishing one's personal identity brings with it the second and most profound aspect of *mortal* fear: the fear of ego disintegration and loss of integrity—the terror of one's total vulnerability in a fathomless cosmos without boundary or meaning. This is nonbeing: nothingness.

The death of the ego swallows up not just our own perceived physical life but any hold on reality, any reliance on meaning that has sustained us, as well. For many, physical death through suicide is a welcome relief from the fear of disintegration of the ego. This loss of identity, personal boundary and self-mastery is inevitably accompanied by a sense of utter confusion, helplessness, despair, humiliation and hopeless panic. It is to be lost in a psychedelic vision of terrifying and totally incomprehensible energies and forms. To glimpse the utter insignificance of oneself in a cosmos which, until this moment of illumination, one was entirely ignorant of, must be a horrifying experience to one who is unprepared for it.

It is one thing to face the annihilation of our own individual existence, knowing the world will go on without us and that those we love and care for will recover from their grief to live out their own lives. After all, we know that every human being in the history of the world has met the same fate. And for some of us, there is even the hope of another kind of existence following the conclusion of our physical one. Yet still the fear and avoidance of death pervade most of our lives. How much more terrifying, then, to contemplate not just the removal of ourselves from a world that we were once part of, but the annihilation of the world itself. Not as in some cataclysmic event, but as the refutation, the negation, of everything we have known, felt, believed in and stood for.

"Oh, the horror!" said the character Kurtz a moment before his death in Conrad's *Heart of Darkness*. The insight that all of life has been a delusion encompasses everything. Family, friends, loved ones, career, cherished traditions, institutions and beliefs . . . all are swept away in one terrible moment of revelation. Such insights, occurring spontaneously, have left their mark on enough people that if the reader has no personal experience of the phenomenon, he may have encountered it in literature or biography. In *Varieties of Religious Experience* William James wrote of Aldous Huxley's elderly father experiencing such a revelation, from which he never quite recovered.

How natural and understandable it is, then, that we avoid this kind of contemplation. Unless they spring out at us from the dark, catching us unawares, we keep our eyes averted from these Medusa-like insights. But the delusion of which they would tell us is real. It is, of course, the fundamental concept underlying virtually all the world's religions. Or rather, it is the dark side whose other face is radiant with the promise our religions have always held out to mankind: immortality. It seems we can't have one without the other.

And so the resistance. The two-fold fear of facing mortality and of risking ego disintegration perpetuates the delusion of duality. We hide from reality, becoming so absorbed in life's fleeting superficialities that we are almost totally insensitive to the mind-boggling mystery of creation and the miracle of our own existence. We seem completely unable to properly gauge the relative importance of these aspects of life.

Scriptures from every religion cite this pervasive blindness to the great mystery of our brief moment of consciousness in an infinite universe. What is its meaning? What is our purpose? What is death? Where will we go beyond this life? When you stop to think for a moment, isn't it strange how we almost totally erase such basic questions from our mind in favor of the insignificant pursuits which occupy us instead?

In the *Mahabharata*,[1] there is a conversation which goes like this:

Q. What is the road to heaven?

A. Truthfulness.

Q. How does a man find happiness?

A. Through right conduct.

Q. What must he subdue in order to escape grief?

A. His mind.

Q. When is a man loved?

A. When he is without vanity.

Q. Of all the world's wonders, which is the most wonderful?

A. That no man, though he sees others dying all around him, believes that he himself will die.

Why is it, even though we know intellectually that we're here for only a brief period of time, that we proceed as if we'll live forever — almost completely losing sight of the miraculousness of our creation . . . seeming totally unaware of the obvious pressing question, "What is this all about?" This blindness is an extraordinary psychological and spiritual phenomenon obvious to anyone upon even brief reflection. Yet within seconds it escapes us and we are caught again in the grasp of *maya*.

Why should something so obvious be hidden from awareness? Why don't we give it proper attention? Because to do so would be a direct assault on the integrity of our ego. Anything that challenges the feeling of security and certainty of our separate individuality brings us face to face with the great existential abyss, the terror and despair of facing an inconceivable void, a meaninglessness and nothingness beyond imagination.

Notes

1. A Hindu epic consisting of about 100,000 verses, the *Mahabharata* is considered the longest poem in the world. It is set at the time of the life of Lord *Krishna*, approximately 5,000 years ago, and is about the battle between good and evil.

The Value of
Mortal Fear

CHAPTER FOUR

IF WE have the courage to look closer, we may find that this great fear is also our saving grace. For while the delusion of separateness causes suffering, suffering prompts the search for an ultimate cure, transcending separateness. Thus fear may be a necessary and powerful spiritual insight—a beacon illuminating the path to immortality. This, of course, is much more than psychology's concept that facing irrational fear leads to its resolution and, ultimately, greater freedom.

The spiritual message is that confronting "real" fear—the fear of facing the aloneness and isolation of duality and the even greater terror of seeking transcendence at the cost of losing personal ego identity—leads to openness, innocence . . . and immortality. And what exactly is immortality? To be very concrete, lest we mistakenly assume that it is merely some theoretical or abstract idea, immortality is a realization of our essential eternal nature, with all its inherent qualities of divinity—including omniscience, omnipresence and omnipotence. We're speaking of the dynamics of transcendence—to a level of consciousness outside the domain of mainstream psychology.

Becker points out Kierkegaard's recognition of fear as being the main obstacle to, as well as prompter of, this transcendence, setting up "the possibility of cosmic heroism":

> He who is educated by dread (anxiety) is educated by possibility.
> . . . When such a person, therefore, goes out from the school of possibility, and knows more thoroughly than a child knows the alphabet that he demands of life absolutely nothing, and that terror, perdition, annihilation, dwell next door to every man, and has learned the profitable lesson that every dread which alarms may the next instant become a fact, he will then interpret reality differently. (Kierkegaard)[1]

Becker writes:

> And so the arrival at new possibility, at new reality, by the destruction of the self through facing up to the anxiety of the terror of existence. The self must be destroyed, brought down to nothing, in order for self-transcendence to begin. Then the self can begin to relate itself to powers beyond itself. It has to thrash around in its finitude, it has to "die," in order to question that finitude, in order to see beyond it. To what? Kierkegaard answers: to infinitude, to absolute transcendence, to the Ultimate Power of Creation which made finite creatures.

> > This is the salvation through self-despair, the dying to be truly born, of Lutheran theology, the passage into nothing of which Jacob Behmen (Boehme) writes. To get to it, a critical point must usually be passed, a corner turned within one. Something must give way, a native hardness must break down and liquefy. (William James)[2]

> Once the person begins to look to his relationship to the Ultimate Power, to infinitude, and to refashion his links from those around him to the Ultimate Power, he opens up to himself the horizon of unlimited possibility, of real freedom. This is Kierkegaard's message, the culmination of his whole argument about the dead-ends of character, the ideal of health, the school of anxiety, the nature of real possibility and freedom. (Becker)[3]

Becker points out how a psychology unaware of this dimension of reality promotes the "characterological lie"—the false sense of safety and security in ego—and thus leads to entrapment, isolation and suffering. It is here, he warns, that modern psychology is making its most serious, perhaps fatal mistake:

> Psychology narrows the cause for personal unhappiness down to the person himself, and then he is stuck with himself. But we know that the universal and general cause for personal badness, guilt, and inferiority is the natural world and the person's relationship to it as symbolic animal who must find a secure place in it. All the analysis in the world doesn't allow the person to find out who he is and why he is here on earth, why he has to die, and how he can make his life a triumph. It is when psychology pretends to do this, when it offers itself as a full explanation of human unhappiness, that it becomes a fraud that makes the situation of modern man an impasse from which he cannot escape . . . .

> If you fail to understand this you risk making the neurotic even worse off by closing him off from the larger world-view that he needs. As Rank put it:

> . . . it was finally the understanding psychoanalyst who sent the self-conscious neurotic back to the very self-knowledge from which he wanted to escape. On the whole, psychoanalysis failed therapeutically because it aggravated man's psychologizing rather than healed him of his introspection. (Rank)[4]

Ken Wilbur is a leading exponent of the rapidly developing transpersonal school of psychology, which focuses on man's higher transcendental nature beyond sense of personal self or duality. He sheds light on the nature of *mortal* fear, the way different schools of psychology, including the existentialists, deal with it, and the means by which it is transcended. He writes:

> The existentialists pointed out that wherever there is a separate self, there is angst, suffering, the terror of being, and the terror of death. "The essential, basic arch-anxiety," wrote Boss (1973), "is innate to all isolated, individual forms of human existence." In the basic anxiety, human existence is afraid *of* as well as anxious *about* its "being-in-the-world." That is not neurotic terror, but a given

terror, and the perception of that terror is not sickness but truth. In fact, the failure to apprehend that inherent angst, is achieved only by denying or repressing the actual and precarious nature of existence itself. Not anxiety but complacency is neurotic. The happy self is the diseased self, the self that "tranquilizes itself with the trivial," as Kierkegaard put it; or the inauthentic person, who, said Heidegger, is precisely one who has not the awareness of lonely and unexpected death.

Even Freud would soon come round to this understanding, for, as he finally put it, "It is anxiety that causes repression and not, as I had thought, repression that causes anxiety." In other words, angst is the primary mood of the separate self, and the separate self then instigates repression in response to angst in order to shield itself from the terror of death, of non-being, of nullity. "Consciousness of death is the primary repression, not sexuality," as Becker (1973) put it. Primary neurosis is thus not caused by a reliance on mental crutches, but by an inability to fashion enough crutches in the first place. As Rank put it, neurosis "is at bottom always only incapacity for illusion"—incapacity to pretend there is no death, incapacity to hide the skull that, as James said, will soon grin in at the banquet.

The existentialists, then, as the epitome of personalistic theory, had seen precisely the nature of separate self-existence. They had diagnosed humankind perfectly, and the diagnosis was angst. But seeing that anxiety came first and then repression, they could no longer pawn off angst as merely neurotic or abnormal. Rather, it was primary; it was first and foremost something inherent in the separate-self sense and not something caused by bad toilet training or something the separate self could escape if only mommy and daddy were nice to it. It was existential and not merely circumstantial. Likewise, neurosis (or primal neurosis) was not caused by repression but by a failure to repress; not "the more repression, the more neurotic and unhappy," but rather "the less repression, the more unhappy," simply because less repression meant a person was coming closer to the actual nature of reality and existence, and that nature is angst, the sour-life, the unhappy self, the self that is inherently anicca, anatta, dukkha (impermanent, insubstantial, painful).

Now the mystical or transpersonal traditions agreed with this diagnosis—the separate self, the subject set apart from objects, is indeed necessarily faced with dukkha, or sour-angst. "Wherever there is other, there is fear," say the Upanishads (see Hume, 1974). "Hell is others," said Sartre. But the transpersonal traditions maintained that there was a way out of suffering, sin, and the disease called self. It is true, they maintained, that wherever there is other there is fear, and wherever there is self there is angst, but one can transcend fear and angst by transcending self and other. Nothing the self can do will put an end to angst, because the self *is* angst; rather, one transcends angst by dying to self—they rise and fall together.

Ultimate reality was therefore said to be "nondual," which may be thought of as either beyond the dichotomy of subject and object or a union of subject and object. The point is that the discovery of this ultimate unity or Supreme Identity was a liberation from the fate of being a separate self. Seeing that self and other are one, the individual is released from the fear of living; seeing that being and nonbeing are one, the individual is released from the fear of death. At this point—but not before—the individual no longer needs to repress death; for "death has lost its sting." Discovering the Whole, he or she is released from the fate of a part.

Thus, not only did the transpersonal traditions understand the diagnosis of humankind—angst, dukkha, death-terror—they went beyond the existentialists and discovered the prognosis of humankind, the cure for the disease itself. Now the word for prognosis, in Sanskrit, is prajna (prajna = pro-gno/sis), and it is prajna, or transcendent insight, that is said to smash to pieces the chains of samsara, of dukkha, of suffering and angst. And it is prajna—prognosis, gnostic insight, jnana—that is activated and engaged in all true forms of meditation and contemplation. The transpersonalists, then, went beyond but included the existentialists.[5]

Becker, then, cites meditation and contemplation, while Kierkegaard identifies faith as the crucial ingredient needed for freedom:

> One goes through it all to arrive at faith, the faith that one's very creatureliness has some meaning to a Creator; that despite one's true insignificance, weakness, death, one's existence has meaning in some ultimate sense because it exists within an eternal and infinite scheme of things brought about and maintained to some kind of design by some creative force.
>
> Without the leap into faith the new helplessness of shedding one's character armor holds one in sheer terror . . . . The truly open person, the one who has shed his character armor, the vital lie of his cultural conditioning, is beyond the help of any mere "science," of any merely social standard of health. He is absolutely

alone and trembling on the brink of oblivion—which is at the same time the brink of infinity. To give him the new support that he needs, the "courage to renounce dread without any dread . . . only faith is capable of," says Kierkegaard . . . .

"not that faith annihilates dread, but remaining ever young, it is continually developing itself out of the death throes of dread." (Kierkegaard)[6]

TRANSCENDENT LOVE

From my experience with Sathya Sai Baba I have found love—an extraordinary selfless love, little-understood by the behavioral sciences—as being the primal cure which transforms consciousness and removes *mortal* fear. Sai Baba teaches that love is far more than a poetic idea or a psychological experience. It is in fact the very nature of creative energy, creating and sustaining everything in the universe in balance. Love underlies the cosmic force of attraction between electrons and protons, as well as the gravitational force governing oceanic tides and the celestial paths of stars. It is the force, the power, the process, the means by which we reach beyond our furthest boundaries to merge and become one with others. In its purest unconditional form it created all of "this." Suffering is the existential challenge—love is the answer.

Love is a much misused word. Any positive response or attraction is called love; any feeling of attachment, however trivial or transitory is characterized as love. We must certainly coin new words or set aside specific words to indicate different forms of love.

The attachment of parents to their children or of children to parents is called affection. The response to sexual attraction is best described as fancy, fascination or delusion. The feeling of kinship or comradeship evokes dearness. The pleasure one gets through a sense of possession, especially of material objects can be known as satisfaction. The yearning to reach for the sublimity that lies inherent in truth—this alone is entitled to be called by the holy word, love. For, that is the sweetest, the most charming, the most satisfying possession of man. Love is strong and steady enough to overcome all obstacles, confront with equanimity all changes of fortune and defeat all attempts to delay or deviate.[7]

Love is fostered and cultivated through giving, says Sai Baba. Real education, spiritual practice and good experiences make the heart tender so that the natural impulse to serve others arises. This precious impulse to give is a divine trait, God's primal impulse, given to man as a spark which must be cultivated into the blazing fire of selfless service rendered to all mankind without desire for reward. Sai Baba teaches that in this way love expands, *"unto the farthest regions of the universe,"*[8] to become one with cosmic love, culminating in the transcendence of separateness and the realization of Universal Consciousness.

The mind first creates, and is then humbled by, profound suffering and the stark vision of our aloneness. Searching to transcend mind, we are driven to plead from our hearts for mercy, as we sense no way out of the existential dilemma but by God's special grace—the gift of love that engenders love. Love soothes, love cures, love transcends all boundaries and separations, enveloping all in oneness.

I said earlier that if God hadn't created *maya*, there would be no drama. But then what is the purpose of the drama? Sai Baba has said that all of creation is by and for one purpose: the expression of love. One way of understanding this is the traditional allegory that before duality, God was lonely, needing an object in order to express His love. There had to be both giver and receiver, so He created the delusion of the other. All of creation is built on the strength of this delusion, and transcending it takes an act of grace—an infusion of divine love so great as to awaken our own deepest love and gratitude. Love merges into love; separateness vanishes: God—pure, infinite, unconditional love—is realized.

See in Me yourself . . .
for I see Myself in all of you . . .
You are My life, My breath, My soul . . .
You are all My forms.
When I love you, I love Myself . . .
When you love yourself, you love Me . . .
I separated Myself from Myself so that I may be
Myself . . .
I separated Myself from Myself and became
all of this
so that I may be Myself.

I wanted to be Myself . . . that is
anandaswarup⁹—premaswarup¹⁰ . .
that is what I am,
and I wanted to be that . . .
How can I be anandaswarup —and premaswarup . . .
    and get ananda . . . and give ananda . . .
    and get prema . . . and give prema . . .
and to whom am I to give ananda . . .
and to whom am I to give prema . . .
so I did this . . .
I separated Myself from Myself and became all this.
                    (Sathya Sai Baba)

Can all of existence be a grand play in which consciousness strives to overcome a self-imposed delusion of duality —by, through and for love? Are we capable of realizing a superhuman identity, a power and glory beyond anything imaginable? No one has been able to prove by the mental process of reason that spirit is the most basic and fundamental reality upon which all creation is based. "Proof" is realized at another dimension of consciousness where faith and devotion predominate and lead to direct experience. But let's start our journey with as much reason and intelligence as possible. And in order to examine the following concepts, phenomena and the extraordinary personality of Sathya Sai Baba, great openness and courage will be needed as well.

Notes

1. Ernest Becker, *The Denial of Death* (New York: The Free Press, 1973), p. 88.

2. Ibid., pp. 88-89.

3. Ibid., p. 90.

4. Ibid., p. 193.

5. Ken Wilber, "Odyssey: A Personal Inquiry into Humanistic and Transpersonal Psychology," *Journal of Humanistic Psychology*, Vol. 22 No. 1 (Winter 1982), pp. 62-63.

6. Becker, Op. cit., pp. 90-91.

7. *Sathya Sai Speaks*, Vol IX (Tustin, CA: Sri Sathya Sai Baba Book Center of America), p. 95.

8. See Sathya Sai Baba's discourse in Chapter 27.

9. *Ananda* is bliss; *swarup* means embodiment of. *Anandaswarup* is the embodiment of bliss.

10. *Prema* is divine selfless love. *Premaswarup* is the embodiment of divine selfless love.

The
Avatar

CHAPTER FIVE

SATHYA SAI Baba is considered by some 30 million people worldwide to be a full *Avatar*[1]—in Western terms, a spiritual teacher of the stature of Krishna, Buddha or Jesus Christ. His reported miraculous capabilities, which have been well-documented by thousands of credible witnesses, and his Christ-like way of life have attracted the attention and following of a large number of scientists and educators from around the world. Many of them believe he is the clearest living proof that our human potential is unlimited and that our essential human identity is pure spirit, unbounded by time, space or a material body. His message challenges many of the basic beliefs widely held among behavioral scientists.

The significance of an *Avatar* should be emphasized at the start, for the full meaning of the word is difficult for many Westerners to grasp with any degree of credulity. It would be a great mistake to consider such a being simply a charismatic spiritual teacher, *guru* or even saint. The *Avatar* is not just a cultural phenomenon either, having

37

special significance only for India or the East. After all, the influence of Jesus Christ and Buddha has been global in scale. The appearance of an *Avatar* is an extremely rare and monumental event in the history of mankind; his appeal is universal. He represents the highest expression of man's potential: consciousness without limit, love without boundary. He is all power, all love, capable of accomplishing anything imaginable, a being who dictates history and whose activities benefit all mankind. He speaks all languages of the world; is a source of all knowledge, knowing past, present and future; and is in all places at all times. The *Avatar's* life is a clear sign that will, consciousness and love are the source of all creation—that spirit transcends matter. He is proof of our divine inner nature.

W.H. Mackintosh, a seasoned British writer, described the significance of the *Avatar* in a review of my book *Sai Baba: The Holy Man and the Psychiatrist*:

> I found this a very disturbing book. For surely one cannot be otherwise than disturbed to learn that in this day and age God had assumed human shape. The author claims that Sri Sathya Sai Baba is an Avatar, which in Hinduism signifies the descent to earth of a divine being.
>
> This embodiment of deity in human form is a rare event, it happens only when the human condition has deteriorated to such an extent that nothing else can bring about redemption. It cannot be denied that the present situation seems to demand an Avatar's appearance.
>
> Dr. Sandweiss, an American psychiatrist, is very much a man of his time. He is trained to regard the scientific method as the most consistently reliable way of reaching the truth, and is imbued with the tenets of modern psychology, which lays so much stress on the need to avoid repression.
>
> He seems to be an unlikely advocate of the spiritual discipline, which rejects the most cherished beliefs of contemporary materialism. Yet again and again he has made pilgrimages to Bangalore to sit at the feet of Sai Baba and partake of this holy man's seemingly infinite wisdom. He found in Sai Baba a being whose nature and power were utterly incomprehensible to him. This was no ordinary guru, no publicity-seeking swami, but a Master about whom stories were told strangely reminiscent of Jesus, Buddha and Krishna.
>
> Is Sai Baba an Avatar? An incarnation of God? This is an

important question and demands a considered answer. If he is an incarnation of God he is the greatest being in the world and indeed the greatest being who could possibly exist.

Like others born and bred in a humanistic environment, I find the idea scarcely credible. I am bewildered and perplexed by the implications. I have lived long enough to learn a few lessons, not many perhaps, but sufficient in number and magnitude to convince me of the limitations of my understanding. I know too little either to affirm or deny the possibility of a miracle — and the incarnation of God would certainly be a miracle. We have no right to assert that the infinite intelligence cannot assume a finite embodiment of itself. For if the attributes of divinity are omnipotence, omnipresence and omniscience, God's assumption of human shape is a very simple exercise of his power.

However much my skeptical but limited intellect may want to reject the notion of an Avatar, the deeper insight into reality afforded by imagination and intuition does not allow me to deny that Sai Baba may indeed be an incarnation of God. Many witnesses testify to the extraordinary effect which Sai Baba's presence has on them. It is not merely the subtle influence of a God-intoxicated man but a much more powerful and direct emanation and outflow of indescribable bliss which transforms the consciousness of those present.

As I have never been in Sai Baba's presence I cannot assess the effect to which I have referred. But, as this book includes numerous quotations and extracts from his teachings, I can comment on their content and quality. The style in which they are written is clear and concise. As I read them I was conscious of an immediate impact which seemed to penetrate the very depth of my mind. The emphasis is always on God and his inexhaustible love.[2]

The concept of the *Avatar* will undoubtedly seem unbelievable, foreign, perhaps primitive, even repugnant to the intellect of many behavioral scientists. Some may consider it an example of not just wishful but magical thinking. Add to this the resistance I feel many have to spirituality[3] in general — at a time when we have been enticed by a long line of charismatic spiritual figures from both East and West, claiming large followings and extraordinary powers yet in a while proving to have feet of clay, or worse — and it is easy to see why the sophisticated intellectual would be highly skeptical of yet another claim.

Nevertheless, I ask the reader to put aside, for now, any critical, perhaps biased mental sets in order to investigate seriously the possibility of an *Avatar*, and to consider the impact of such a being not just on the behavioral sciences but on our very way of life. For many, being open to this material will not be easy. Until recently, behavioral scientists have virtually ignored profoundly relevant discoveries by saints and sages—the scientists of consciousness in the spiritual world.[4] But taking the risk of openness may bring with it considerable reward.

This is Sai Baba's challenge to the behavioral sciences' capacity for openness and change. For if we find that an *Avatar* is possible—that man's true potential encompasses no less than divinity—then obviously the textbooks defining our human condition and identity would have to be completely rewritten. While this represents an exciting possibility for the truly adventurous, it may be precisely the cause of resistance in those who dread losing a sense of certainty when old concepts tumble.

Upon returning from my first trip to India, in June, 1972, it seemed to me that the first order of business was to confront this professional resistance. Can you imagine how naive I was? I returned from that visit knowing that I had experienced something profoundly important about the dynamics of man's consciousness, and feeling that everyone would be immensely interested. Here was evidence that consciousness, not matter, formed the basis of all creation. Here were insights into how consciousness expanded—how it was interrelated with love and morality . . . how spiritual attitudes and practices like meditation, prayer, detachment, renunciation, devotion and faith related to the development of character—and how they deepened empathy, intuition and creativity and could therefore influence the therapeutic process. And here was a chance to broaden our awareness, to consider the possibility of previous lives influencing our present one—the continuation of consciousness after death.

And then the question of God: is He to be taken seriously after all? Could there be a Universal Consciousness and love that created the cosmos—and are we capable of realizing our connection with this greater dimension?

> Psychology is primarily the science of consciousness . . . Psychologists are now returning to the essential questions of our discipline: How does the mind work? What are the major dimen-

sions of human consciousness? Is consciousness individual or cosmic? What means are there to extend human consciousness? These questions have not yet had a full treatment within academic science, having been ruled out of inquiry by the dominant paradigm for the past 60 years.

Yet there is a cultural and scientific evolution, if not revolution, in process. Academic people, being members of their culture, reflect the general interest in "Altered States" of consciousness, meditation, drug states, and new and old religions . . . . There is, therefore, a continuing need to re-establish the basis of psychology and to link current research with that of other students of consciousness such as William James and Carl Jung, and with the "esoteric" psychologies of other cultures such as Sufism, Yoga and Buddhism.[5]

Soon after I got home I threw a party. I wanted to tell everyone about my amazing adventure in India—and that was my undoing. Three hundred and fifty friends and colleagues were invited. There were impressive speakers, including doctors, lawyers, an internationally known *yoga* teacher, down-to-earth business people. An extraordinarily moving film was shown. The party was well-organized, the food was good—but something fell flat. I lost my credibility and most of my friends. Psychiatric residents I taught in medical school were contacted to see if I had gone crazy. It was then that I began to realize how hot this issue was. I would have recognized it earlier had I remembered my own ups and downs—my own soul searchings and resistances in India.

Actually, looking at the situation from another point of view, I could see the humor in it. I left for India as a modern, successful psychiatrist going on an adventure—and returned almost as if in rags and covered with ash. I had served on the abortion boards of two large respected hospitals, and upon my return resigned on the grounds of the incompatibility of abortion with my new spiritual beliefs. I was aware of being in a very awkward and humorous position, as in the film "Oh God." Here I was, trying to maintain my professional posture while suspecting that I would eventually end up in front of colleagues, stating something like, "Yesterday God sent a message between the leaves of a cabbage, saying that He exists, wants us all to know that He loves us and that we should appreciate His creation."

Even so, I tried as hard as possible to open up communication within my profession. I proposed papers about Sai Baba to the 1973, 1974 and 1980 annual meetings of the American Psychiatric Association—and was turned down all three times. Colleagues in the community seemed totally disinterested.

To me this represented understandable but professionally untenable resistance to material which was of profound importance. I decided to look at this problem in more detail by arranging an interview with a respected San Diego psychoanalyst whom I felt represented the mainstream of psychiatric thinking. He was sensitive, bright, experienced as both teacher and administrator, with a broad range of interests, including psychosomatic and hospital psychiatry. I hoped to define and examine resistances that he might hold to this material. After the interview he asked to remain anonymous.

Notes

1. See definition of *Avatar*, Note 1, of Introduction.

2. W.H. Mackintosh, nine times president of The Spiritualist Association of Great Britain, has written articles and reviews for numerous publications. He is the author of *The Essence of Spiritualism* and *The Unwilling Healer*.

   Mackintosh's review appeared in the December 31, 1977 issue of *Psychic News*, a spiritually-oriented London newspaper.

3. Spirituality is defined here as that dimension of consciousness—either personally experienced or intuited—related to our existence outside of time and the physical body, in which we realize that our deepest and most meaningful relationship is with and by means of the divine, or God.

4. Eliade Marcea, *Yoga, Immortality and Freedom* (Princeton University Press, 1958)

   T.M.P. Mahadavan, *Ramana Maharshi, The Sage of Arunacala* (London: George Allen & Unwin, 1977)

   Swami Nikhilananda, *The Gospel of Sri Ramakrishna* (New York: Ramakrishna-Vivekananda Center, 1969)

5. Robert D. Ornstein, Ed., *The Nature of Human Consciousness: A Book of Readings* (San Francisco: W.H. Freeman, 1973), p. xi.

Psychiatry's Resistance, An Interview

CHAPTER SIX

SANDWEISS: PSYCHIATRISTS have learned a lot about normal personality development and effective treatment approaches by studying severely disturbed people. Do you think we could gain even deeper insight into the human condition by studying highly evolved people—people who show heightened awareness or higher levels of consciousness? For instance, do you think that learning about higher levels of consciousness with in-depth studies of the lives of saints or mystics might be relevent to modern day psychiatry?

Doctor A: Relevant to me as a person, yes; as a psychiatrist, no. I suppose that the phenomenon of higher levels of consciousness is an important human phenomenon, but as a psychiatrist I don't think it relates to my clinical practice. Lots of things don't, of course. I can think of other things that I don't understand that interest me as a person, from extrasensory perception on one hand to astronomical speculation on the other, and they really have nothing to do with psychiatry. I just accept them as things I can't understand although they interest me as a person.

S: Does religion have anything to do with psychiatry?

Dr. A: It has a lot to do with me as a person but nothing to do with me as a psychiatrist, I guess—or very little.

S: Why should that be?

Dr. A: I guess that I see psychiatry as a clinical specialty which tries to help people with disordered behavior to function better, and people who are not highly disordered to learn something about themselves. When one reaches the so-called normal point, one is finished with psychiatry. Psychiatry brings a person from minus to zero. To go from zero to plus you'd use another method.

S: So you see a separation between the fields of psychiatry and religion: there is no interrelationship?

Dr. A: Yes.

S: Do you think that this is a commonly held belief in psychiatry?

Dr. A: I don't know.

S: Is it something that you have thought about a lot?

Dr. A: Not a great deal. I have speculated about it just as part of being human and wondering about the world, but not in a clinical sense—not in the sense of trying to relate my psychiatric knowledge to religion.

S: Why do you think that you and perhaps many psychiatrists don't consider how psychiatry relates to spirituality?

Dr. A: I suppose everybody tries a little but finds it unprofitable. I know that I did. Other people may find some profit in investigating a relationship and so pursue it; I just couldn't do anything with it. It became too much a change in my thinking style. So I kept the two fields separate.

S: You said that at one point you did try to relate the two. Just how did you try?

Dr. A: Well—I've reacted to the naive religionists who say things like: "If this person only had faith he wouldn't have mental illness." I don't think that that's true. Religious people have as much mental illness as anyone else. It seems that faith is neither causative nor curative. I assume it is not related.

S: This inner state called "faith" hasn't been clearly defined by psychiatry—so how do we know what we're talking about?

Dr. A: I feel that faith has to do with one's own personal inner exploration, but I don't think it has anything to do with clinical psychiatry as I use it. It doesn't seem related to my clinical practice.

S: Faith implies a sense of hope—a feeling of optimism about the future. It would seem to be an essential part of a successful treatment.

Dr. A: We are tripping over the word "faith." You are using it as a kind of optimism toward the treatment process. But I see religious faith as not always being hopeful or positive. It can be frightening or it can be, in the *Old Testament* sense, very restricting. It involves the acceptance of the irrational as an important part of life, and there is a danger in the attitude of believing, "because I have faith," and not, "because it makes sense."

S: I agree that some people may use this attitude to avoid taking responsibility for making their own decisions. But surely that's not to say that the attitude of faith is never to be trusted—that it is a primitive reaction that is always inappropriate in any and all situations. Because there are many sophisticated thinkers—philosophers and scientists—who conclude that the mind cannot totally grasp the world in its entirety, and, like the spiritually oriented, feel that our deepest insights about the meaning of our existence are grasped intuitively and through the experience of love—not by means of the intellect. I think this is where many scientific and technologically oriented people feel resistant to spirituality—when the intellectual mind as ultimate authority is challenged.

I'd like to change direction because we may be getting a bit too cerebral. What do you suppose would happen if you met someone who was clearly at a higher level of consciousness—who had the power to materialize objects and heal people, who demonstrated boundless clairvoyance and saintly love and was in a perpetual state of bliss. How would you feel if he told you that spirituality and psychiatry were very much related and that spirituality's view of reality was more profound and all-encompassing than psychiatry's?

Dr. A: I don't know how to answer that because, I have never met such a person. You are telling me about something that doesn't register—I don't react to it—I don't know what it means. Perhaps I'm not capable of responding to anyone in this way. I assume that you have had an experience with such a person. Yet I can't understand it. I can't empathize with you—which has happened with me occasion-

ally. Patients have talked about a mystical experience and as they described it, I felt it also to a small extent. But it wasn't put in such
elaborate and farfetched terms.

S: Is it possible to consider this hypothetical situation at all—
accepting that it's highly unlikely? What do you think would be your
response if you met a great teacher with boundless knowledge and
unlimited powers—who said that spirituality is very much related to
psychiatry?

Dr. A: We are already in trouble—because it is inconceivable to
me that a great teacher with boundless knowledge could exist.

S: Why do you suppose you have such resistance at this
point? Granted, this is certainly out of the ordinary, but why are
you unable to even conjure up fantasies and thoughts about the
possibility?

Dr. A: When such people have supposedly appeared on earth,
their disciples couldn't recognize them, and if they couldn't—people
who lived and worked with them daily—how on earth am I to
assume that I could?

S: Have there been such people on earth—people whom others
have recognized as having great wisdom and power?

Dr. A: No, I don't think there really have been such people.

S: Let's say Jesus Christ.

Dr. A: Jesus' disciples didn't recognize him for what we would
recognize him for. Judas couldn't see him at all and he was there all
the time.

S: Didn't Peter recognize him?

Dr. A: Sort of.

S: Who do you think had a better vision of Christ, the disciples
who were there with him daily, or we, today?

Dr. A: Apparently we do, but I don't know.

S: Didn't the disciples have to see something grand to follow
Christ through thick and thin?

Dr. A: Eleven men followed him through thick and thin. One
didn't even know what was going on; he followed him fairly well and
then finally decided he had better get this guy stopped. But the record—
inadequate as it is, being two millennia old—doesn't show that they
really recognized who he was. He had to tell them, "I am the way," and
this sort of thing. There is no real evidence that they could understand

what he was saying. And if they did, it took them years and years to get to that point.

This really isn't an original idea; you often read that if Jesus walked in today, we wouldn't recognize him. The authorities would probably lock him up.

S: I'm a bit confused. First you say that you couldn't conceive of a person with the power and wisdom that Christians believe Jesus Christ had—and now you seem to acknowledge that this type of greatness could exist even though we might not recognize him if he appeared today.

Dr. A: Maybe I should expand on that. I think that my human mental capacity is limited. We cannot evaluate anything beyond our level of consciousness.

We formulate the universe in terms of ourselves. We project ourselves onto the outside world. Astronomical theories, for instance, may be no more than extensions of what we feel and touch on earth—and may have nothing to do with what is really going on in space. What we really have is a projection—probably not a whole lot better than a paranoid projection of ourselves onto what we observe.

It would be hard for me to conceptualize something as far-removed from my own experience as a person with boundless knowledge or pure selfless love. I wouldn't trust my ability to evaluate a capacity so beyond my own. I don't think I would be able to recognize such a person. Now if I could get beyond that limitation—but I don't know how to do that.

S: What I hear—and correct me if I am wrong—is that there are a number of concepts and ideas that you hold on an intellectual and rational level that serve to stop you from thinking about this kind of situation. You have decided that this whole subject cannot be comprehended by the human mind—and so you decide to shut yourself off from even considering possibilities.

Dr. A: I would think I had reached the outer limits of my mental capacity and everything that I thought beyond that would be spinning wheels mentally. To a certain extent I think the logical positivists, the Viennese philosophical school, really did away with metaphysics in one stroke on the basis that since we can't think about it in a logical fashion, let's not think about it at all because it is a waste of human effort. Let's think about something we can actually grasp with the rational mind. This approach has a certain attraction.

S: Then in your way of thinking, it's futile to consider the possibility of a God-man with boundless power and love?

Dr. A: Yes, we don't know whether such observations of a phenomenon so far outside our experience are really valid or psychotic.

S: This is very interesting. I think that a lot of psychiatrists feel the same.

Dr. A: It's like the question, "What's beyond the most distant star?"

S: In college, I remember how discussions about God seemed unending. Nobody could prove anything because there was no rational proof of God's existence. The discussions seemed senseless because people believed whatever they wanted anyway—whatever supported their needs. It was like spinning wheels. Is that what you're saying?

Dr. A: Yes, that would be the positivists' point of view as I understand it. I think that they carry it a bit too far though, because you can at least have some fun playing with these ideas.

S: Well, perhaps that's not a bad way of looking at mysticism. But speculating about what is beyond the most distant star and holding abstract discussions is quite different from actually seeing what's beyond the farthest star. For instance, let's consider the hypothetical situation where all of a sudden we have a clear, concrete experience of an extremely bright light in the room, and from that light Jesus Christ materializes.

Let's say that this isn't just a thought or an abstract argument; we are actually with the physical Jesus, right here and now. And you and I confirm it and even take motion pictures which confirm it. Let's say that he tells you that he is giving you a concrete transcendental experience out of his love, in order to teach you a lesson—and then he disappears. And what if we both saw him and that it showed up on film? How would you react? Would you still say, after such a concrete experience, that the mind cannot comprehend such phenomena and so it would be inappropriate to even think about it?

Dr. A: My initial impression would be that I was crazy—stark raving mad. How long it would take me to get around that one, I don't know. And the fact that my colleague was crazy too would be no help initially—even though it might be of some security later on. I would think that I was hallucinating—or at least delusional about the consensual validation. I would take it as psychopathology.

S: What if while you were thinking it was psychopathology, Jesus came again to give you another experience?

Dr. A: Now I would say that the world is part of my delusion. I would begin to think that I was delusional about Christ giving me another sign. I'd think that I was going crazy.

S: What if you didn't go crazy, and were still able to function well?

Dr. A: If it happened to me too many times I'd be sure that I was crazy. But if it happened only once I might be able to consider that it wasn't psychopathology. Because I don't think that psychopathology usually comes as an isolated blip out of the void. The more often it happened, the more I would be sure it was psychopathology, I suppose.

S: Let's say that you went to your desk and all of a sudden, on your writing pad, there was a magnificent picture of the vision that you had just had with a message underneath saying, "I understand what is going on in your mind and the difficulty you are having grappling with it. I want you to know that this is real and not an hallucination. I am giving you a deeper vision into reality."

Dr. A: If he really wanted to help me he'd better not do that. He'd better let me wrestle with the experience and not do too much confirming. In other words, I suspect that my tolerance for an idea that has this much disjunction from my ordinary experience is going to be very low; I could stand only a little piece of it without assuming that I had lost my capacity to separate primary process[1] from secondary process.[2]

S: I'm feeling your resistance right now.

Dr. A: This has happened to me once. I had a brief religious experience about twenty years ago. It lasted two to four minutes, I suppose. And my initial assumption was that it was psychopathology. I was a psychiatric resident and I thought, "Oh no, finally it's happened to me—I've blown my tubes and that's it." It literally took some weeks before I felt more comfortable. I happened to be in analysis at the time and fortunately my analyst didn't assume right away that it was psychopathology, so I began to accept it as a very brief mystical experience.

S: What was the experience?

Dr. A: I'll tell you—I suppose it's all right, I told my analyst. Actually, after this many years it doesn't seem like such a marvelous event. Of course it did at the time. It had the quality of disjuncture and the feeling that I was changed permanently, and then a great positive lift and the feeling that I had kind of seen through to another level, or whatever you want to call it. Then after I had decided I really hadn't come to pieces, I wanted to repeat it—but the repetition didn't come. Then the feeling that I had been permanently changed slowly quieted and I kind of came back to baseline in a couple of months or so. I wasn't able to repeat it.

S: What happened?

Dr. A: Well, I was sitting in the Riverside Church in New York with my wife, and during a service I looked up at the cross—which is a big one, about life-size. I don't know if you know Riverside Church but it's enormous—built by Rockefeller—and it must be four stories high. It is a huge replica of a French Gothic cathedral, a magnificent building. And I had the idea that I could understand why Jesus had to go to the cross in order to express his love for man—because to me that doesn't make sense at all. But somehow at that moment this illogical—totally illogical as far as I'm concerned—phenomenon made sense.

It made kind of a universally important sense and I felt a feeling of love myself, and a kind of warm glow came over me. It lasted about half a minute and the immediate assumption I had was that I had gone crazy. And I was surprised that I had gone crazy, especially in a religious way—I hadn't expected it to occur that way.

But that is what happened. And it has not happened again—just the one time. It did, however, increase my interest in religion. I have since found out from patients that these experiences are not common but they are also not rare. It was a positive experience.

S: Did it make you more or less interested in religion?

Dr. A: More, much more. I always had been. I had been a practicing Christian essentially all my life, but I had difficulty with the irrationality of religion and the fact that I somehow had to suppress my own critical faculties in order to continue—because, you know, a lot of this stuff doesn't make sense. But at that moment it didn't matter—I had faith. I suppose I might have called it a conversion experience in a way. But it wasn't, because it didn't change anything I thought about religion. It did increase my interest and my feeling that "there is something there"—although I know we are loaded up with all kinds of garbage and projecting all over the place, so that in fact the perception might have been 90% wrong. Still, I felt there was something there.

S: Did you want to repeat the experience?

Dr. A: Yes, but it didn't happen. I understand now that this is often the case with mystical experiences. There is a great effort to repeat it and the experience may not happen again. I can remember in college reading Saint Bonaventure's *Journey of the Mind to God*, which as I recall, was a kind of recipe on how to have a mystical experience. It involved fasting and standing out in the rain and cold, and all kinds of things such as not sleeping and running oneself down physically. It seems that he put himself in what amounts to a toxic psychosis in order to create this experience. Maybe that worked for him. It certainly showed how much he wanted to repeat the experience: to subject himself to these tortures to get it again. I didn't do that; I just waited. It didn't happen. And thinking about it now, I'm not sure—I'm ambivalent—about wanting it to happen again.

S: Why?

Dr. A: Because I am sure I would think the same thing I did the first time. I'd think that I probably had gone to pieces.

S: When faced with a profoundly moving mystical experience, the most appropriate response might be devotion. Could it be that you fear being devotional because it would mean giving up your scientific, rational approach to reality? Do you feel that being devotional is dangerous?

Dr. A: Not dangerous—uncomfortable. I don't know as I would damage myself in that sense, but I would discomfort myself.

S: If by being devotional you opened yourself to a profound feeling of love—a love that brought great strength and courage—would that feel uncomfortable? Suppose you knew that this experience was something given out of love as a gift of grace by divinity. If you were filled with bliss and love—with appreciation, gratitude and devotion toward God—wouldn't you like that?

Dr. A: I am rather sure that I wouldn't.

S: I'm surprised. Because if that's so, then I see you resisting achieving and realizing the highest state of consciousness described by man.

Dr. A: I keep coming back to the same thing. I wouldn't trust the experience. Point one, I think that it is not possible for anyone to enter a state of prolonged bliss; I don't think that is within one's mental capacity. And point two, I would be sure that I had gone into some kind of ecstatic psychosis.

S: That's what you think—but can you be sure that it's absolutely impossible for one to achieve a state of constant bliss: unbounded power and unconditional love?

Dr. A: Even when described in the lives of saints, such as St. Francis of Assisi, I can't recall a case in which the state of bliss was continuous.

S: From my point of view, the question is much more than a hypothetical exercise—because I believe that I've seen such an individual. Distinguished people—reputable trained observers—people from all over the world—are convinced. If there were a great deal of evidence to support this unlikely possibility, don't you think that psychiatrists would be interested? Or do you think that some of the resistances we are talking about would be so strong we would avoid him and shut the phenomena from awareness?

Dr. A: I think I would shut it out. I would say it was a hoax or he was a charismatic leader—but not genuine. I would assume that it wasn't so and wouldn't even add, "until proven otherwise," because I assume that it couldn't be proven to me.

Human beings are continuously changing. If you said that someone is in constant bliss and shows unbounded power—whatever he is, he isn't human.

S: If the most respected scientists, after extended observations, concluded that a particular human being did appear to be in a state of unwavering bliss—wouldn't that interest you?

Dr. A: Let me put it this way. When I was in high school, the answer might have been "yes." I was at a point in my view of cosmology and humanity that was flexible enough, I suppose, that I could entertain that kind of speculation. But at this point in my life the answer is "no." I think that in the intervening thirty years of not having observed such a phenomenon, I assume that it just doesn't exist, and I am at a point where if I did see such a phenomenon, I would interpret it as an aberration in my observation.

When I was 15, I was looking for a man on a white horse who was going to save us all, politically or otherwise. I would assess each presidential candidate on the basis of whether he was an Abraham Lincoln who would lead us into a better world. Since then I have changed. Instead of looking for such qualities in a leader, I almost go the opposite way. If he looks too good, like the man on the white horse, I am going to vote against him. Now I feel we have to be saved from the men on the white horses because they usually lead us to destruction. Charismatic figures usually wind up doing something wrong—or worse. Hitler is an example.

S: Do you think that Christ and all the stories about his divinity are actually real?

Dr. A: I don't doubt that there was an historical Jesus. Whether he was Christ or whether we made him one, I'm not quite so sure about. I don't know how much of what we ascribe to him now is thrust upon him by our own need to have such a figure. What we say about him and describe about him now probably doesn't bear much resemblance to the historical Jesus.

S: If he actually walked on water, would that interest you?

Dr. A: I wouldn't believe it. I wouldn't believe my own eyes.

S: If others saw it and it was documented in photographs—then would it have any meaning?

Dr. A: Photographs mean nothing to me.

Notes

1. Primary process—Freud's term for the kind of primitive, non-logical, wishfulfilling and magical thinking found in childhood, dreams and psychopathology.

2. Secondary process—Freud's terms for the kind of intelligent, logical, reality testing and problem solving thinking necessary for successful adaptation to the outer social world.

Bhagawan Sri Sathya Sai Baba

TELE NO 30
BRINDAVAN
WHITEFIELD-560 067
TELE NO 36
PRASANTHINILAYAM P O
ANANTAPUR DT 515134

My Dear's! The time will come when the whole of This dream will vanish. To everyone of us there must come a time whent the whole universe will be found to have been a mere dream, when we shall find that the soul is infinitely better than its surroundings. In this struggle through what we call environments, there with come a time when we shall find that these environments were almost-zero in comparison with the power of the Soul. It is only a question of time, and time is nothing in the infinite. It is a drop in the ocean. We can afford to wait and be calm.

With Blessings

Sri Sathya Sai Baba

(Baba)

Points
of View

CHAPTER SEVEN

IS MAN body and mind, or spirit? Is the purpose and meaning of life to be found in the successful gratification of desires, or in the transcendence and renunciation of them? Is the material world real or a delusion—a mere hint of a much vaster eternal reality? What about morality on the other hand? Is it relative and changing—or absolute, a narrow path to salvation? Can we honestly say that we are really content, living in the transient and evanescent? If not, could it possibly be because we yearn for union with the eternal, for the salvation of everlasting life and eternal peace? Is doubting divinity more realistic and intelligent than believing in it—or is this doubt conceivably a self-destructive defense against one's *mortal* fear?

Is Sai Baba authentic; could he be a vivid reflection of our infinite, eternal and divine nature? And is there a level of unconditional love, not yet defined in psychology, which is powerful enough to dissolve all our fears and limitations and lead us to liberation, total freedom from the tyranny of self-consciousness? Is man animal . . . or God?

I believe that the way psychotherapist and client answer these questions greatly affects the approach and outcome of therapy. The following is a case in point, and in this and the next three chapters we may see more clearly just how universal and important spiritual issues are, and to what extent and with what kind of approaches they should be addressed. Names of people and places have been changed to protect anonymity.

THE CASE OF A.T.

In 1979 when A.T. began treatment she was a bright 27-year old married graduate student in biology. Five feet, six inches, 145 pounds, sturdy and athletic in build, tanned and loving the outdoors, with a natural earthy attractiveness, she usually dressed casually in jeans, dress or shorts. She related to people in an interesting, sensitive, responsive, verbal, at times a bit overly intellectual manner. Intelligent, educated and excelling in the best American schools, admired and respected by peers who elected her president of the graduate student body, happily married to a physician—she had, you would think, all that life could offer.

Although showing no apparent personality or emotional weaknesses, clear-thinking and expressive of a full range of emotions, at times A.T. showed an unusual, misty far-away look in her eyes and complained of an ill-defined void in her life. She entered treatment also complaining of a lack of motivation in pursuing her spiritual life. To my way of thinking she was expressing the yearning to contact a deeper, more meaningful level of love, but was blocked by some fear.

As treatment progressed it was apparent that she used her intellectual and verbal skills to control her interactions with people and distance herself when she felt threatened. She was over-concerned with being reasonable and rational and hesitated to show childish feelings, as she felt they expressed "unreasonable" needs and wishes. Instead of expressing feelings she would describe and explain events in elaborate detail, in a manner which controlled and quieted her emotions. At times when she appeared sad to me, with tears welling up and her lip quivering, she would deny this feeling, saying, "There's no reason to be sad. Dwelling on sadness is a morbid self-indulgence that leads nowhere. Why are so many people sad when all they have to do is force their mind elsewhere?" So along with her over-control and distancing was occasional sadness. Why did she have to exert such intellectual control? What was she defending against?

To answer this question we'll first look at how A.T.'s intellectual defenses were related to her childhood and her relationship with her parents, and then see if perhaps there is even a more fundamental spiritual reason for them.

BACKGROUND INFORMATION

A.T. was born in a rural area outside a comfortable small Massachusetts town—in natural surroundings, with a small brook that ran close to her home. She was the second of a sibship of four, having an older sister, younger sister and younger brother in that order. All sibs grew up excelling in school and finding responsible and productive professions.

A.T.'s parents were bright, creative people. Her father was an electrical engineer doing research and development. Her mother interrupted her education close to finishing her master's degree in biochemistry in order to start the family and has now reentered the field, doing research as a field technician. A.T.'s older sister is a graduate of an eastern college with a B.S. in biology; her younger sister, a Ph.D. psychologist with a children's day treatment center. Her younger brother has a B.S. degree in mathematics from Yale and is a consultant for a research lab.

A.T.'s early memories are wholesome and pleasant. She remembers her family as close and loving, free of drug problems, excessive aggressiveness or parental separations. For her first eight years the family was strongly Christian fundamentalist, but they became Unitarians when A.T.'s father felt uncomfortable teaching hell-fire and brimstone.

Although both parents were emotionally healthy, each was exposed to an element of psychological pain in childhood, resulting in some narrowing of consciousness. Later in life, A.T.'s father expressed this narrowness by dismissing as nonsense any subject that could not be clearly conceptualized in terms of forces, forms and mechanisms. Although having a strong spiritual side, he discounted most mystical thought as fuzzy, unclear, and unworthy of attention.

A.T.'s mother was born in Japan where her father was a Christian missionary. Her early years were lived in a strict and authoritarian setting, and later in her life she developed osteoarthritis, leading to double knee replacements.

A.T. was always bright, inquisitive and creative. She graduated from high school with a straight-A average and during her high school years showed remarkable sensitivity to the plight of the poor. About age 15, while at a one-week Unitarian young people's conference retreat, she and her friends were moved by Ralph Abernathy's Poor People's Campaign. She fasted three days and went with friends to Washington to visit Tent City and take part in the protest. The next summer she volunteered her time with a Head-Start program.

At age 16 she was an exchange student for three months in South America, becoming fluent in Spanish and developing a continuing interest in South America. Then followed a heightened awareness regarding broader world problems. She became involved in student rights activities and anti-war protests even while living in a conservative community. Following her graduation from high school at age 17 she entered Brandeis University, majoring in biology.

Over the next few years she met and married her present husband, a physician, and graduated from Brandeis in 1975. Then she and her husband moved to a small California town where, for the next two years, she worked as an instructional aide for a migrant educational program, helping migrant high school students adapt to school. Her sensitivity to the issues, fluency in Spanish, intelligence and humanistic interest brought her success and led to her involvement in curriculum development.

While teaching there, she developed a friendship with a substitute teacher who introduced her to new spiritual ideas and gave her my first book upon her leaving in 1978. She and her husband then came to San Diego, California, where he entered practice. Approximately one year later, in 1979 and at age 27, she entered treatment to investigate her inner world and improve communication with her husband. There was no history of drug abuse, trouble with the law, marked depressions or sexual problems.

EARLY YEARS

Although A.T.'s family was basically healthy and strong, as in all families there were some discernible problems in the relationship between children and parents. Foremost among these, and the one about which A.T. complained the most during therapy, was her feeling of a lack of unconditional love and that parental love and attention were *earned* by intellectual performance. For the most part, this was fine with her, as she was innately bright and could readily win the affection of her parents by mental quickness. But the belief that self-worth is dependent upon intellectual performance was to cause her some grief later in life—and during treatment, when her intellectual performance wasn't rewarded.

Doubting the existence of unconditional love, she developed a heightened need to control situations by means of her intellectual performance, to assure herself that she was loved. Intellectual control brought a sense of well-being.

Of course it is always nice to excel and feel in control, but A.T. needed this sense of control to a degree that limited her openness. Not to feel it meant experiencing the possibility of being unloved. In therapy, when her intellectual responses were not rewarded, she became threatened and tried to regain mastery by an exaggerated use of her intellect. She would overly explain and discuss to impress me or hide from feelings, and quickly forgot painful emotions from one session to another.

Also remarkable was her lack of memory for early childhood and adolescence. She wondered why she had less recall of these memories than did her peers, and began to see how she hid from her own feelings of anger and sexuality lest she feel out of intellectual control and hence experience awkwardness and vulnerability. But in defending against these feelings she kept herself distant from other important feelings as well—deep feelings of love for her parents and others, as well as deep spiritual impulses. Now she wanted to overcome these barriers and seemed willing to risk the pain to do so.

THE DREAM

A.T. had learned of Sai Baba from reading my first book, given to her by a friend prior to moving to San Diego. Even though we hadn't discussed Sai Baba much, early in the treatment she expressed the wish that he would help her find deeper meaning in life. Soon after verbalizing this she had the following dream.

I was in a large hall, something like a gymnasium. I think it was registration day because of the commotion. People were scurrying about and lining up at tables as if preparing to register for classes. I was approaching a table, carrying my books in my left arm. Under my right sleeve I felt an unfamiliar object, and then noticed that I was carrying a wooden statue of Sai Baba there. I thought it strange —I was embarrassed and wanted to keep it hidden from sight. While waiting my turn at one of the tables, I heard a voice coming from my right side. *"What do you have up your sleeve, A.T.?"* I tried to ignore the voice, but to my embarrassment it continued even more loudly. And then for the third time it repeated, *"I said—what do you have up your sleeve?"*

I was embarrassed to uncover the statue. Turning to face the person on my right, I was amazed to find that it was Sai Baba! My eyes were caught by a smile which was full of mischief and joy. Immediately I was ignited with the same feeling. With high-intensity excitement and glee he said, *"It's me, it's me, IT'S ME!"* I was caught up in his energy and joyful beyond description. He had come to me!

Is this a dream about A.T.'s hidden love for her father? Does it express transference feelings toward me? Is it about control and her fear of revealing herself, or about her yearning for union with God and her mind's struggle with this yearning? Or could the dream represent all these themes—and if so, then which issues should be dealt with first?

Although this, of course, is determined by what is specifically happening in the treatment, one therapist's choice may differ from another's depending on their particular schools of thought. Ken Wilbur, whose thoughts about the nature of anxiety I've presented in Chapter 4, defines 10 levels of consciousness (see Appendix IV under the heading *Transpersonal Psychology*). He discusses the differences in theories, approaches and goals between Freudian, existential and transpersonal psychologies,[1] seeing them as reflective of the different levels of consciousness that each addresses. He shows that the existential point of view includes the level of consciousness with which psychoanalysis deals, and goes beyond it, and that the transpersonal school addresses an even broader level of consciousness.

Let's look at the psychological aspects of A.T.'s dream from a psychoanalytic point of view and then examine a possible spiritual interpretation to see the similarities and differences in these approaches, and to begin to appreciate the vast dimension of possibilities and meanings added to a therapy by increasing its scope to include spiritual considerations.

PSYCHOLOGICAL APPROACH

The concept that deepening one's insight, expanding consciousness and enhancing the experience of love can all come from confronting and overcoming one's misconceptions and fears is common to both psychology and spirituality. Freud learned that people separate themselves from fearful parts of the self, protecting themselves from recalling past traumatic events by utilizing defenses such as repression and denial. But there is a price to pay for this safety: consciousness is constricted in other areas as well.

To experience love fully, one must be fully open, like an innocent, spontaneous child. If feared situations no longer exist and the defenses for them are no longer necessary, the therapeutic aim is to challenge these defenses in order to resolve any residual fear, thus allowing the unconscious to become conscious. No longer needing to separate part of the self, one experiences a new openness, an expansion of consciousness and a new sense of wholeness, a deeper contact with life, a greater sense of freedom, more energy for living, and a greater capacity to experience and express love. This degree of "wholeness" must not be confused, however, with the "unity" or oneness with all things, about which spiritual systems talk. The crucial difference is that non-dualistic spiritual approaches aim at transcending *all* boundaries, to achieve a unity without *any* separation or limitation (see Appendices III and IV).

From the psychological point of view, the large school building in A.T.'s dream can be seen as representing her mind, with its intellectual strengths as well as the intellectual defenses that distanced her from both human love and spiritual union. The scurrying of people and the high level of activity indicate that her intellect was being challenged and perhaps threatened by a love demanding more openness—an openness quite possibly accompanied by fear and pain. The dream can be seen as a struggle between her desire to experience greater human warmth and love—perhaps initially arising from her demanding relationship with her father—and her fear of, and intellectual defense against, this kind of love, because such openness would expose her to the pain and fear that occurred in that relationship. I believe the dream also shows that human and transcendental love can overcome defenses and bring greater meaning into human relationships.

SPIRITUAL APPROACH

Focusing on the same idea—that expanding consciousness and love can be realized by overcoming fears that hinder full awareness of the real self—non-dualistic spiritual systems carry this point to the limit, asserting that man must not only become aware of repressed childhood fears, feelings and experiences, and be able to fully re-enter childhood with all innocence—he must also overcome his sense of separateness from *everything* that is considered other. He must overcome the subject-object split: duality itself. To do this, one must fully face and transcend *all* fears—imaginary and *REAL*. With the innocent, spontaneous, sensitive, total openness of a child, one must face suffering, pain, death and *mortal* fear. The only force powerful enough to effect this transcendence is love.

Within this context, then, A.T.'s dream can represent the fundamental spiritual dynamics: the struggle between mind and spirit—the spirit's yearning to transcend all limitations and separations, including duality and mind itself; and mind's *mortal* fear of transcendence and its own possible non-being—as well as selfless, unconditional love's ability to transcend all fears. Along these lines, one possible spiritual interpretation of the dream, based upon my own experience with Sathya Sai Baba, is as follows. Later we'll see confirmation of these dynamics in the course of A.T.'s therapy.

I have heard many Sai Baba dreams. They all seem to have the same quality, expressing humor, excitement and always his great compassion and warmth. I know of no other type of dream that leaves such a lasting glow of delight—even days afterwards. It is not like the symbolic wish-fulfilling dreams with which most therapists deal. Sai Baba's appearance in a dream seems to me an actual clear expression of our own higher consciousness—and the personality of Sai Baba in India is fully at one with this dimension of consciousness. I believe that he is actually, personally in the dream and in fact fashions it to teach, protect, give love and help us overcome earthly fears, as well as the *mortal* fear of transcendence. I have been present during an interview in which Sai Baba not only described a dream in which he appeared to one of our group members, but interpreted it in a most unusual way as well—*before* the dream had been told to him.

To protect herself from *mortal* fear, A.T. had apparently sacrificed her spirituality, carrying it at a distance from her heart, attempting to keep it isolated from awareness. While in treatment and shortly before the dream, she had asked Sai Baba's help in awakening this impulse. He had responded—at first with only a nudge; her intellect struggled, trying to ignore him. But again he intruded, not allowing her resistance to keep him away. Unconditional love finally prevailed, overriding all her barriers, breaking through all her defenses and fears. Finally A.T. could no longer dismiss this intimate and persistant approach, an irresistible invitation into her own heart.

Caught literally with something up her sleeve, she would have to face her defenses and fears and reveal her deepest hidden reality. When she reached for what she thought was a hidden, lifeless statue, she found instead her real center, a penetrating and exhilarating burst of innocence, love and joy, which ignited her heart and soul. Sai Baba challenged her mind—her intellectual defenses and *mortal* fear—made her into an innocent child, and brought her spirituality alive. Love turned fear into love and revealed itself as supreme.

The belief that this dream represents a *real* visit from Sai Baba, who I believe is one with our own higher consciousness and manifests to awaken our inherent divine joy and love, represents a real departure from mainstream psychological thinking. It implies that the spiritual dimension is personal and responsive and concretely affects us in everyday life—that transcendental love (represented here by the form of Sai Baba and which is our own innermost reality) is not bound by the laws of duality and can transcend time and place. Unconditional love affects others instantaneously, no matter past, present or future—or whatever distance away.

Experiencing Sai Baba's omnipresence in this way convinces one of the existence and vastness of the spiritual dimension and quickens one's interest in it. And Sai Baba's *actual* appearance, at the same time both in India and in the mind of a young woman in the U.S., means that at a fundamental level A.T. and Sai Baba are one and the same. Experiencing our inner life and outer world as one in this way brings a whole new insight into the meaning of "oneness." And in this dream we see the struggle of the intellectual rational mind as it opens to this profound insight.

If all of this is true, how important to know! It is vital and crucial information of the highest order, which must be integrated into every aspect of therapy.

In *Zen Buddhism and Psychoanalysis*,[2] Erich Fromm discusses the differences in aims and goals between the psychological and spiritual approaches, in this case Freudian psychoanalysis and Zen Buddhism. He examines the implications and significance of their differences and emphasizes the importance of integrating the two points of view. He writes:

> The aim of Zen is enlightenment: the immediate, unreflected grasp of reality, without affective contamination and intellectualization, the realization of the relation of myself to the Universe. This new experience is a repetition of the preintellectual, immediate grasp of the child, but on a new level, that of the full development of man's reason, objectivity, individuality. While the child's experience, that of immediacy and oneness, lies before the experience of alienation and the subject-object split, the enlightenment experience lies after it.
>
> The aim of psychoanalysis, as formulated by Freud, is that of making the unconscious conscious, of replacing Id by Ego. To be sure, the content of the unconscious to be discovered was limited to a small sector of the personality, to those instinctual drives which were alive in early childhood, but which were subject to amnesia. To lift these out of the state of repression was the aim of the analytic technique. Furthermore, the sector to be uncovered, quite aside from Freud's theoretical premises, was determined by the therapeutic need to cure a particular symptom. There was little interest in recovering unconsciousness outside of the sector related to the symptom formation. Slowly the introduction of the concept of the death instinct and eros and the development of the Ego aspects in recent years have brought about a certain broadening of the Freudian concepts of the contents of the unconscious. The non-Freudian schools greatly widened the sector of the unconscious to be uncovered. Most radically Jung, but also Adler, Rank, and the other more recent so-called neo-Freudian authors have contributed to this extension. But (with the exception of Jung), in spite of such a widening, the extent of the sector to be uncovered has remained determined by the therapeutic aim of curing this or that symptom; or this or that neurotic

character trait. It has not encompassed the whole person. However, if one follows the original aim of Freud, that of making the unconscious conscious, to its last consequences, one must free it from the limitations imposed on it by Freud's own instinctual orientation, and by the immediate task of curing symptoms. If one pursues the aim of the full recovery of the unconscious, then this task is not restricted to the instincts, nor to other limited sectors of experience, but to the total experience of the total man; then the aim becomes that of overcoming alienation, and of the subject-object split in perceiving the world; then the uncovering of the unconscious means the overcoming of affective contamination and cerebration; it means the de-repression, the abolition of the split within myself between the universal man and the social man; it means the disappearance of the polarity of conscious vs. unconscious; it means arriving at the state of the immediate grasp of reality, without distortion and without interference by intellectual reflection; it means overcoming of the craving to hold on to the ego, to worship it; it means giving up the illusion of an indestructible separate ego, which is to be enlarged, preserved as the Egyptian pharaohs hoped to preserve themselves as mummies for eternity. To be conscious of the unconscious means to be open, responding, to have nothing and to be.

Fromm implies that man can move beyond the subject-object split and arrive at total awareness. He implies that the path "includes an ethical aim"—values are centrally important—and that spiritual issues are more basic than the psychological, that they must be faced and transcended before a lasting cure can be effected, that failure within traditional Western psychological approaches are the result of not clearly and directly facing these spiritual issues.[3]

This aim of the full recovery of unconsciousness by consciousness is quite obviously much more radical than the general psychoanalytic aim. The reasons for this are easy to see. To achieve this total aim requires an effort far beyond the effort most persons in the West are willing to make. But quite aside from this question of effort, even the visualization of this aim is possible only under certain conditions. First of all, this radical aim can be envisaged only from the point of view of a certain philosophical position. There is no need to describe this position in detail. Suffice it to say that it is one in which not the negative aim of the absence of sickness, but the positive one of the presence of well-being is aimed at, and that well-being is conceived in terms of full union, the immediate and uncontaminated grasp of the world. This aim could not be better described than has been done by Suzuki in terms of "the art of living." One must keep in mind that any such concept as the art of living grows from the soil of a spiritual humanistic orientation, as it underlies the teaching of Buddha, of the prophets, of Jesus, of Meister Eckhart, or of men such as Blake, Walt Whitman, or Bucke. Unless it is seen in this context, the concept of "the art of living" loses all that is specific, and deteriorates into a concept that goes today under the name of "happiness." It must also not be forgotten that this orientation includes an ethical aim. While Zen transcends ethics, it includes the basic ethical aims of Buddhism, which are essentially the same as those of all humanistic teachings. The achievement of the aim of Zen, as Suzuki has made very clear in the lectures in this book, implies the overcoming of greed in all forms, whether it is the greed for possession, for fame, or for affection; it implies overcoming narcissistic self-glorification and the illusion of omnipotence. It implies, furthermore, the overcoming of the desire to submit to an authority who solves one's own problem of existence. The person who only wants to use the discovery of the unconscious to be cured of sickness will, of course, not even attempt to achieve the radical aim which lies in the overcoming of repressedness.

But it would be a mistake to believe that the radical aim of the de-repression has no connection with a therapeutic aim. Just as one has recognized that the cure of a symptom and the prevention of future symptom formations is not possible without the analysis and change of the character, one must also recognize that the change of this or that neurotic character trait is not possible without pursuing the more radical aim of a complete transformation of the person. It may very well be that the relatively disappointing results of character analysis (which have never been expressed more honestly than by Freud in his "Analysis, Terminable or Interminable?") are due precisely to the fact that the aims for the cure of the neurotic character were not radical enough; that well-being, freedom from anxiety and insecurity can be achieved only if the limited aim is transcended, that is, if one realizes that the limited, therapeutic aim cannot be achieved as long as it remains limited and does not become part of a wider, humanistic frame of reference. Perhaps the limited aim can be achieved with more limited and less time-consuming methods, while the time and energy consumed in the long analytic process are used fruitfully only for the radical aim of "transformation" rather than the narrow one of "reform." This proposition might be strengthened by referring to a statement made above. Man, as long as he has not reached the creative relatedness of which satori is the fullest achievement, at best compensates for inherent potential depression by routine, idolatry, destructiveness, greed for property or fame, etc. When any of these compensations break down, his sanity is threatened. The cure of the potential insanity lies only in the change in attitude from split and alienation to the creative, immediate grasp of and response to the world. If psychoanalysis can help in this way, it can help to achieve true mental health; if it cannot, it will only help to improve compensatory mechanisms.

Notes

1. See Appendix IV.

2. D.T. Suzuki, Erich Fromm, and Richard De Martino, *Zen Buddhism & Psychoanalysis* (New York: Grove Press, Inc., 1963), pp. 134-136.

3. Ibid., pp. 136-138.

You feel that there is something behind and beyond all this fleeting fantasy, something that persists through all the success and defeats, all the tears and smiles, all this mirth and moan, but you are unable to grasp it and realize that it is the same entity that underlies the entire universe. You are one with the most distant star, and the least little blade of grass; you shine as dew on the petal of the rose, you swing from star to star. You are part and parcel of all this manifestation.

(Sathya Sai Baba)

Layers of Fear,
Levels of Love

CHAPTER EIGHT

WE MAY dream of contact with our innermost joy, bliss and love — with the divine (as in A.T.'s dream) — but reaching it is something else again. The road inward may be frightening and lonely, requiring openness and courage as we face layers of fear one by one, calling upon deepening levels of love to dispel the darkness, until we finally realize our core reality — unconditional love. Following is a detailed account of one psychiatric session with A.T., which recapitulates in microcosm the two years of treatment that preceded it. Perhaps, in an insight-oriented therapy like this, where there is a systematic uncovering of layers of defense and pain that constrict consciousness, we may see more clearly the underlying psychological and spiritual issues, their relative importance, and how the therapist's orientation (whether primarily psychological or spiritual) affects the direction and outcome of the therapy.

I'd like to clarify that my intention here is not to offer conclusive proof of any particular theory, but to examine impressions gleaned from my clinical observations, which hint at and help define a reality beyond mind—and to suggest possibilities for treatment beyond our usually accepted ones. Because I want to speak the language best suited for the mainstream and because the psychoanalytic model has been so influential in shaping modern psychology, I'll talk in the language and with the concepts of the psychoanalytic orientation. But I ask the reader to keep in mind the spiritual reality which encompasses all types of therapy and all aspects of life.

Because we will be focusing on her fears one might mistakenly think that A.T. is "troubled" more than most and that these fears are not operative in "normal" people. Quite the contrary. It's important to point out that the fears we will be looking at are not related just to A.T., but are universal and lie within all of us. As I tried to point out in Chapter 7, A.T. is actually a uniquely talented, creative, adventuresome and intelligent person. I chose to use this material *because* of her strengths—because she had the courage to reach under the surface, deep into an inner world which we all share, to places where many of us would be too frightened to tread—and had the capacity and talent to clearly describe what lies there. She represents an aspect of all of us—and the particular struggle she expresses between her intellect and her spirit clearly reflects the dynamics of the conflict that psychology has with spirituality.

FEARS OF SALVATION

A.T. returned hardy and tan from a river rafting trip with her husband. "Being in the wild, on the water six to eight hours a day, shooting rapids through untouched country, was sheer delight. We'd stop, build a fire, have a nice meal and feel at peace with the world," she exclaimed.

She liked to talk about the meaning and joy she found in the outdoors; closeness with it brought her a sense of great exhilaration. Granted, nature is an attractive subject, but I sensed that A.T. was using it in therapy to avoid exploring deeper inner experiences where she would have to encounter more painful issues.

I sensed her distancing and remained silent, allowing her to experience it more fully herself. With awareness would come the choice to remain there or to reach out and reveal more of herself.

"We stopped in San Francisco and stayed with friends, a husband/wife dancing team who had just returned from tour. Some months back, they'd started their tour in San Diego. Because of poor advance promotion, hardly anyone came; it flopped. They were depressed and very worried about money.

"Unexpectedly, I had just received $400 in the mail from an outstanding loan. It seemed to have dropped from the sky. I gave it to my friends. My husband was upset; he thought it was irresponsible, inappropriate generosity, but to me it was spontaneous good will.

"When we met them in San Francisco, they were elated from a successful tour. They had rave reviews wherever they went, especially about a dance they had choreographed themselves. And they were so appreciative of my gift that they had dedicated this dance to my husband and me—even noted it in their printed program. I'm not able to create a dance myself, so I was happy to have contributed in this way."

A.T. had been generous to her friends and was rightly appreciated. But at another level she was telling me how painful it was to be unaccepted when expressing deep, inner feelings, as had happened to her friends when their dancing wasn't appreciated, and how frightened she was of revealing more of herself lest I disapprove. She was expressing her desire for my approval, perhaps symbolically wishing us to be a successful dancing team. At this point in the interview, I again felt her defensive distancing, a sign of her blocking *herself* from her own deeper, inner experience of love as well. What was she frightened of revealing?

In intensive uncovering psychotherapy, the client is encouraged into a systematic investigation of avoided areas. When the therapist senses distancing, he suspects that the client is defending against fears and their underlying wishes and desires. The first clues to these connected fears and desires may be seen in the patient's free associations (the uncensored verbalizations of whatever spontaneously arises in the patient's mind) and dreams, which provide a clearer channel into the unconscious than does the waking state, and in his transference reactions (the projection of feelings, thoughts and wishes onto the analyst, who has come to represent an object from the patient's past).

If the therapist shows his understanding by correctly interpreting the situation and provides a safe atmosphere of acceptance, the client develops the faith and courage to reveal more of himself and face the underlying conflict. He is spurred on by the desire to rid himself of the emotional pain of fear, depression and/or anxiety arising from this conflict, as well as the desire for finding greater pleasure and gratification and more meaningful life experiences.

As past repressed childhood experiences are brought to awareness, the patient begins to relive the experience—regressing to that period of life when the conflict occurred. His reactions, feelings and defenses become characteristic of the earlier developmental stage. For instance, early in the treatment, A.T. showed evidence of a struggle that occurred during the Oedipal stage—that crucial stage of the child's psychosexual development in which developing sexual feelings lead to an increasing interest in sexual gratification with the parent of the opposite sex. Freud described the Oedipal complex as:

> the nuclear concept of the neurosis, that it represents the essential part in the content of the neurosis. It is the culminating point of infantile sexuality, which through its after effect decisively influences the sexuality of the adult.[1]

At one point, A.T. had revealed her developing sexual feelings for me by appearing for a session in a skimpy, seductive leotard and short-shorts. She had fantasies of attracting other men and of being sexually powerful. With awareness of this desire, came increased awareness of her childhood fear of possible rejection from her father or retaliation from her mother—and with this a better realization of why she had created her intellectual defense to keep these feelings hidden.

Her intellectual aggressiveness also served other purposes, allowing her to be like the father she admired—and at the same time, to win his attention, as he admired this quality in others. And her drive for competition and mastery was, in part, a way of expressing anger toward him for not fully gratifying her—as well as a defense against feeling an underlying sense of weakness and fear of retaliation from her mother, who would want to keep her husband for herself.

Freud postulated that little girls fear that they have been castrated because they lack a penis and, therefore, may feel inferior and weak and fear that continuing to pursue the father could lead to further mutilation. In the treatment, this fear of castration and mutilation was confirmed in A.T.'s dreams of tall buildings falling, a large threatening tiger escaping from a cage, someone's being decapitated and having a rotten, spoiled core—all signs of a degree of castration anxiety.

She defended against this fear and weakness by accentuating her strengths—even entering her male-dominated career where she could attract, compete with and challenge men. In this way, she could both gain the attention of the father as well as act out her anger toward him and defend against her fears of further castration and mutilation by being overly masterful and, figuratively speaking, castrating others.

As A.T. became more aware of the Oedipal determinants of her intellectual defenses, something new began to develop: reactions signaling an even earlier conflict characteristic of the anal stage of development. At this state, the child struggles with the parent for control, the child wanting complete freedom and the parent wanting the active youngster to contain himself so responses are socially acceptable—the central theme, of course, being toilet training.

One aspect of love at this level is the parent's understanding and awareness of the developmental task that the child faces. The parent must be sensitive and caring, yet capable of appropriate discipline and rule-setting. If the parent is too overpowering, manipulative and harsh, the child can feel shame and humiliation—with his spirit broken. Or if the parents fail to show the necessary discipline, also a part of caring and love, the child may feel out of control and unloved.

The child struggles—that's part of the natural growth process; but the struggling can be greatly complicated and accentuated if he must also deal with not being understood or loved. He may fight back by refusing to produce a bowel movement or in some other way not responding as parents would wish.

A.T.'s responses and behavior revealed a struggle with anal conflicts. For instance, at one point in the treatment she was quick to feel shame, embarrassment and humiliation—a loss of confidence which made her anticipate failure and criticism with even easy tasks. This is a constellation of feelings and responses characteristic of the anal stage of development. While taking a computer course, for example, she became so afraid of making a mistake that she wanted to drop out. This in a woman who is almost a straight-A student. She became hesistant to show anger, to express emotions of any kind, withholding as one would expect during toilet training. As she was tied up verbally, I encouraged her to express her anger physically by yelling or hitting a pillow. The suggestion just made her feel more foolish and ashamed, and she refused to try.

A.T. defended against these feelings by attempting to regain a sense of mastery and strength with more vigorous workouts at the gym, more frequent vacations to the mountains, by being late and even missing appointments and by falling silent and not producing material. And at this point, I could see the anal determinants of her intellectual defenses; her descriptions, explanations and verbalizations, devoid of emotional content, were used here to provide a sense of mastery, control and strength in the face of her vulnerability.

With growing awareness and acceptance of this constellation of feelings, desires, fears and defenses, and a lessening of her need to struggle with underlying conflict, A.T. began to experience the freeing-up of valued personality attributes such as energy, innocence, spontaneity, joy and love—and a clearer, more immediate grasp of reality.

As this level of reality became more available to consciousness and we could both see the anal determinants of her intellectual defenses, we began to see newer reactions, signaling even earlier conflict. Deeper still, she opened into an awareness of the early oral stage of childhood experience, when the helpless child is fully dependent on the parent. Rather than a sign of illness, opening to this level showed an inherent strength, a faith in her ability to bring into awareness the earliest, most helpless stage in her life. Here the child can feel frightened, confused, overwhelmed and utterly lost if parents are too distant, inconsistent, absent or show a lack of understanding and love at this time.

This level of oral pain is very difficult to face openly, and we began to see how A.T. used her mind to block it out, and to create the illusion of being safe and certain. Her mind became like a parent, creating a sense of protection and certainty—providing nurturing by using ideas as food, to thwart loneliness and helplessness and to attract attention, support and solace from others.

This state of suffering existed prior to her mind's intellectual development, and to return to it again, she had to have the courage to lay down mental defenses all together. A.T. had begun to recognize that her intellectual defenses, although useful in the past, were a poor response to her unfulfilled oral needs and was now willing to try to find the real answer—a solution that only the deepest kind of human warmth and love can provide. She was now willing to face the infant's awful feeling of separation from parents—and was humbled, confused and lost. This was the point to which we had come in this current session—a session in which the therapeutic work of two years was recapitulated as we moved from Oedipal, to anal and now oral defensive positions.

A.T.'s first awareness of her oral conflict came by way of recognizing how her intellectual defenses constricted consciousness. "You know, my dancer friends, even people on the trip, talk about another kind of reality that seems so foreign to me. When people talk like this I feel left out. One evening on the raft trip, I had a long conversation with a lady who told me how she reexperienced her birth and a new awareness of early memories after taking psychedelic drugs. She felt more open to life afterwards.

"I know that's not for me, but I wonder if it's really possible to have such a powerfully meaningful experience that can change attitudes about reality. Why don't I have these insights and experiences that bring deep meaning?

"My dancer friends and others speak of *chakras*, centers of energy that they feel in the body; it sounds like Greek to me. Yet some of this must be real; everyone can't be just imagining this— these are productive and creative people. Why can't I see it? Why am I stuck in this intellectual, rational way of being?"

She fell silent. Her body posture weakened; she no longer had the look of confidence in her eyes. During this interview, she had gone from her initial defended position when talking intellectually about her trip . . . to expressing Oedipal feelings and looking for my approval when recounting the story about her appreciative friends . . . to guarding herself against an anal feeling of loss of control . . . to an experience of oral deprivation in which she felt a deep sense of separateness from others: "What's wrong with me? Why can't I feel closeness and contact with you—why am I different from everyone else?"

Rather than intellectually talking herself out of this feeling, A.T. settled into it. I knew that if she allowed herself openness to this pain she would also open to the kind of human warmth and love that could resolve it. As long as she had to block awareness of this helplessness and separateness from an insufficiency of nurturing, she would also limit her ability to experience the full innocence and openness of the young child and her ability to receive the full power of nurturing love as well.

As I watched this reaction develop, I recognized a distinct change in the quality of her expression, signifying a different order of inner experience. It was an experience more fundamental than even her earliest oral experiences with her parents, or fears arising out of any conflicted interpersonal relationships. It seemed that she was now beginning to perceive a dimension of *real* existential separateness. I am referring to that fundamental vision of our *real* aloneness, our mortality, our intuition of mind and ego disintegration, of non-being and of meaninglessness without boundary.

This vision of *mortal* fear, as described in Chapter 3, is what is tapped by our most terrifying horror movies, in which we seem unable to make sense of reality and helplessly teeter on the edge of annihilation while lost in a vast, terrifying and incomprehensible mystery. Who can stand before this moment of authentic spiritual insight in calm and peace? It is understandable that we would want to hide from this terrifying vision, and that we attempt to escape from it into a dream fantasy. The American writer William Saroyan recognized how pervasive this hiding is when he said at the time of his death: "When I was young I never thought that I would die—and now that I'm dying, I don't know what to do."

For most, this insight that is both a vision of terror and a chance for transcendence comes only fleetingly and is sealed over quickly. It can come during any phase of any type of therapy, or at any time in life for that matter. Pain, the chief reminder of our limitations, seems to be the necessary catalyst, opening us and making us more available to both the *mortal* fear and the transcendental love which is its answer.

William James noted that the emotionally ill have authentic and positive mystical experiences more frequently than the "normal" population. And it may be that in the course of intensive uncovering psychotherapy, when defenses are weakened and one becomes more innocent and open, when we are more sensitive to our vulnerability, we are then also made more ready for a transcendent experience. We may not only have a clearer vision of *mortal* fear, but also of unconditional love, a sense of union with, and trust in, a transcendental loving omniscience. And as Ken Wilber writes,[2] it isn't repression that causes anxiety, but anxiety that causes repression. When the repression process is weakened one has a clearer vision of the *real* world, and it is then that *normal* existential anxiety is experienced.

This is what I believe happened in the case of the psychiatrist who was interviewed in Chapter 6, who in the course of his analysis had a profound spiritual experience of the selfless and unconditional love of Christ. To me this meant that he had become so open in the course of his therapy that he was able to identify a Christ-like love within himself, which he recognized had been the motivation for Christ's great sacrifice.

I believe that this is the innermost reality which we are all yearning to rediscover. But to do so we must risk looking more deeply into our life and facing the *mortal* fear of the possibility of mind-ego death. We must be willing to walk through the valley of death as A.T. was doing here. As terrifying as it seems, we must be able to tolerate this dark vision if some day we are able to see it for what it really is: a grand delusion.

Notes

1. S. Freud, *Three Contributions to the Theory of Sex*, 1930.

2. See Chapter 4, p. 30.

TELE NO. 30
BRINDAVAN
WHITEFIELD-560 067
TELE NO. 36
PRASANTHINILAYAM P.O.
ANANTAPUR DT 515134

Bhagawan Sri Sathya Sai Baba

30- 8- 75

After long searches here and there, in temples and in churches, in earthes and in heavens, at last you come back. Completing the circle from where you started, to your own soul and find that He, for whom you have been seeking all over the world, for whom you have been weeping and praying in Churches and temples, on whom you were looking as the mystery of all mysteries shrouded in the clouds in nearest of the near, is your own self. The reality of your life, body and soul. That is your own nature. Assert it, manifest it. It is Truth and Truth alone, that is one's real friend. relative. Abide by. Truth tread the path of righteousness and not an hair of your body will ever be injured.

Meditation is nothing else but rising above desires Renunciation is the power of battling against evil forces and holding the mind in check.

With Love and Blessings
Sri Sathya Sai Baba

A Therapeutic
Dilemma

CHAPTER NINE

"HOW ARE you feeling now?" I asked after a while.

Looking utterly defeated, A.T. replied, "I feel terrible, I feel like bursting, shouting and yelling. And then my mind tries to blank it out—it says not to think about it, to get away from it any way that I can, it's not good to feel this terrible. But what can I do? You tell me to be open to these feelings, that it's important not to hide from reality. I don't understand the purpose, but I don't seem to have any choice anyway—I couldn't get rid of it if I tried." Then she fell silent.

There comes a time in therapy when the mind stops and nothing comes—because there is nothing more to come. This silence is the empty stillness of defeat, different from the tense silence of resistance. Likened to the profound effect of a Zen Koan,[1] it is the stillness of a mind humbled by a vision beyond its comprehension, and which no amount of earthly relationship can resolve. What is needed is a transpersonal relationship: *a relationship with divinity*, which allows for releasing one's fear of nothingness into an ocean of infinite love, so that nothingness is transformed into love.[2]

I had a decision to make. We were at a crossroads. Here, I felt, was a central spiritual issue calling into question my profession's basic assumptions about therapy. If one believes exclusively in the philosophical implications of psychoanalytic theory—that duality is a fundamental characteristic of reality and that we are basically mind—then the goal in treatment is to develop a greater sense of a *separate* individual identity and a greater capacity for unconflicted gratification of basic animal drives and impulses.

This silence, then, is seen as resistance resulting from unconscious conflicts which interfere with the normal gratification of basic needs. The therapeutic approach is to uncover unconscious childhood fears and interpersonal conflicts by the process of free association and the analysis of dreams and transference, so that they may be relived within the safety of the treatment process. Finding no reason for continued fear, the patient becomes free to experience a wider range of activities and greater personal gratification.

This, of course, is only one way of conceptualizing the dynamics of psychopathology and treatment. One may, just as well, view continuing distress as a sign of a thinking-pattern problem to be treated by cognitive therapy aimed at developing a more positive outlook on life; or a biological problem—a clinical depression that should be treated with antidepressant medication—or even worse, a problem of ego and personality decompensation to be treated with antipsychotic medication. But no matter what point of view, these methods of treatment all have in common the belief that duality is fundamentally real, and thus leave out the possibility of spiritual transcendence.

On the other hand, if we accept a reality beyond duality and see Universal Consciousness as being more fundamental than separate mind—if we accept that we *can* merge with the infinite—then we can see the possibility of a higher-order spiritual *yearning* to transcend all limitations and boundaries and to merge *back* into the ocean of Universal Consciousness.

We can then accept that there may be a legitimate time in therapy when this yearning expresses itself. And the first sign may be the awakening of that *mortal* fear which reflects the mind's struggle with incomprehensible spiritual visions and which also heightens the yearning for transcendence. Attempts at finding an earthly solution only avoid the problem. This is a yearning of a higher order, beyond the gratification of drives and instincts, beyond the stage of interpersonal relationships or strong personal identity, beyond pleasure and pain, beyond the objective world of the senses, and beyond mind and duality itself. It can be stilled only by a transcendental experience of unity.

What is required to address this spiritual issue is a revolutionary new approach to psychology and mind in light of *spirit*: knowledge about the way to transcend duality, an appreciation of the dynamics of mergence, the process of transforming pain and nothingness into love through the cultivation of devotion.[2] Taught by all the major world religions, this path to transcendence is described briefly below.

But first let me comment on why I want to be specific here. There are many therapists who recognize that this information is vital and should be communicated in some way to their clients, yet don't know how. Not having a firm enough grasp of the material themselves, and not knowing how to communicate it within the context of therapy, they opt for not mentioning it at all. Therefore, I've tried to present the material as specifically, clearly and unequivocally as possible so that therapists have some source to which they may refer their patients, without having to take full responsibility for these ideas until they feel ready to do so. The material will no doubt have an impact on patients and form the basis of inquiry and discussion concerning its relationship to their specific problems, helping both them and their therapists enter this centrally important area more directly.

TRUTH

First we must have confidence in the truth: that the spiritual dimension exists; that Universal Consciousness exists; that man is capable of merging with divinity; that duality is transcended through love, that love is cultivated through morality, devotion and service. We must have faith that there is a dimension beyond mind and that its nature is boundless, unconditional love—love which is much more than just an emotion or feeling. The love we're talking about is the power that created the universe and keeps it in balance; the force that protects and sustains us; the process that inspires and enables us to reach out to the other with compassion, to give without desire for return; the path that allows us to break the bonds of self, merge with the other, and become one with the infinite ocean of love which is Universal Consciousness. This is the path to transcendence, with its own dynamics and mechanisms for unfolding.

FAITH

Faith in this love, faith in divinity, proves an awesome stumbling block for many scientists. So it is extremely fortunate if one has *direct experience* of this love, for like nothing else, it convinces and deepens one's faith in its reality. Sai Baba may have his greatest impact here, for I am convinced that he is the most compelling evidence of Universal Consciousness seen since the time of Christ. Sai Baba's Universal Consciousness, compassion and love are experienced so clearly, dramatically, convincingly and poignantly that he can awaken another's love instantly and turn one to a life of devotion.

DEVOTION

Once one recognizes the truth that duality can be transcended through devotion and love, then one realizes how important it is that knowledge about the devotional path be taught. Devotion is an essential element in the cultivation of selfless love. It awakens the deepest spiritual centers, allowing a much deeper vision into reality than the mind can afford (and I use this word in both its meanings). Through devotion the world is seen as a holy expression of divine grandeur: everything is perceived as God's will. This vision of God's omnipresence and of His manifestation as all of creation, brings with it the perception of unity in diversity, a deeper vision of the oneness of all creation.

There are definite and practical steps to take in the cultivation of devotion. Prepare a devotional area in your home and in your heart, and keep it sacred and clean. There, in reverence and respect, begin your devotional relationship with God—in whatever name and form with which you feel most familiar and comfortable—through the quiet and stillness of silent sitting. Rise and go to bed with His name on your lips, and repeat His name as often as you can during the day. Read the scriptures—of any religion—daily and look for their meaning in the fabric of your daily life. Seek the company of the pious and of serious spiritual aspirants, and spend time in study and worshipful devotion with them.

MORALITY AND RIGHT LIVING

Lead a just and moral life. Teach your children about the deeper meaning of life and the importance of morality and devotion. In praise and adoration, sing to God with your family and with a devotional group in your community. Spend time in service to others, giving charitably of your time and love. Take pilgrimages to holy places. Speak softly and sweetly, be kind and loving to everyone. Feed the poor. Prepare for your last moment, when you will leave this world and stand before God—ready to show that you knew the deeper purpose and meaning of the precious existence given to you and that you used your time well.

Devotion brings the strength and inspiration to carry out the necessary spiritual work that leads to salvation. This spiritual work consists of a new appreciation and more intense practice of morality and the leading of a just life—in a way not yet comprehended by Western psychology.

The true practice of morality means constant awareness of what is important and what is not and requires the courage and discrimination to renounce the temporary and trivial in favor of the eternal and everlasting. It is a struggle between self-gratification and self-sacrifice, between selfishness and selflessness. It is in the heat of this struggle that pain, fear, desire, ego and duality are transcended: self-gratification and bondage to the pleasure/pain principle are renounced in favor of establishing righteousness and selflessness. Hence morality and its expression in selfless service purifies character, expands love and is the path to transcending duality.

Sai Baba says that morality and right living are the expression of love in action:

> *Love is central. Love in thought is truth—that which is always the same and beyond beginning and end. Love in feeling is peace, bliss—being unaffected by the sorrows or joys, the ups or downs in life. Love in understanding is non-violence and respect and reverence for all creation. Love in action is morality and right living—the giving of selfless service to all in need without desire for reward.*

When this love takes the form of selfless service, and selfishness is sacrificed for the good of others, love expands and becomes one with everything. *"The way to immortality,"* says Sai Baba, *"is by eliminating immorality."*

PEACE AND EQUANIMITY

In order for the subtle spiritual qualities of peace, expansion, light and love to be experienced, the mind must be stilled from the agitations of the outer world. While spiritual energy is purified and intensified by moral practices, body postures and breath control exercises help align the energies which sustain us and prepare the inner dimension for higher spiritual visions.[3]

The focus of attention must be brought inward, away from the coarse agitating energies of the outer world and into the vast, peaceful and subtler spiritual realm where one can glimpse a personal vision of the miracle of existence. If consciousness is allowed to dwell in contemplation here, a new sense of equanimity and oneness intensifies the yearning for mergence with the divine. The inner experience of divinity allows for a vision of holiness in the outer world as well. As this process deepens, the yearning becomes so intense that one finally bursts beyond all limitations. The small "individual" self merges in supreme triumph and transcendence into the oneness of divinity.

THERAPY

These dynamics are timeless and universal. They are the fundamental truths that form the basis of all the world religions. And I believe they must become the fundamental truths of psychology as well. Techniques and practices for teaching them—such as described in Appendices III and IV—must be developed in a way that is at least as effective as those which address mental psychological growth.

The process of spiritual growth must lose its undeserved stigma of being a sterile, constricting, sermonizing, even punitive "lesson," as if in a dry, lifeless Sunday school classroom. We must come to understand that the process of spiritual evolution by means of devotion, detachment, renunciation, compassion, selfless service, meditation, prayer and morality is every bit as intriguing and exciting—every bit as innovative, creative, challenging and sophisticated—as the process of psychological growth, through such techniques as free association, verbalization, guided imagery, relaxation techniques, desensitization, emoting, catharsis and dream analysis, etc.[2] Spiritual growth requires training and discipline on every level of human experience, including the physical, emotional and mental.

SELF-CONFIDENCE

How is this brought alive in therapy? First the therapist must have confidence that the spiritual dimension is *real*, and he must be committed to this reality in his own life. First, says Sai Baba, is self-confidence, the confidence that there is a higher self—that divinity exists and is a real living presence which must be appreciated every moment of the day. Then comes self-satisfaction—the satisfaction and confirmation that come from actually experiencing the higher life through the spiritual process outlined above. Then when confidence is acquired and strength attained through spiritual practice, the therapist is ready for self-sacrifice through the deeper and more intense practice of morality and the renunciation of the false and trivial. And then the final triumph—self-realization: the direct experience of divinity, of oneness.

EDUCATION

With confidence in the higher self, and a deeper appreciation of morality, comes the courage to challenge ignorance whenever it arises in therapy. The first responsibility of the therapist is one of educator. This is not new; in the early stages of therapy all clients must be educated to the process, whether it be in free association, relaxation or behavior modification techniques. Education in the rules and dynamics of the spiritual dimension is a constant, continuing undertaking, because it is unnatural to be constantly aware of the unitive state. We are so drawn by the powerful forces of the mind—to the senses, desires, pleasures, pains, wishes, fears and ego needs—that we believe duality is real. This misconception, in whatever form it takes, must be challenged in all facets of the therapy, in methods integrated with the psychological techniques used to teach mental truths.

Yes, repressed sexuality and aggression must be uncovered and experienced, to the point where one has the choice to express them or not. And at the same time, while the psychological work is proceeding, through the time-tested approaches of psychotherapy, time tested spiritual approaches such as morality, meditation, devotion, service, and the eventual goal of renunciation (experiencing emotions and thoughts while remaining fundamentally unaffected by them) must be taught. It is not a matter of one or the other, it is a matter of both disciplines having their time and place.

What is needed, then, is integration—insightful, sensitive and appropriate integration of psychological and spiritual approaches to an individual's health, well-being, personal fulfillment and growth—and always, *always* remembering the fundamental reality beyond duality. In so many subtle ways a vision of the more profound truths underlying our contemporary view of "reality" must be developed in those seeking treatment, even while mental and emotional fears are being addressed. Beyond the false is truth; beyond doubting, faith; beyond darkness, light; beyond death, immortality.

Beyond gratification is renunciation; beyond the physical, the transcendental. Beyond jogging are *yoga* postures; beyond crying is breath control; beyond catharsis is calm; beyond the outer world, the inner. Beyond free association is meditation; beyond desire, devotion; beyond defiance, respect; beyond anger, bliss; beyond violence, peace.

Beyond chaos is morality; beyond agitation is stillness; beyond verbalization, silence; beyond tears, equanimity. Beyond memory is mergence; beyond mind is spirit; beyond selfishness, selflessness; beyond bondage, liberation; beyond hatred, love.

"GOOD-JUDGMENTAL"

The therapist himself must appreciate and *practice* morality at a new level of understanding. Beyond education by word, he must set an example by deed. His life must reflect a unity in thought, word and deed, or the words become empty and useless. With his consciousness firmly centered in the higher life, his devotion, equanimity and love must be reflected in a just and moral character.

His character and morality are vitally important. Unlike what is now commonly accepted in psychoanalysis, his central attitude must not be *non*-judgmental, but *good*-judgmental (discerning). I see one of the major goals of treatment as the development of good judgment concerning one's responsibility for morality. Presented in a non-demanding, completely open, accepting and compassionate way, the development of good moral judgment must be at the very core of therapy.

PAIN AND SUFFERING

Also needed is an entirely new approach to pain and suffering, the chief experiences which bind us to duality. Through the strength gained by the practice of morality, devotion and detachment, the first step is to be *open* to pain and suffering and not to run from them. Sai Baba tells us that suffering should be welcomed as a valued teacher, as it humbles us, shakes us from attachment to the outer world, and quickens our yearning for transcendence. Pain and suffering represent attachment to the emotional body, to duality, and the only way to escape it, to become unaffected by it, is through renunciation and detachment.

RENUNCIATION AND DETACHMENT

Renunciation means resisting being affected by the outer world of duality by restraining consciousness from flowing to it through the senses, desires and ego (see Appendix IV, the challenge of *chakra* 5). It is not a negation of all creation, only a resisting of the influence of the senses, desires and ego on consciousness. Through this process the outer world ceases to be seen as comprised of separate and distinct entities, but rather as one glorious and indivisible whole—the embodiment of God.

Detachment is quite a bit different from repression or denial. It is not a defense mechanism, which hides feelings and fears from conscious awareness. It is the process of being open to feelings and fears, yet relating to them in a new way—surrendering them to God through devotion, in a way that renders one unaffected by them.[2]

By saying "yes" to pain as we do to pleasure, by not desiring one over the other, by being unaffected by pleasure or pain and unattached to the fruits of our labor, by offering it instead to God in an act of faith and devotion, we pull ourselves from the mind-ego complex—and from duality.

I'm not recommending the courtship of suffering, or even rushing into the process of detachment from ego, desire and pain. Nor am I advocating that retreat from the world that is justly criticized as "quietism." The process of detachment is slow and requires patience and persistence. It's like shaving: press too hard and you'll be cut, too lightly and nothing happens. It is vitally important to know the amount of "tension" that's right for each of us.

The mystery of man's existence is that he must live simultaneously in two realms—in body-mind and in the spirit. Like Sai Baba, we too must transmute sky into earth (by bringing spiritual reality into manifestation on earth) and earth into sky (by transmuting the outer world and mind into spirituality). We must try to be happy, to fulfill our needs and desires—which is part of the nature of our life on earth—yet simultaneously we must work to transcend them.

LIVING ON TWO LEVELS

This living on two levels is a complicated process in life and in therapy. How does the therapist deal with both earthly fears and desires related to interpersonal relationships and, at the same time, to *mortal* fear if it arises simultaneously. Both issues require attention, perhaps using different approaches and techniques. The problem may, in fact, be beyond the mind's comprehension and is answerable only to the higher consciousness afforded by meditation and devotion.

MEDITATION

Here is where the therapist as well as the patient can benefit from spiritual knowledge. Instead of relying on a dualistic approach such as psychoanalytic free assocation, with its valuing of fantasies and emotions, both therapist and patient can benefit from the process of devotional meditation leading to union. Through any number of meditation techniques—such as observing the breath or visualizing light—the mind is quieted.

Detaching from all personal desires and needs, as well as thoughts, feelings, distractions and biases—becoming an unaffected witness, open to all possibilities—brings a marvelous freedom in which intuition, creativity and real caring and love flourish. In this inner stillness, mind is directed by the will of the observer to rest on an aspect of the divine. In this way, one may experience God's omnipresent, infinite love and, eventually, the merging of the witness and the witnessed— the "I" and the "that." Jesus referred to this as "the peace that passeth all understanding."

Nurtured in this way, consciousness reaches out and merges more deeply with the other, affording expanded knowledge of the other. This kind of listening and being, for both therapist and patient, allows for detaching from and mastery over the mind, and the use of it as a tool rather than the other way around: being enslaved by mind's emotions. It allows for the deepest kind of true insight—an insight which clearly intuits which issue, earthly or spiritual, must be dealt with first, and how. And it brings deep and abiding peace.

A DECISION TO MAKE

Now we're ready to return to my patient, A.T. I had a decision to make: was she facing a psychological or a spiritual problem? Was I to concern myself with helping A.T. protect her psyche by finding a defense against her stark vision of finiteness? Or was she strong enough now to be left alone, face to face with it, to accept it and to open to the divine more deeply through it?

I decided that she was facing a legitimate spiritual experience and that her psyche was strong enough to accept this vision and its possible invitation to transcendence. We had been here before—through her mental fears and desires, through our discussions about spirituality and my suggestions of techniques and approaches for her to follow. We had gone over the ways to prepare consciousness for its expansion into the spiritual dimension.

In order to take the next step, she would have to make a decision herself. Was she willing to face her own *mortal* fear and relinquish her mind for a possible transcendental solution? Was she ready to leave the security of her old attachments to mind for the possibility of an instantaneous flash of insight into the real nature of existence? Was she ready to take more seriously to the spiritual path?

> *You must have not only freedom from fear, but freedom from hope and expectation. Trust in my wisdom; I do not make mistakes. Love my uncertainty! For it is not a mistake. It is my intent and will. Remember, nothing happens without my will. Be still. Do not want to understand; do not ask to understand. Relinquish understanding. Relinquish the imperative that demands understanding.*
>
> *Meditate upon the feeling between waking and sleeping, knowing how immediate, how close, how deeply compatible it is. There is the feeling of really giving up: the body is limp. Awareness too is limp. Let the feeling of God overcome you like sleep.*
>
> (Sathya Sai Baba)

For one so centered in mind, this would be an awesome step. Harder than surrendering to the technique of free association, more difficult than revealing the secrets and fears of mental life, is the surrender to the experience of *mortal* fear, and the decision to seriously adopt the spiritual life for lasting peace. I could see A.T.'s mind being shaken by turmoil, as in her dream. She was being coaxed into awareness of the devotion that lay dormant, literally up her sleeve as in her dream. But first she had to take a frightening step. Was she ready now to make this contact with her innermost love? I waited, knowing that a solution at this depth of inquiry doesn't come easily.

Notes

1. Zen Koan—A paradox used in Zen Buddhism as an instrument of meditation in training monks to despair of an ultimate dependence upon reason and to force them into sudden, intuitive enlightenment.

2. The surrendering process has its own dynamics by which deeper levels of conflict and ignorance are opened and released. See Appendices III and IV regarding the organization and dynamics of *Prana* and *Kundalini* energy and Patanjali's *Eight-fold Path*. Central to the process is developing a relationship with God, whose compassion accepts all suffering.

3. See Patanjali's *Eight-fold Path*, Appendix III, pp. 292-293.

Confirmation

CHAPTER TEN

A FEW months later, in March, 1982, A.T. stopped therapy. She didn't like feeling vulnerable, especially since she was so successful in life in general. Besides, she was now six months pregnant with her first child and wanted to prepare herself for childbirth without having to struggle with therapy.

Eleven months later she returned to therapy, happy with the birth of a lovely son, but having trouble deciding how to split her time between career and child. As before, we met for one 45-minute session weekly. The psychological and spiritual themes described in Chapter 8 reappeared. Then, during a session in June, an unusual reaction occurred.

In preceeding chapters I have presented ideas about a *mortal* fear which I think profoundly affects everything we do in and out of therapy. Some people may question the validity of such a fear, hidden from consciousness yet profoundly constricting awareness and hiding us from spiritual reality. The following reaction seems to me to bring this fear into vivid focus and to be strong confirmation of its existence.

A.T. related a dream in which she was at the controls of a plane when all of sudden it turned and dove out of control. Helpless and panic-stricken, she was unable to stabilize it. As she had been dealing with spiritual themes in the treatment, at one level the dream suggested her *mortal* fear of non-being of ego, if her consciousness soared to a height beyond mind.

As I listened, I had the impulse to relate a Sai Baba miracle that had occurred recently, thinking that it might serve to deepen her appreciation of, and faith in, higher dimensions of consciousness and even, perhaps, calm her fear of exploring these dimensions. But after I had related the story, to my surprise she reacted not with calm and confidence, or even intellectual curiosity—but with stark panic. I didn't expect to see this fear in such vivid relief. Quickly preparing my recorder, I captured her initial startling reaction. Below is a brief section of this reaction and, following it, a transcript of the session one week later, when she was able to discuss the incident under better control and with more insight. The transcript is slightly edited for clarity.

One thing more: the specific miracle I related is, I feel, not important. I had told her of many others before without this kind of response. And when she mentioned it to her husband, he had no different response than when hearing of other Sai Baba miracles. Both she and her husband recognized that the difference lay with her. For some reason, A.T. was ready to hear in a new way, apparently having gone through some subtle change in consciousness which prepared her for this reaction.

THE REACTION

Seeing A.T. speechless and frightened, I asked:

S: What are you afraid of?

A: I don't *know* what I'm afraid of! I feel jumbled. It's like my mind's gone on tilt. Nothing computes.

S: Was your mind jarred?

A: Yes.

S: Can you describe what happened to your thinking?

A: I felt suspended—I was just sitting there. I wasn't moving. My mouth wasn't open. I wasn't blinking—it was like I had been arrested at some point. And I couldn't move forward or backward—or anything. It was like everything stopped. Have you read the books by

Carlos Castenada, the Don Juan books where he talks about stopping the world? I felt as though the world had stopped . . .

S: Did your mind stop?

A: I was astounded. All these figures of speech that people use—"stopped dead in my tracks"—that's what I was. It stopped me dead in my tracks. I was rooted to the floor (pause) but it wasn't as if my mind stopped. It was like it was racing so fast that you can't see it—like a propeller going around—so fast that it may as well not be there.

ONE WEEK LATER

S: Do you remember much about the reaction that you had last time?

A: I was in a state of panic—or terror. I've been thinking about it, and I can't really describe it. I don't experience panic very often, an occasional test panic or something like that—"Oh, my God, I'm not going to do well." But I don't think I've ever experienced anything you would really call terror before—I mean, fear for my life or that something really terrible was going to happen. But the reaction last week was something else. It was just a mental tilt. It was more the feeling of being in the grip of something that I didn't understand, and I experienced that with fear. I experienced it as terror or panic or something like that.

I can't think back and say what it was that I thought was going to happen to me, it isn't as though if I do "x" I will die or I'll be destroyed or something like that; it was much less specific than that. But I think what freaked me out so much was that it was so physical and it was so real and it wasn't something I had made up or was trying on for effect. I went through all of these things in my mind during the week. What was I trying to prove? Was I trying to make an impression on someone? Was, you know, was I trying to make an impression on you? Was I trying to be obedient for you for some reason or another. But no, I don't think it was any of that. It was very real, very gripping, and it was very, very sudden. I had come in here at the beginning of the session and was blabbering on about this, that and the other thing and I wasn't prepared for what happened.

S: Did you experience it as a fear like a fear of some kind of bodily harm—did you feel you were in danger?

A: Yes, but, again, I couldn't have said in danger of what.

What was threatening me? I have this mental image of something that happened a couple of years ago when my sister graduated from her Ph.D. program. My father, sister and I took a trip up to Yosemite. We backpacked down Yosemite Creek from the whatever road it is, and then we hiked down the next day to the very top of Yosemite Falls. Have you ever been there?

S: No.

A: I mean it's incredible. You've been to Yosemite Valley perhaps?

S: No, never.

A: That's too bad. It's enormous. I'd only been in the valley before and you look up at the falls and you look up at Half Dome and you look up at all of these mountains all around you. Well, here we were looking down on everything—and this falls, this river, just comes shooting out of this gorge and goes leaping out into space. At the time I had eaten mushrooms. My sister had brought along some mushrooms, and so she and I were kind of quietly hallucinating. You don't really hallucinate on mushrooms, but it was definitely a psychedelic drug.

And I had wedged myself into this little crack on the face of this wall where I felt that I was safe, that I couldn't roll off—so that while I was going though this half hour of very intense drug experience nothing would happen to me. There I was, looking at this water just leaping out into space. And there were swallows, these little cliff swallows. They skim along the ground and kind of go darting out over the cliff to chase the insects that I guess are brought up on the updraft. I don't know too much about their feeding habits but they do chase insects and they would just go swooping down over my head in front of my face and out into this abyss. I mean there are two big miles of air out there in front of you, it's awesome—and that's a little bit the way I felt.

I was sort of looking out over something that was plummeting out into nothingness, into space, and it was terrifying—it was anticipatory, it was riveting. I mean I sat there for half an hour and didn't move. I probably barely even blinked, just contemplating this space in front of me.

I wasn't seeing it as a panorama, like people take pictures and they say, "Oh, how beautiful!"—you know, all of this scenery. It wasn't scenery, it was space, and that's the closest I can get to it. I don't know if I've described it very well, but it was terrifying. For if I had rolled off, I would've been killed instantly on impact. If anything would have happened to one of these swallows in the air, it would've plummeted 3,000 feet to the valley floor.

S: That's the kind of danger you felt last week?

A: A little bit. But it wasn't that something was really going to happen to me. I wasn't really afraid of falling. It was more being confronted with the enormity of something in front of me, that had I been there—in the space—I would not have survived. Do you know what I mean? It wasn't so much that I was in danger of being forced out there, but for the first time I really saw it.

S: You think for the first time in your life you really saw that enormity last week?

A: Yes. The first time that I can remember. I don't ever remember having felt that way. The drug experience is different. It's fleeting, you know, your mind races when you eat these kinds of mushrooms or else it just sort of stands still and you can sort of stare at something for a long time and not really be aware of what you're seeing. But I've never really freaked out on drugs. I've never panicked on them or anything. I just sort of have experiences that seem sometimes marginally profound.

S: Do you take drugs a lot?

A: No, I don't think so.

S: How often did you take hallucinogens?

A: Oh, I haven't taken them in years, since I got pregnant certainly. When was the last time I ate mushrooms? I don't even remember, it was awhile ago, it was two or three years ago.

S: Do you miss it?

A: Well, you know, I sort of do but I've got a bunch of them in the freezer and I haven't eaten them. It's like you need the right time, and I certainly wouldn't want to do it when I had my child around. I wouldn't want to be responsible for anything.

S: Do you think the reaction that you had was similar to a drug experience?

A: Well, yes and no. When you're on drugs, at least when I'm on drugs, I always know I'm on drugs. I've never lost it so much that I really thought that I was somewhere else. I guess maybe some people get deeply enough into a drug experience that they really forget that it is a drug experience. That's never happened to me. I've always been aware at some level that whatever was going on was because of this thing that I had eaten or smoked or whatever. This was different because I wasn't on any drugs and something very profound and very emotional happened to me and there was only me. There was only me, and if there was something else from outside, some kind of spiritual force, whatever, it isn't anything I know about. It sort of snuck up on me, I didn't take it willingly. I didn't take it deliberately the way I do on drugs. So in that sense it was very different.

S: Did you also consider that the drug experience is not real, is something false and manufactured by the drug itself?

A: I think it is real—just different real. I remember one time when I was in the desert in Utah and sitting and staring at this wonderful red sandstone cliff that has these patterings on it from the way the chemicals weather on it. The whole cliff was moving, it undulated and it moved up and down and the whole world seemed to be alive. At some level it made me feel oneness with the universe— that yes, everything is alive and I am part of this. The rocks, although they don't appear to move to me, are part of a living, breathing, organic world, and I think at some philosophical and some real level that it is true. It's not part of my everyday reality. I don't treat the rocks as though they are alive, but I think that drug experiences can open you up to what are probably fairly profound truths. But they don't really last.

S: What's the difference between that and what was happening to you? Was there much of a difference in terms of the quality of the experience or the sense of its being real and lasting?

A: Well, I don't know. I haven't thought about that very much. I mean, I had been talking with Jim (a fellow researcher) about how you can learn a lot from drugs and that they are selective disinhibitors, that they sort of turn on parts of your mind that are usually left off, and allow parts of your mind to shut down that maybe screen you from other experiences. To that extent the drug experience is real, and I don't think the drug puts anything in your mind that wasn't there already. It just—you see it differently.

S: But the sense of realness—is there a difference in this sense of realness in the drug experience compared to the feeling you had—was there a different quality to it? Or doesn't that seem important? I'm asking because Sai Baba says that the drug experience looks authentic but isn't—it's like plastic grapes.

A: I don't know. The difference in quality was that I couldn't place the blame for it anywhere. It's like having a dream. I have my dreams and sometimes I really wish I could blame somebody else for my dreams. It was something I ate, or (laughter)—I didn't really dream that dream, it was somebody else, it wasn't really me. But you can't turn around and say the drug put it there or somebody suggested it to me and therefore it came.

S: Did you have a dream this last week?

A: I had a couple of dreams but nothing that sticks with me except a dream last night in which I had sort of laboriously pushed myself up a hill on a skateboard or some such flat device and came to a stream. And the way that it seemed to be—isn't this funny, this is the same image of the waterfall that I just told you about. It was a waterfall, which fell some fairly large distance down and the water was moving very rapidly and I just sort of shoved myself into the stream and plummeted over the waterfall. I don't remember landing at the bottom, but the dream continued. I sort of climbed out of the stream and went to wherever it was I was going.

S: Do you remember the latter part of the dream?

A: Not really, except that I think that the people who were there were my women's group whom I'm going to be meeting with tonight.

S: Had you thought about this image of Yosemite, the example you told me earlier, between last time and now, or did you—

A: It just came to me right now.

S: What might these symbols mean about you? Do you have any idea?

A: Well, that there is something about me that's rushing headlong to an abyss and it's just going to plunge over it and presumably I'd survived. I mean I always felt this wonderful, not identification exactly, but you know—these swallows. If I were going to be a different creature in this world I should think I would want to be one of those swallows. This ability to just soar out—but they don't soar; they swoop, they dive, they're quick, active little creatures and they're just utterly in command of all of this space, because they don't fall out of the air.

S: What of the possibility of moving like this water and shooting off into space and then all of a sudden—boom! becoming the space, just becoming infinite. Would that frighten you? Or does that even have any meaning to you?

A: No, it doesn't, it's an abstraction. I don't feel anything when you say that, except sort of memories of having had dreams about flying or something.

S: So you just think that once you're up into the space without anything to hold to, you would plummet down?

A: Yes. I guess. In the dream, when I went over the waterfall nothing happened to me.

S: Do you remember falling?

A: Yes. I remember kind of going to the edge of this thing. I think there was a log jam there or something, and I was riding on a log. I remember thinking, "My God, I'm going to go over this water-fall—it's a long way down." But then there wasn't anything I could do about it. I mean, not going over the waterfall was out of the question. There was nothing to grab onto. The river was going much faster than I could possibly hope to swim and buck the current so I just let it take me over the waterfall, and I said, "Well, here I am."

And in the dream—it was one of those dreams where I am aware that I'm in a dream. I've done this a couple of times: I sort of say to myself, "Well, it's only a dream, I can go over this waterfall because it's only a dream." I mentioned that to myself and then went over the waterfall, and that was that. Like I gave myself sort of an out from my panic. See, I kept trying to give myself outs like that all during this last week. What happened to me in here? Was it only "a this," was it only "a that," was it only a something or another thing, and I haven't figured out what it was, only . . .

S: Well, what were some of these "only's?"

A: I mentioned them before: Was I acting? Had I conjured it up myself?

S: To please me?

A: Yes, maybe. I guess mostly to please you. Or to be dramatic—to make an impression.

S: But it continued even after you left here. Jim saw it.

A: Oh, yes. I drove up to my field site and he was down at the other end of the site looking at something. So I sat down on the ground and started to set up the tape recorder and I couldn't remember what I had to do. It's like I couldn't focus on the recorder and remember which buttons to push and how to put the tape in and how to go through the motions of starting the program running. So I just put it down and sat there. I kind of put my head in my hands and just tried to collect myself so that I could continue.

And at that point Jim came up and I looked up at him. He took one look at my face and said, "You're furious," —because I had been mad at him a few days earlier. And I said, "No, Jim, I'm not furious." He sort of tried a few more things: "You're this, you're that," —and finally I said, "Well, you know what we were talking about yesterday about having these experiences that kind of shake your world? Well, I just had one."

And he fished on that one for awhile, I guess giving me the chance to talk about it if I wanted to. "Well, did you feel this, did you feel that?" I said, "No, it's none of those things." I told him that I didn't want to tell him about it because I was afraid of appearing ridiculous. I mean it sounds ridiculous to somebody who doesn't know anything about this. I couldn't bring myself to tell him.

He said, "Well, you can appear as ridiculous as you want to me, I'll like you just the same." And I said, "I appreciate that but I really couldn't talk about it now." So I didn't, and we continued to work. I asked him a little bit later in the day, "Jim, how did I look to you when I came in this morning? Did I look really freaked out?" He said, "You looked really freaked out, I've never seen you like that before."

S: What did it do to your mind? You say you couldn't concentrate or push the correct buttons on your tape recorder, that your mind went on tilt, that your thoughts speeded up, that there was a sense of not being able to grasp something. Are those some of the ways you felt?

A: Everything except the business of my thoughts speeding up—everything stopped. I felt as though I was sitting in this chair without moving a muscle, without blinking, without—I was riveted.

S: The idea of your mind standing still, what is that? The mind doesn't know where to go?

A: No, it didn't know where to go. It's like it had been given information, sort of like a computer program, I guess. You give a computer program information that it can't process and it usually gives you an error message and then it stops. They call it "bombing out." The program just bombs out. It's stopped and it will wait there indefinitely for further instructions. (laughter)

S: Well, did you feel spacey?

A: No. Space is infinite. I felt one-pointed—I felt the opposite of spacey, I felt totally contracted and focused. There was nothing else in the world at that point.

S: Was no thought going on, just being riveted to that moment?

A: For a while, yes; then I sort of realized what was happening to me. I said, "What am I doing, what am I feeling, what's happening to me?" But asking myself these question didn't stop it. When I told you that I didn't feel like I could get in my car and drive somewhere, I said to myself, "I can just snap out of this; I can just stop—I can just stop and be my usual self and walk out of this office."

But I couldn't. I didn't want to try. It was like I was afraid if I tried and failed, then I would really be freaked out. I've felt that way on very, very rare occasions and not for a long time—when I would get really, really depressed about something. And I would just sit in my chair and not move. I would think, "I should get up and do something." Then I would say, "What if I can't, what if I try to get up and I can't?" I'd be scared, so I'd just sit there until the mood passed.

S: And this thing you couldn't get out of—again I'm just trying to clarify it. Was it that your mind was stunned by that moment and that it stayed stunned? And even though you tried to divert yourself, thoughts didn't have much impact on that feeling of being stunned?

A: Yes, yes. Thoughts were there and I could sort of see myself thinking, "I have to go, I have to be in the field, I can't afford this indulgence right now; what must Sam think of me?"

S: What must I think of you?

A: Ah, I don't know. I mean you were probably as surprised as I was—maybe you saw it coming. I don't know, it was you who brought out the tape recorder.

S: Do you think I think any less of you or that I think any more of you?

A: Well, you seemed to be pretty pleased about it. I mean, what with whipping out a tape recorder and all that. What could be a more positive reinforcement for anybody—after three and a half years of therapy, something I said was worth putting down on tape. (laughter)

S: Did you think you'd please me with this reaction?

A: Well, I thought about that. That was one of the things I thought about this week.

S: Afterward.

A: Yes. But not beforehand.

S: Did you conjure it up?

A: I don't think that I did. I mean it's possible, I suppose, but that didn't feel like a real alternative.

S: You were stunned—were you also intrigued by it all?

A: I was very intrigued by it and went through the rest of the day with some kind of calm settling over me. It seemed a very beautiful day, and I wasn't worried about getting finished with the work and . . .

S: Well, how could you have both reactions, the fear—like going over the waterfall—and yet calm?

A: The only thing I could think was what we've talked about before—what I've always said I have no experience with—which is surrender. Once I had sort of understood that I hadn't created this thing for myself, that I hadn't done it for any purpose, I just surrendered to it. It just was, and it had picked me up and taken me. There was nothing I could do but just, in a way, surrender to it. The phrase that kept coming all day long and all week long is something the Quakers say: "What is it that you require of me?"

But it was more like, "What is it that is required of me?" I felt that I didn't have the answer to that question. And all of the thinking about it in the world wasn't going to give me the answer. Was it required of me that I go to your house for a Sai Baba meeting that evening? I couldn't bring myself to do it, partly because I would have had to cancel a date with my husband. I didn't feel up to explaining to him. I would have owed him an explanation and it would have been very uncomfortable—partly that kind of scared me.

I wasn't sure that seeing any more of it would have any impression on me, and I wanted to kind of leave myself with what had happened and not force it in one direction or another. I felt that what was required of me was to surrender, to have had this experience, to try to look at it, to try not to force it into any direction and to try and remain open to it. That's pretty hard for me because I'm not used to that kind of thing. But that was where the sense of calm came from:

"This has happened to me; I've got it, I can't fight it, there isn't any-thing I can do with it. Maybe I'm just going to have to live with it for awhile."

S: Anything like resigning yourself to going over the waterfall when you were on that log in the dream?

A: A little bit.

S: Did you think, "No more struggling," because you knew that struggling wasn't going to help—the water was too fast, so you were resigned to just riding it?

A: Yes.

S: And was there a calm that went along with that surrender in the dream?

A: I don't remember; it was too quick.

S: How long did it take you to get back to your regular thinking?

A: I guess after Jim came over to me and asked all these ques-tions. I sort of articulated a little bit what I thought had happened, and then we started doing the data collection. It's all very routine and requires concentration to make the right codes on the computer. It kind of wrenched me back.

S: Did you talk to Jim about your experience? Did you tell him what had happened?

A: No, I still haven't. There really wasn't time.

S: Did you tell your husband?

A: I talked to him about it, yes.

S: And what was his impression?

A: He was interested because it happened to me. It didn't make an enormous impression on him. I described all of this and he said, "Well, yes, it's interesting, but we've heard this kind of thing before." He said that what appears to be the difference between this time and the others is that I never before felt as though it had anything to do with me. And somehow this particular experience struck me more personally than the others. I said, "Yes, I guess that's it."

I've seen movies at your house where Sai Baba appears to be materializing ash from a big upturned urn, and somehow it never made an impression on me. My psychological or spiritual state at this point allowed me to think that it had something to do with me. My talking about it to my husband didn't have any affect on him, except that he was real interested that this had happened to me. It really seems to me as though it's less what actually happened than being in the right place at the right time. It was like a state of grace. You can't go around asking for faith or religious experiences or anything like that; it just descends upon you.

S: Do you consider that grace? Do you consider that that was a religious experience?

A: I don't know what it was.

S: Do you feel frightened by it now, or do you feel glad that it happened?

A: We-e-e-e-l-l-l-l (laughter) Glad? Um, I don't mind it so much. What I fear is that it will just sort of evaporate and . . .

S: Would you like it not to evaporate?

A: Yes. I feel that having gone through it, I'd like it to go somewhere. But I think that it's going to require some patience on my part and trying to keep it in my mind—to really try and be aware. I don't know how to do this, it's all kind of new to me.

S: Let's talk about this next time if you'd like. Right now time is up and we'll have to stop.

A: Okay.

UPDATE—JULY 26, 1984

Shortly after her profound experience of terror, A.T. had a remarkable dream. It represented to me a moving example of what Jung called the emerging central archetype (see Appendix II)—deepening spiritual awareness manifesting in the form of a special geometric figure, a mandala.

The Dream: Playing a captivating melody on the piano, A.T. suddenly recognized that she was not playing notes on a sheet of paper. Instead, settled gently on the stand in front of her was a lovely four-petalled flower. At one with the reality of this delicate flower, actually experiencing herself fully merged with its petals, she was able to transform its inner message into music.

Although *yogis* describe the heart *chakra* as having twelve petals (see Appendix III), the petals are divided into four quadrants, and so this *chakra* has been described by some clairvoyants as being a four-petalled lotus. Could this dream represent her conscious awareness awakening more deeply to the love in her heart? The theme was strikingly similar to that of the dream she'd had about Sai Baba earlier in therapy. The first seemed to promise exquisite love if she accepted spiritual reality. Could this present dream represent her having acquired an element of that love after facing her fear and now opening more to her spiritual self?

Soon after the dream, on July 26, 1984, A.T. stopped treatment. As she drew closer to terminating she dealt with the same themes — faith, trust, openness and surrender — but now on deeper mental and spiritual levels. More fully in touch with biological impulses and drives, at the same time she became more aware of the need to enter spiritual practices to gain deeper peace. She has continued to be successful in the outer world with work and family, as wife and mother, and has a wonderfully close and loving relationship with her son.

She now spends time daily, sitting quietly in contemplation and meditation. She is more willing to be vulnerable in sharing fears. She is seriously involved with church and community service projects and is more intense in her search for spiritual meaning and insight in dreams and daily life. She appreciates the importance of facing joy and sorrow, pleasure and pain with equanimity — with openness and courage — and with faith in the possibility of realizing a grand transcendental reality in this lifetime.

Death's
Lesson

CHAPTER ELEVEN

Although the mind is our most powerful tool for adaptation to the outer world, it may also be the source of our greatest obstacle to awareness of inner reality. It has almost infinite power to hide from awareness our most profound spiritual and mystical experiences. Why is it that more of us don't have a vision of cosmic unity, or cannot grasp the reality and awesome mystery of our imminent death until we are facing it? How many of us have a clear vision of our finite mortality in a cosmos whose bewildering dimensions defy measurement?

To find immortality, we must face the *mortal* fear of mind-ego death with openness and innocence. Out of fear we hide for the brief moment of our life—avoiding, resisting—until one day suffering and death come to shake us from slumber, brushing aside the mesmerizing delusions of insignificant mind with a passing shrug—to reveal the unfathomable. For what do we know of death? Only that it is, and that before its awesome reality, our soul trembles. To confront this great mystery directly and honestly is to be humbled, to be unmade, to be readied for the possibility of becoming fully open to all possibilities. Before it the entire "real" physical world dissolves, and we come face-to-face with either nothingness . . . or God.

In October, 1978, a month before my tenth trip to India, I received a phone call from Dr. K., a respected San Diego orthopedist. He had heard of my planned trip and asked to come along. I was surprised; most of my professional friends treated Sai Baba with skepticism and kept their distance.

Although not knowing him well socially, I respected Dr. K. professionally, and we occasionally referred patients to each other. He was a brilliant doctor, with great warmth and compassion. Just one year before, I had consulted with him when my wife Sharon developed a chest pain. We never found the cause of the pain (it was probably muscular in origin and due to a virus), but his thoroughness and warmth were comforting and greatly appreciated. I was delighted to hear of his interest and welcomed his company. He was not absolutely sure, however, and said he would get back to me in a week with his final decision.

Two weeks passed before his call. "Sam, I've really been thinking seriously about this trip. After a lot of struggle, I've decided not to go. You know, I am undergoing an analysis and my psychiatrist and I see my interest in this trip as a way of avoiding dealing directly with my depression. I think it's best to stay and face the problem. Perhaps I can join you some other time."

I wanted so much to say to him, "Why dismiss this yearning for God as neurotic, why consider belief in Him only a crutch or an opiate? Why take your depression so seriously, letting it deny the possibility of a genuine and uplifting spiritual experience? Where is your sense of adventure, your curiosity, your spunk, your imagination—your vision? Please don't discount your yearning for God—your intuitive grasp of the infinite: your dreams, your hopes, your aspirations. Please don't explain away these precious aspects of your humanity as avoidance behavior due to a depression."

But I didn't say any of this to Dr. K.; I wished him well and promised to share my experiences with him when I returned.

Two years later, I received a call from Dr. K.'s secretary. He was very ill; would I visit him? He had been thinking of Sai Baba and wondered if the *vibuthi* ash would help his illness.

I had heard some months before that Dr. K. was ill, supposedly from the recurrence of a slipped disk in his lower back. I understood he had severe back pain and had to take time out from his practice and stay flat in bed. "Is it anything more serious than this?" I asked the secretary.

"Sam, this is in confidence and not to be repeated, but Dr. K. has metastatic cancer and may be terminally ill. He has severe pain in his back and spine from the spreading cancer and can't get out of bed. He's depressed about the illness. He knows that traditional medicine can't give much hope and is willing to try anything that might offer some relief." I immediately called Dr. K. and arranged a visit.

Walking past the Volkswagen camper bus and boy's bicycle parked in the drive, I approached an open expanse of lawn shaded by tall stately trees. Dr. K.'s house was a spacious, modernistic structure of wood and glass. His young family was growing up in a fine part of sunny San Diego. But inside the house there was a solemn stillness; there was no laughter here, although I could hear the rustling of a child in a nearby room. In a moment, I was sitting next to my bed-ridden friend.

His familiar beard gone, his hair thinning and falling out from toxic chemotherapy, Dr. K. lay flat and still from pain. In his soft eyes, I could see sorrow and strain. A claustrophobic stillness enveloped the room.

"I'm mostly sad about having to leave my loved ones, and not being able to share love with patients and family anymore," he said with a voice now weak and shaking with sadness. "I never thought this would happen to me; I can't believe it. Why me—now, after so many years of study and work—just at the strongest point of my career? I could do so much to help people. I could give so much to my family." He paused, his gaze turning inward for a moment.

I was shocked by the suddenness myself. The last time I had seen Dr. K., he stood out as one of the most competent medical doctors in the city. In his mid-40's, he was the strength and pride of his family, a leader in his community. Now he lay weak and failing, feeling destroyed and humiliated at being a burden to his family, and in constant pain, terribly depressed and unable to care for himself.

"The doctors at the University haven't given me much hope," he whispered. "The primary cancer is from the lungs. What an irony;

I've always been so health conscious and I've never smoked. I see people who smoke packs of cigarettes a day with no trouble at all—why me? My white blood count has dropped; the chemotherapy has damaged my bone marrow, and the cancer is probably there too. I know I'm depressed, but I can't get myself out of it. I know I won't be alive much longer."

Silence fell again in the room. My eyes moved slowly across it, observing the beautiful teak furniture, plush carpeting, the style and elegance of fine furnishings, architecture and design. Large windows overlooked a wooden deck and spacious open yard filled with flowers and trees. But the scene lacked joy. A dark shroud covered what had once been a garden of Eden.

Dr. K. stirred. Eyes moist and with a strained smile, he continued: "You know, Sam, lying here in the quiet, hour after hour, I don't have much else to do but think—and read if I have the strength. The world looks very different from here. It's so hard to appreciate how the world looks from the death bed. When I was working, I dealt with death day in and day out, hour after hour. It was constantly before me, every minute a part of my work. But even though I dealt with it constantly, I never really saw it clearly. I never saw it the way I do now. It's so real now, so present. So close—so frightening."

Now face-to-face with the omnipresent death that can take any of us from this dream world forever, we stopped—mute. In this deafening silence, we stood open and vulnerable before the vast, awesome presence of a mystery beyond comprehension. Before this terrifying vision, all worldly realities dissolved. Only fear and stark questions remained. Where will I, myself, be going? Will I be no more; will I be lost in the void forever? What is this brief existence in consciousness? Is it a mistake, a meaningless chance occurrence? Where . . . *where* will I be going?

In this terrible trembling silence and in the midst of this open, suffering vulnerability, our souls met. "Sam, there are no answers left in this world. Do you think *vibuthi* would help?"

The
Trial

CHAPTER TWELVE

MAN TRIES to avoid suffering. But could there be a purpose to suffering, some role it plays in the unfolding of consciousness? It may be presumptuous to try to understand the deepest meaning of this profound human experience. Suffering can be so penetrating, so total and profound, that concepts and words which try to explain become empty and meaningless. Beyond thought, beyond understanding, suffering reaches beyond mind to the center of our being. And perhaps this may be the key. By thus humbling our mind, it destroys the presumptuousness of mankind's "wisdom," earned by avoidance of the unfathomable. It forces us to face our *mortal* fear and reveals a reality deeper than mind. And if we can find a power great enough to soothe that suffering—to bring strength and peace in the face of unendurable and incomprehensible pain— then we may have found our innermost reality.

The great Jewish story-teller and philosopher, Elie Wiesel, who was in both Auschwitz and Buchenwald German concentration camps during World War II, tells this story which occurred at Ausch-witz. Although the theme comes from Professor Wiesel, and the inci-dent and outcome actually happened, I'd like to emphasize and make clear that I am telling the story in my own words with imagined dialogue. I am sure that my rendition does not exactly reflect what happened and would not be the way Professor Wiesel would tell the story.

It was at a time when Jews were subjected to the most grotesque atrocities and underwent the terrible suffering so widely documented now. Herded like cattle, starved, beaten, tortured, left bare against harsh winter elements, and slaughtered—they tried to endure and survive. Who can explain the meaning of such an ordeal to the one who is suffering?

There seemed no end to the inhuman treatment, the bizarre and sadistic experiments and mutilations. Here was an unthinkable attempt to exterminate a whole race of people, and for what possible reason? In all, about six million people were slaughtered in this enor-mous eruption of evil and destruction. Elie Wiesel was one of many well-educated and sensitive Jews left helpless in these hell-hole camps, screaming out to God: "Where are you? Where are you? Put an end to this torture!"

Among the captives were some of the most brilliant minds in Europe. Distinguished scientists, scholars, artists and professionals in all fields experienced this carnage together. Together they cried out at the atrocities. But pray as they might, God didn't seem to be listen-ing. They screamed out in agony . . . into what seemed more and more likely to be nothing but an empty black void.

"Oh Lord, God in heaven," they cried out, "how can You do this to us? We are broken and dying in a grotesque chamber of horrors. We are humiliated, hunted down and slaughtered with no rhyme or reason. Each day brings anew a hopeless struggle without relief, filled with pain and agony and the terrifying degradation of seeing our-selves turn into subhuman animals: dominated by the need to sur-vive, filled with feelings of hatred, revenge and jealousy; even wishing that our own kin would fall so we might steal a piece of stale bread or shred of clothing from them.

"Is this the cruel plan you conceived for him who is made in Your image? For what reason, oh Lord, are we herded and bludgeoned like swine—to be penned tight and bleeding by barbed wire, frozen by cutting, icy winds with nothing for protection but a worn layer of cloth on our bare skin? Oh, our Protector, what have our innocent children done to deserve starvation and brutal beatings—to be maimed, crushed, split open and gassed—to be made a mockery and a plaything for the fury of the devil?

"Oh Lord, why must I see my baby, innocent and without guilt, picked up by the heels, swung and crushed into a headless bloody pulp? Why do you allow the young girls to be raped, and men beaten until all their bones are broken beyond healing? Why do you permit the severing of limbs, the puncturing of eyes, the grotesque experimentation with human flesh? Why don't you respond to the murders, the laughter and sadism of the torturers, the gruesome thud of thousands falling at once in the gas chambers?

"Why must I hear the screams of my mothers and fathers burning to death in open pits of fire, or buried alive before receiving even the mercy of a bullet between the eyes? All the time cursing, You, oh God, day in and day out. For what purpose this infernal exercise in hopelessness and suffering without end—and consciousness filled with constant condemnations of Your name?"

At last they decided to put God on trial, accusing Him of allowing unforgivable crimes and of neglecting His people in time of their most urgent and terrible need. "He must be tried as a criminal for the guilt of unimaginable and inexcusable cruelty!" they cried out. "And we must do it with the utmost deliberation and care, for those who live on will look back at this day. They must understand and take us seriously. We are intelligent, wise, good God-loving and God-fearing people and aware of exactly what we are doing. Yes, this must be carried out with diligent, patient care—deliberately, objectively and with as honest a search for justice as possible."

So they held court for three days and three nights. The wisest men in the Jewish community willingly took sides for the contest. There were those who considered God's inscrutability beyond man's comprehension, and who were willing to assume the atrocities to be, in some strange twisted way, an expression of His love.

And on the other side, the opposition: those who could only weep in pain and defiance. "No, no, no! No loving God, no God at all, could accept or allow such evil." Arguments were presented and explored—points seriously made and as diligently debated and refuted—to assure that every possible effort was made to plumb the most profound depths of this epic and unexplainable mystery.

"Are we guilty for some wrongdoing in this lifetime? Could this be a punishment for earlier transgressions, when Jews defied their covenant with the Lord? Are we suffering now for the sins of our forefathers? Are we Jews somehow being cleansed and purified—or perhaps even taking on the pain of others? And by our death will we be granted special grace to live with the Lord for ever and ever in heaven?"

And the other side: "No, no, no! Nothing can justify this cruelty, this unprecedented manifestation of evil."

"But who can understand God's ways? His ways are mysterious and immeasurable, His omniscience never to be questioned, His holiness so great we're not worthy even of saying His name aloud. Our role is only to bow before Him and accept all as His loving grace; that all creation and evolution are realized through His exquisite omniscience, in perfect order; and that His actions and ways are always pure, always ineffably right, always infinitely perfect."

But on the other side: "No, no, no! What God can take the prayers of the helpless, the tears of the pious and innocent and use them as a hangman's noose, a whip—to beat, strangle and snuff out life without mercy? No argument can justify an evil so dark, unforgiving, pervasive, repugnant, perverse and grotesque as this!"

"But our God and the God of our fathers has been merciful to us in the past. He has led our people through the valley of death before and in time of suffering has come to protect and bring peace. Somehow we must accept this newest experience with gratitude and love. We must *never* lose faith, for He has always been with us in time of need, even when we felt abandoned—and He must be with us now. He has brought us out of Egypt, He has strengthened and purified us through the ages, and even now He must be toughening us for another great mission in the future. Yes, His ways are beyond question, beyond our judgment—His mystery is impenetrable. Everything given us must be accepted as a holy gift from Him.

"The only response we rightfully have is: 'Yes, yes, yes! I accept all as your grace, no matter the depth of the mystery or the degree of the suffering and pain.' Test me, oh Lord—as deep and profound a test as you wish. Nothing will turn me from my love and praise, my adoration and supplication to You. You are the creator of all that is. Ours is not to judge or presume to understand even an iota of Your mystery; ours is to say with open hearts, in full acceptance: 'Yes, yes, yes!'"

But the other side remained adamant. "No, no, no—this perversion, this sadism, this holocaust is a blight on Your name. No amount of twisted reason can condone it. It is totally beyond acceptance and must be repulsed, refuted, refused, repelled, condemned. It must be defied with every ounce of strength that human decency can muster. This level of evil must be wiped off the face of creation no matter what the effort or consequences; it cannot, must not and will not be accepted. This reality is the devious and nightmarish imaginings of a mind gone mad; it must perish and be no more. God is guilty of being not just imperfect but merciless, cruel and unjust!"

For three days and three nights, charge, countercharge and defense were deliberated, point by point. Finally weary and spent, the jury convened. When the verdict was in, the judge rose to face a courtroom spilling over with grim-faced spectators hushed with expectation. Looking down solemnly over the gathering, he read: "After long deliberation and consideration the jury has found God . . . guilty as charged." They had actually found God guilty. So deep and impenetrable was their ghastly record of suffering, that this group of learned, wise and well-intentioned people could not accept it, no matter what the circumstances or explanation, no matter what possible hidden inner meaning or reality.

Guilty was the verdict and guilty it would remain. Now, worn from the deliberation, the group sat stunned, without direction. After a long silence the judge again rose to address the court.

"Now let us pray," he said.

Bhagavad Gita

CHAPTER THIRTEEN

W E TRY to hide from our mortality, but in vain. Suffering and death catch us one day or another to teach us their lesson. Though we struggle, minds and egos are finally humbled and reduced, until we stand vulnerable and trembling like innocent, open children. Only when shaken from our attachment to the outer world, do we finally cry out for the inner strength to transcend it. Thus, have the dynamics of rebirth been described in the scriptures of all the great world religions. Let's look to the most sacred of Hindu scriptures for a deeper appreciation of these dynamics.

The *Vedas* are believed by devout Hindus not only to have come directly from God but, because their message is difficult for mortal man to understand, to have been dramatized by Him later in real life, to make it more comprehensible. The *Bhagavad-Gita* (the Song of God), considered by many the gospel of India, supposedly chronicles this event. In it, *Krishna*, who has been called the Christ of India, and *Arjuna*—the apotheosis of purified man, ready for profound spiritual insight—are the personalities in an historical drama in which the teachings of the *Vedas* are brought to life.

Why is the first chapter of this epic poem called "*Arjuna's* Despondence"? Here is the setting: two large armies face each other across a large battlefield. On one side is an army led by the *Pandava* brothers symbolizing righteousness; on the other, a force of evil led by the tainted *Kaurava* family. The *Pandavas*, full of love, compassion and mercy, have been inexorably drawn into war by the selfish and provocative acts of the *Kauravas*. As the drama unfolds, *Krishna*, the embodiment of God, approaches the leaders of each side with a choice. "You may have the help either of the mighty army of my kinsmen, or of me alone—though I myself will not lift a weapon."

Both sides have already witnessed the marvel and majesty of *Krishna*, but the evil side not so clearly as the righteous. They immediately choose the full, battle-ready army. With a vision as clear and pure as their character, the *Pandavas* choose *Krishna*. *Krishna* will drive *Arjuna's* chariot.

As the armies stand facing each other, poised for combat, *Arjuna* speaks:

> Krishna the changeless,
> Halt my chariot
> There where the warriors,
> Bold for the battle,
> Face their foemen.
> Between the armies
> There let me see them,
> The men I must fight with,
> Gathered together
> Now at the bidding
> Of him their leader,
> Blind Dhritarashtra's
> Evil offspring:
> Such are my foes
> In the war that is coming.[1]

Arjuna has grown up with the *Kauravas*. After the death of his father King *Pandu*, his father's brother *Dhritarashtra*, who succeeded to the throne, educated him and his four brothers. King *Dhritarashtra* was the head of the *Kaurava* family, and in their ranks *Arjuna* now sees his blood relatives, friends, companions and teachers. As he views the scene from between the two armies, his spirits fall. He can see that thousands of his kinsmen will be killed and maimed. No matter how evil the foe, what can justify the gross carnage to families on both sides? No, *Arjuna* will have no part; he would rather die. Filled with profound sorrow, he cries out to *Krishna*:

> Krishna, Krishna,
> Now as I look on these my kinsmen
> Arrayed for battle,
> My limbs are weakened, my mouth is parching,
> My body trembles, my hair stands upright,
> My skin seems burning.
> The bow Gandiva slips from my hand,
> My brain is whirling round and round,
> I can stand no longer:
> Krishna, I see such omens of evil!
> What can we hope from this killing of kinsmen?
> What do I want with victory, empire,
> Or their enjoyment?
>
> O Govinda,
> How can I care for power or pleasure,
> My own life, even,
> When all these others,
> Teachers, fathers, grandfathers, uncles,
> Sons and brothers, husbands of sisters,
> Grandsons and cousins,
> For whose sake only I could enjoy them,
> Stand here ready to risk blood and wealth
> In war against us?
>
> Knower of all things,
> Though they should slay me how could I harm them?
> I cannot wish it:
> Never, never,
> Not though it won me the throne of the three worlds;
> How much the less for earthly lordship!
>
> Krishna,
> Hearing the prayers of all men,
> Tell me how can we hope to be happy

Slaying the sons of Dhritarashtra?
Evil they may be,
Worst of the wicked,
Yet if we kill them our sin is greater.
How could we dare spill the blood that unites us?
Where is joy in the killing of kinsmen?

Foul their hearts are with greed, and blinded:
They see no evil in breaking of blood-bonds,
See no sin in treason to comrades.
But we, clear-sighted,
Scanning the ruin of families scattered,
Should we not shun this crime,
O Krishna?

We know what fate falls on families broken:
The rites are forgotten,
Vice rots the remnant, defiling the women,
And from their corruption comes mixing of castes:
The curse of confusion degrades the victims
And damns the destroyers.
The rice and the water no longer are offered;
The ancestors also must fall dishonoured
From home in heaven.

Such is the crime of the killers of kinsmen:
The ancient, the sacred, is broken, forgotten.
Such is the doom of the lost, without caste-rites:
Darkness and doubting and hell for ever.

What is this crime I am planning, O Krishna?
Murder most hateful, murder of brothers!
Am I indeed so greedy for greatness?

Rather than this
Let the evil children of Dhritarashtra
Come with their weapons against me in battle:
I shall not struggle, I shall not strike them.
Now let them kill me, that will be better.[2]

This first chapter, "The Despondency of *Arjuna*," is the foundation of the *Bhagavad-Gita*.[3] His is a special kind of despondency: a
state of mind that we all must experience sooner or later as a result of
attachment to this outer world, which is frustrating by nature and

filled with injustice and suffering. This despondency makes us aware of our mistakes—it intensifies our yearning for an answer to the riddle of our mortal existence and for the ability to transcend. By humbling our minds and egos, this despondency—Kierkegaard's dread or despair, modern man's existential anxiety—readies us for our journey inward. It brings us from our mind to our heart—from selfishness to selflessness, from loneliness to love, from separation to union. *"The Gita which begins with despondency, ends with realization—despondency is the seed and realization the fruit."*[4]

What is the basis of our suffering?

> *Whoever the individual, however scholarly, he cannot escape delusion and so he is subjected to grief, which acts as a break upon activity. Arjuna, the great hero, capable of great renunciation and great wisdom, is deluded by the awful needs of war, and his grief handicaps his activity too. He confuses the body and the self; he starts identifying the two. He imposes on the real self (the atma[5]—ever untouched by the characteristics of the moving, changing world) the unreal and ephemeral nature of the world and takes this delusion to be as true. This is the tragedy not only of Arjuna alone but of all humanity![6]*
>
> (Sathya Sai Baba)

Can we transcend suffering—overcome the delusion that we are only the body, bound by time and space? The *Bhagavad-Gita* teaches a number of attitudes and approaches to this consummate human dilemma. The most basic are those extolled in all the major religions: those of faith and devotion leading to surrender to God's will, the dynamics of which we in the behavioral sciences are almost totally ignorant. Perhaps appearing simple and naive to the scientifically minded, *Krishna's* most profound declaration in the *Bhagavad-Gita* is also the essence of Christ's teachings.

> Fix thy thought on Me; be devoted to Me; worship Me; do homage to Me; thou shalt reach Me. The truth do I declare to thee; for thou art dear to Me. This is My teaching, My grace. This is the path to come to Me. Give up all lesser actions and duties; surrender to Me; do not grieve; I shall liberate you from the consequences of all your acts.[7]
>
> (Krishna)

Let us not get scared off by words like faith, devotion, worship and surrender. There is a mystery much deeper than meets the eye in these few simple lines. We must take the time to inquire more deeply into their inner meaning if we are to appreciate the relevance of this mystery to the behavioral sciences. The words may actually relate to a level of reality which many of us have mistakenly discounted as primitive or unreal.

In my experience, understanding the dynamics of devotion—the miraculously transforming relationship between man and God—leads to a deeper understanding of the dynamics of love, in a way which nothing in the field of psychology can equal. Yes, *Krishna's* declaration may at first appear simple; it seems so because we behavioral scientists haven't accepted the possibility of divine intervention effecting miraculous transformations of consciousness through the devotional process. Since it is beyond the mind's comprehension, the only way of understanding this transformation is through the direct personal experience of devotion and love itself. Devotion and love are the path . . . and the goal. This process leads to a whole new inner world of strength and peace and toward the transcendence of the material world and the realization of our own inner divinity. Modern mainstream psychology is largely unaware of this extremely subtle inner dimension, at best glimpsed fleetingly in the words and images of mystics and saints. In the Hindu tradition, this *attainable* universal self, whose central attribute is selfless love, is called the *atma* and is described by Sai Baba as follows:

> The atma is the unseen basis, the substance of all the objective world, the reality behind the appearance, universal and immanent in every being. It is inherently devoid of attachment, is imperishable and does not die. It is the witness, unaffected by all this change in time and space, the immanent spirit in the body, the motivating force of its impulses and intentions. It is one's own innermost reality, one's divinity, the real self—the soul.
>
> The atma cannot be grasped through metaphors and examples. No form can contain it; no name can denote it. How can the limited comprehend the unlimited; the now, measure the ever; the wayward understand the stable?
>
> The atma persists unchanged, however many changes the thing

motivated by it might undergo. It contacts the senses of perception and affects the mind; it awakens the intellect to discriminate and decide upon the lines of action. It activates the instruments of thought, speech and action, of expression and communication. The eyes see; but what force prompts them? You may have ears but who endows them with the power of hearing? Words emanate from the mouth; but what urges us and frames the manner and content of the speech? That force acts like the cells in a torch which provide the bulb with the current to illuminate it. Doctors know that the body consists of cells, billions of them, alive and alert, busy and active. Each cell is motivated by the atma; it is immanent, all over. The atma is in each of them, as well as in every spot of space. When we realize it as such, it is experienced as effulgent, total, splendorous light: endless, incomparable, unique light."

(Sathya Sai Baba)

Notes

1. Swami Prabhavananda and Christopher Isherwood, Translators, *Bhagavad-Gita* (New York: The New American Library Inc., 1944), pp. 30-31.

2. Ibid., pp. 31-34.

3. Sathya Sai Baba, *Geetha Vahini* (Brindavan, Whitefield, Bangalore, India: Sri Sathya Sai Publication and Education Foundation), p. 5.

4. Ibid., p. 5.

5. See last quote of this chapter.

6. Ibid., p. 2.

7. Ibid., p. 7.

Love is God, God is love. Where there is love, there God is certainly evident. Love more and more people. Love them more and more intensely. Transform the love into service. Transform the service into worship. That is the highest spiritual discipline.
(Sathya Sai Baba)

Sai
Love

CHAPTER FOURTEEN

THE ANSWER to suffering is love. Unfortunately, in its everyday usage, this concept has become oversimplified. What exactly is love? Can we understand it—can we grasp it? Here is precisely where spirituality teaches a profound lesson to psychology, because the love of which spiritual systems speak extends beyond the concepts of Western psychology.

The psychological self says, "I want to survive; I want to master, to be successful; I want pleasure, I don't want pain—I want, I want!" The spiritual self says, "What is this mysterious game—this incessant movement between up and down, sadness and joy, pleasure and pain? What is there beyond this constantly changing world, this transient fleeting moment that is soon forgotten? Is there *anything* beyond it?"

Yes. Love is constant, unchanging, selfless—transcending separation and duality, revealing the oneness underlying and unifying all things. It is a state of consciousness in which giving needs no reward. Love reaches out to and encompasses the other. It is the source of our intuition, our creativity, our empathy. It is the most basic and primary tool of all therapists, allowing us to extend beyond ourselves to merge with the other, experience the other's pain, and finally dissolve that pain with love's life-giving force. Love is far more than a psychological feeling; it is said by Sai Baba to be the most basic principle of all creation—the principle that created, preserves and sustains the entire cosmos. This basic universal principle is also our own inner nature; it triumphs over suffering; it survives the grave—it extends us into eternity.

The following letter, written in English by Sathya Sai Baba to the students of his men's Science and Arts College at Brindavan, describes in poetry a closeness not conceived of by Western psychology— a pure form of love experienced as oneness beyond duality. This oneness has an intriguing dimension. Although Sai Baba has had no formal education past age thirteen, and has lived all his life in a remote Indian village, observers report that he speaks all the major languages of the world. Sai Baba says that this represents his oneness with all knowledge. In this poem we see his profound grasp of the English language.

My dear boys,
Accept my blessing and love.
The footstep is the token of arrival
    and departure:
and every farewell echo rings with expectation.
Wakefulness and slumber lie in the eye together;
and then when blindness comes
deeper grows the vision.
In the mind cohere thing
    and nothing both;
and on this bank of blankness
    memory tells . . . beads.
Life is a drawing-in of breath
    and a giving-up:
the footstep is the token of . . . .
My boys,
The bird with you,
    the wing with me.

The foot with you,
*   the way with me.*
The eye with you,
*   the form with me.*
The thing with you,
*   the dream with me.*
The world with you,
*   the heaven with me.*
So are we free,
So are we found,
So we begin, and so we end,
You in me,
*   and I in you.*
Be happy
*   With Blessings*
Study well and be good
God is with you
*   Baba*

In late December, 1978, during my tenth trip to Sai Baba, a videotaped interview was held on the grounds of *Prasanthi Nilayam*, his *ashram* in southern India. The moderator asked me about the place of spiritual love in Western psychology.

Question: In your book [*Sai Baba: The Holy Man and the Psychiatrist*], Dr. Sandweiss, you described in your chapter on psychiatry a new element that Sathya Sai Baba has added to your understanding of human nature—that of divine love. Can you tell us a little bit about how that's affected your work back in the United States?

Answer: Baba's love touches us at such a depth and with such intensity that one can only describe it as omnipresent, unconditional, boundless—divine. It is his greatest gift to us, a gift which transforms the devotee—and I'm sure will transform the world as well. My first experience of his love was so profoundly moving that I saw in it the basic force which supports and sustains us all. Since then I have come to see my life's work as trying to purify my own capacity to love, to express this love with those who come to me for help, and to help modern day psychotherapists come to know of this love that heals all illnesses.

Perhaps I can begin by describing the impact and meaning of my first experience of Sai love. Throughout my personal and professional life, I had been searching for peace of mind, how I might achieve this for myself, and help with its achievement by others. After treating thousands of people and going through my own treatment in the course of my education, I came to realize that basic questions still weren't answered by Western psychology. Although many patients were brought through crises and felt better emotionally, there was still uncertainty, worry and unresolved suffering in their lives. Still unanswered were such basic spiritual questions as, "Who am I in the vastness of this infinite universe? Why am I here? What is the purpose of my life? How shall I lead it?"

I could see that Western psychiatry did not know the answers. Neither I nor my patients had the deep sense of peace and protection in our lives that one would hope to find in a close relationship with a loving, caring God. Of course, very little is said about God in Western psychology; to entertain the possibility of His existence is generally regarded as just a pipe dream.

I began to see the confusion in my field evidenced by the super-abundance of therapists and the multiplicity of competing techniques and approaches. Many psychological theories developed within the past seventy-five years challenged central spiritual teachings that had survived for thousands of years. New therapies seemed to come and go like adolescent fads, and though some appeared to help in the short run, how would they stand the test of time? I began to wonder if there was a genuine authority around: someone who really knew, some safe place to put one's trust. Was there a Master amongst psychotherapists, someone at a higher level of consciousness who could satisfy my thirst for answers about spiritual questions? Had anyone really ever seen a miracle?

"Have you ever seen a miracle?" People I asked simply scratched their heads, and I don't doubt they thought me a bit off balance. But I was seriously looking for a concrete sign that would be more reliable than the empty theories of noted scholars.

It wasn't long after I began asking for a miracle that I heard about Sathya Sai Baba. How sweet he is to respond to the genuine pleading of his devotees.

I came to India full steam ahead, enthusiastic and set to demand my own personal miracle. What a surprise! I don't know how he did it, but he quickly wore me down to a frazzle. Like so many people, I came to Baba with a fantasy that he would immediately recognize me, welcome me with open arms, show me the meaning of my life— and along with it perhaps reveal one or two aspects of his divine form. But what one usually finds is something quite different. He made me sit and wait; I became angry and frustrated; I began to think myself crazy for coming all this way, hoping for a glimpse of God. And then all of a sudden—in the moment of my most intense pain— he came to me like the sweetest parent. One of his attributes is perfect "therapeutic" timing.

I related this incident in the book Baba allowed me to write about him. In short, after I became aware that Baba had the capacity to materialize objects, after I had witnessed my miracle, I began to seriously listen to what he had to say. And what he said disturbed me. Baba spoke about the place of discipline and morality in our lives. Coming from a background where permissiveness and doing what one wants is valued, it was upsetting for me to hear Baba say, "It's not important to do what you want to do, but to learn to like to do what you have to do." When I heard him tell his students not to get caught up in transient, meaningless fads—long hair, tight pants, sensual and violent movies—I mistook him as being repressive and punitive. I was deeply disturbed by his message of discipline, control, respect and morality.

One evening after hearing Baba speak to his students in this way, I retreated dejected and almost broken. I stood a great distance away from him, many walls and many people separating us. I was in the moment of my greatest pain, attracted by Baba's immense vitality, love and sheer beauty—yet wanting to retreat. I felt that he challenged the basis upon which my life was built. If I listened to him I would have to change the direction of my life, my relationship with family and friends, and even the way I practiced my profession. I pictured myself being a penniless outcast.

As I stood steeped in this dark cloud of pain I looked up to find the most precious, tender healing light of love I had ever witnessed. Baba came directly to me, smiling tenderly and playfully—capturing me in the radiant burst of sheer bliss which sparkled in his eyes. I was immediately immersed in his great joy—and happy beyond measure.

Up to this point he had hardly noticed me; why was he coming to me in this manner now? He had been with his devotees and I was angry with him; why should he have come to me and how did he find me?

He reached out and gave me a small piece of candy—but the spiritual gift was immeasurable. What an immense revelation to me: his understanding of another being, deeper than anything I'd ever realized before. In an instant he showed me he was nearer to me than my very breath, that he actually resided in my heart, and, what's more, that he responded to my pain. He had waited for the moment when I would be ready to understand—and accept. In this tender, intimate act of compassion I saw the glory of his omniscience and omnipresence, the mighty transforming and healing power of his unconditional love. And he wanted nothing in return.

How to get that love, to sense it in the universe, to realize it in ourselves, to express it in everything we do—those questions followed. Baba answered: Love is cultivated, purified and expanded through the process of devotion, offered to humanity in the form of selfless service. It is about the importance of this reality that he had come to teach.

How unfortunate that the process of devotion—love for God—is so poorly understood by many Western scientists and intellectuals and is actually viewed as primitive and regressive. At first I, too, was embarrassed by my impulse to prostrate before him, to touch his feet, to direct every thought, word and deed to him; to sing and pray to him. But his love made that all so natural, allowing me to see that the expression of devotion is one of the most innate instincts of the heart. What a great mistake to dismiss this inner holiness as a regressive trait! Freud thought that neurosis was caused by overly harsh repression of natural drives. But what greater ill is caused by the repression of our most sacred instinct—our heart's yearning for God. To deny this is to turn our back on our own precious liberation.

Modern clinical psychology has given rise to so many different theories and practices. Some are interesting and some obviously nothing more than a joke, such as the short-lived "tickle therapy" which gained some recognition in the U.S. until its originator was sued and lost credibility. (It was ruled that more harm than good was done to a client who had been tickled for hours without letup. It seems as if this science is struggling to find its center, a safe mooring place from which to receive steadiness and strength—and tickling isn't what's needed.)

I've come to see that the Western behavioral sciences represent a young spiritual movement which has not yet realized its true identity. Its investigators, therapists and clients seem to be spiritual aspirants searching for truth but still unaware of the reality of God—or even of their own souls. The rapid growth of so many seemingly opposing and divergent attitudes and techniques speaks of the lack of a unifying underlying principle. This young science seems to sense the darkness and to be crying out for its own spiritual awakening much as in the vision of W. B. Yeats in his poem "The Second Coming":

> Turning and turning in the widening gyre
> The falcon cannot hear the falconer;
> Things fall apart; the centre cannot hold;
> Mere anarchy is loosed upon the world,
> The blood-dimmed tide is loosed, and everywhere
> The ceremony of innocence is drowned;
> The best lack all conviction, while the worst
> Are full of passionate intensity.
>
> Surely some revelation is at hand
> Surely the Second Coming is at hand.

Such a coming will occur in the behavioral sciences when it awakens to the central importance of God, devotion and the soul. And Baba has come for this purpose—to teach us through love, by love and for love, how to dwell in the paradise of divine love forever.

In February of 1977, soon after *Mahashivarathri*, a holy day dedicated to Lord *Shiva* and to winning a transcendental vision of unity, I accompanied two American psychiatrists to see Baba. He said, *"I'll see you soon,"* and then kept us waiting. It is surprising how quickly Baba can get to the mind through the behind. Patience, patience— sitting, sitting—and within two days these respectable psychiatrists were reduced to a grumble. It was then that Baba invited us in for an interview, showing us another example of his impeccable timing.

Looking at us with a gentle smile he said: *"Psychiatry doesn't know the way to God-realization; it only studies the mind. But there is a reality that is boundless, beyond time, infinite in dimension. The color of that which cannot be measured is blue—like the blue of the sky and the blue of the ocean. Blue is cool and calming; see, the three doctors are all wearing blue."* Everybody chuckled as we noticed that we three were indeed all wearing blue shirts.

Baba continued, *"Shirdi Baba[1] wore a ring at the time of his death. The color of the stone in the ring was blue—the color of the infinite and boundless—and in the stone was engraved the symbol of OM, the inner reality of that which is fathomless. See . . ."* And with that he circled the air with his precious hand and produced the treasured *Shirdi* ring.[2] What a marvelous moment to behold—not only to hear from Baba himself about his own inner reality, but to see in the tender joyful giving of this miracle, that his love *is* that boundless reality. We all had a chance to touch the ring, to place it to our foreheads and to revel in the glory of that moment.

I pray to be a worthy instrument of Baba's love—that boundless, fathomless, glorious reality which he shows us we are. I see my life's work as trying to express his love to my utmost—bringing his reality, our true reality, into my work, and sharing it with colleagues.

What a lovely challenge. Just recently I gave a talk at the largest psychiatric hospital in San Diego and saw so many psychiatrists wiggling their feet and tapping their fingers on the table, restless and uncomfortable having to listen to spiritual matters. After the talk, as I was leaving, two young psychiatrists approached me and seriously asked, "Do you mean there really is good and bad, right and wrong?" Thank Baba! He has come just in the nick of time—helping us awaken to the importance of our role in upholding morality and *dharma* (righteousness).

And even though people were wiggling their feet and tapping their fingers on the table, I saw through the apparent restlessness and nonattention a marvelous gift that Baba has come to give his devotees at this time. It is a most wonderful time to be here on earth. Because while our Lord is still not well-known or well-understood worldwide, we have so many wonderful chances to talk about him. We have the opportunity for some small role to play, some work to do, in bringing his love into the world. And the knowledge that he cannot fail is exciting. Even though there are taps of fingers and wigglings of feet, with so many people not paying attention, I know that underneath the surface many hearts are barren, crying out for the nurturing mother and father to touch them and caress them and bring them alive. There are so many people crying out for this great light, and he has come to give us life.

Notes

1. An Indian holy man who died in 1918 and who Sathya Sai Baba says was his previous incarnation.

2. Photo of the *Shirdi Baba* ring is on p. 264.

Love is
God

CHAPTER FIFTEEN

*L*OVE IS *the solvent for the hardest of hearts.*

Love can confer peace, joy and wisdom; cultivate love, express love.

Let love be your breath, let the sun of love help the lotus of your heart to blossom.

Love is my highest miracle. Love can make you gather the affection of all mankind.

Love will not tolerate any selfish aim or approach.

Love is God, live in love.

Expand your heart so that it can encompass all. Do not narrow it down into an instrument of restricted love.

Man is love embodied. He thirsts for love and he finds real joy in loving and receiving selfless love. Love all as embodiments of the same divine principle.

The bliss that you give, the love that you share, these alone will be your lasting possessions.

Love. Love alone can bind you to others and to God, who is the embodiment of love. Love knows no fear, no untruth, no anxiety, no grief. I am love; I shower love.

I share love; I am pleased with love; I bless that you may bring more and more love to more and more beings.

Love can transform man into a divine being, it helps him to manifest the divine which is his core.

Love can tame even the most ferocious of beasts.

Start pouring out love to all the members of your community and gradually expand that love to include all mankind and even the lower creatures.

Soak every moment in love, that is to say in God.

Be born in love, die in love, live in love, that is to say emerge from God and merge in God. Be a wave in the ocean of love.

You should not die, you should merge and fulfill yourself. That is the destiny, that is the destination.

Spread love; be full of love. If you cannot love man, how can you hope to love God?

Love must see the best in others and not the worst. Love cannot ignore the divinity in others. The greatest of the virtues is love. Love is the basis of character.

God is love and can be won only through the cultivation and exercise of love.

Love is expansion and expansion is divine life. Sow love, it blossoms as compassion and tolerance. It yields the fruit of peace.

Unless you cultivate love, tolerance, humility, faith and reverence, how is it possible for you to realize God?

Love activates. Love fulfills. Fill your hearts with the sweet fragrant water of love. Then every act of yours, every word of yours (which are like the water drawn from the tank through the taps, tongue, hand, brain, etc.) will be sweet and fragrant. If the tank is polluted how can the word be helpful or the thought beneficial or the deed commendable?

When you know that you are but a spark of the divine and that all else are the same divine spark, you look upon all with reverence and true love. Your heart is filled with supreme joy and the canker of egoism is rendered ineffective. Man is seeking joy in far-off places, in quiet spots, not knowing that the spring of joy is in his heart, the haven of peace is in himself. Love is God; God is the embodiment of perfect love. So, He can be known and realized, reached and won only through love. You can see the moon only with the help of moonlight. You can see God through the ray of love.

One kind of love expresses itself as attachment to things, affection towards kith and kin, desires for objects. Another kind reveals love in human relations, reverence towards the great and devotion to God. Cultivate love and all its aspects will be fed and fostered. There is only one royal road for the spiritual journey—love. Love all beings as manifestations of the same divinity that is the very core of yourself. Love all beings, that is enough.

See God in everyone, even in persons whom you regard as your enemies. Practice that broad all-inclusive type of love.

Remember, when love is installed in the heart, jealousy, hatred and untruth will find no place there.

Expansion is life. Expansion is the essence of love. Live in love.

Love expresses itself as service. Love grows through service. Love is born in the womb of service. And God is love.

Right conduct must be surging from the heart as the cool energizing water of love and peace.

The goal can be reached only through the purification of character and the cultivation of unselfish love.

To attain God, love is enough. Love is the key to open the door, locked by egoism and greed.

Love for all should spontaneously flow from your heart and sweeten all your words. The best spiritual discipline that can help man is love. Foster the tiny seed of love that clings to "me" and "mine"; let it sprout into love for the group around you and grow into love for all mankind and spread out its branches over animals, birds, and those that creep and crawl and let the love enfold all things and beings in all the world. Proceed from less love to more love, narrow love to expanded love.

Expand into universal love, unshaken equanimity and ever-active virtue. That is the path which will bring out the divinity in you to the fullest.

Man's native characteristic is divine love, his nature is divine love, his breath is divine love.

God is the source of all love. Love God, love the world as the vesture of God, no more no less. Through love you can merge in the ocean of love. Love cures pettiness, hate and grief. Love loosens bonds. It saves man from the torment of birth and death. Loves binds all hearts in a soft silken symphony. Seen through the eyes of love, all beings are beautiful, all deeds are dedicated, all thoughts are innocent, the world is one vast kin.

Love . . . love . . . love first. Love as long as life lasts.
My life is my message.
My message is love.

(Sathya Sai Baba)

Notes

1. *A Recapitulation of Sathya Sai Baba's Divine Teachings* (Tustin, California: Sathya Sai Book Center of America, 1982), pp. 87–90.

PART II Psychiatrists Meet Sai Baba

Dancing Shiva (Nataraja) on a ring materialized by Sathya Sai Baba for a devotee

Shiva

CHAPTER SIXTEEN

ONE DAY in October, 1976, I was scurrying around the house searching for a lost article. Looking in the wastebasket, I came upon a form letter that my wife or I must have filed there. It was from Dr. Jules Masserman, the upcoming president of the American Psychiatric Association, informing psychiatrists of a trip to India that he and a colleague, Dr. Schwab, would be co-sponsoring.

I got excited. Having wanted to share my experience of Baba with colleagues for some time, I felt this might be a sign—a way of Baba's granting me this wish—no matter that news of the event was coming by way of my wastebasket.

I called Dr. Masserman, sent word to Baba asking for permission to bring the doctors to the *ashram*, and managed to arrange for a meeting. I would talk to the group upon their arrival in New Delhi and make final arrangements regarding how many would join me, at that time. This would take place soon after *Mahashivarathri*.[1]

Shiva, the God of beneficence and compassion—the renovator, guardian and father of the universe—is worshipped and revered, propitiated and prayed to for mercy on the auspicious eve

139

of Mahashivarathri. Shiva, the destroyer God of the Hindu trinity (Brahma, creator; Vishnu, protector; Shiva, destroyer)—he who adorns himself with the cloak of an elephant skin, symbolic of the elemental bestial primitve traits which his grace destroys and makes powerless and harmless—he who is impervious to temptation and is in perfect balance always—is implored, beseeched and prayed to for the self-control and even-mindedness which destroys desire—the root cause of delusion.

(Sathya Sai Baba)

During *Mahasivarathri* Baba clearly shows his union with *Shiva* by performing two major public miracles in the presence of a crowd of thousands: the miracle of the *Vibuthi Abheshekam,*[2] and the holy act of *Lingobhava,*[3] the materialization of the sacred *Shiva Lingam.*

I was coming to Baba this eighth time to witness the creation of the *lingam,* for it and the holy and monumental act of its creation have profound spiritual significance. Indeed, the whole of Baba's message is contained in this sacred form, and the major focus of this book is an attempt to grasp the *lingam*'s inner significance.

The *lingam* has more to do with dimensions of consciousness than with its material substance. It is the symbol of duality emerging out of, and merging back into, the one. The sphere, a symbol of unity, has one centerpoint—but the *lingam,* ellipsoid in shape, has two centers, emerging and merging in and out of one another. Here is the symbol of the two (duality) coming out of and returning into the one—the one being the source, the sustenance—the basis of the two.

The purpose of our life, says Baba, is to purify our heart so that love expands and broadens our consciousness until we see beyond the consciousness of duality—beyond the difference of subject and object—until we are able to see the underlying unity. We must not only see this reality but merge with it through love as well.

You have had the good fortune of looking at the divine vision. You have also seen the divine significance of the lingam and that will grant you complete salvation. So far as you are concerned, you have attained complete salvation and there are no more rebirths for you. It is a piece of great good fortune for you. Some of you have seen this manifestation as a specific form, some as a light and some only as a streak or a flash of light; but it does not matter in what form

you have seen the generation and manifestation of this lingam.
What you have really seen is the secret of creation.
(Sathya Sai Baba)

No wonder one would want to see this great event for himself.
And as an added incentive, it so happened that that year *Mahashiva-*
rathri fell at the time of my 40th birthday. I could think of no better
way of bringing in my new decade. I would fast and sing myself into
oblivion and with luck merge myself into the Godhead as a birthday
present.

I was also prompted to make the trip by feelings that this could be
the last time Baba would preside over the public observance of this
holy day. So many thousands were pouring into *Prasanthi Nilayam*
for the event that it seemed unlikely Baba could continue it for long.

Then too, there was the initial reason for going. I had so
wanted to share my experience with colleagues, knowing that Baba
would have such meaning for them. By some "coincidence" a group
of respected American psychiatrists would be going to India at this
time, and I had arranged to meet with them to talk about Baba and
take some to him for a visit. There would be no better time for this to
take place, as *Mahashivarathri* was all about the strengths and limitations of the mind. And although Baba's teachings directly challenged
modern psychiatry's thinking about the mind, this was a subject in
which psychiatrists should have great interest.

Notes

1. *Mahashivarathri* — A Hindu holiday devoted to the worship of Lord *Shiva*.

2. The apparent miraculous creation of a shower of materialized ash from an empty
   upturned urn, in a ritualistic bathing of a sacred statue. The inner meaning of this
   act relates to the kinds of purified inner personal qualities, devoid of selfishness,
   which we must offer to the Lord.

3. The apparent miraculous materialization of a *Shiva Lingam*, an egg-shaped stone
   considered a symbol of *Shiva*, and containing within its form the attributes and
   power of Lord *Shiva*. This act is a symbolic reenactment of the creation of the
   cosmos by an act of God's will.

Bhagawan Sri Sathya Sai Baba

TELE NO 30
BRINDAVAN
WHITEFIELD-560 067
TELE NO 36
PRASANTHINILAYAM P O
ANANTAPUR DT 515134

My dears! Accept my Blessings and love
Each one from ego takes his birth and clad in
ego dies and comes and goes, Gives and
receives and earns and spends, and deals
in lies or speaks The truth, In ego all the
while. Heaven and hell and incarnations.
All these from ego are not free. Those who
do aways with Their ego attain salvation.
The Lord is ever true, and higher than The
highest is, But you must crush your ego
and realize Him. He is in you, with you
and around you, Be happy.

With Love and Blessings
Sri Sathya Sai Baba
(Baba)

Mind

CHAPTER SEVENTEEN

THE NOTION that we may exist beyond mind—
that the mind, in fact, may be an obstacle to liberation, or cosmic
awareness, is usually mistakenly seen by psychiatrists as a suppres-
sion, repression or denial of our basic identity, as being a nihilistic
and self-destructive attitude. But the process of detachment, by
which we transcend mind, is different from repression or denial, an
important point which I discussed in my last book.[1]

Let's look at spirituality's attitude and approach to mind through
the teachings of Sai Baba, in order to gain a deeper appreciation of
mind's limitation.

* * *

*The study of the mind and the science of perfecting conscious-
ness has not developed because man seeks peace and joy in external
things and objective pleasures. The attention all along has been on
the outer senses and methods by which they can be used to collect
information and pleasurable experiences. The vast regions of inner
consciousness have been left fallow; the fact that the mind is the
creator of the multiple world of the senses is ignored. When a thorn
enters the sole, it has to be removed by another thorn, and*

143

after that is done, both thorns are thrown away. So too, the world of things that the mind has projected has to be negated by the clarified and concentrated mind, and then both the universe and the mind disappear. The thorn it is that pricks; the thorn it is that removes the thorn. The mind binds; the mind releases.

*   *   *

Transform the mind into an instrument of progress for liberation. Clarity of mind can be earned only by withdrawing it from external objects and teaching it through meditation to concentrate on the One behind the many. When you see the One and not the many, you are liberated from the coils of delusion. Egoism is a doctrine that binds; but the ego as the reflection of God in you liberates. However many trials and tribulations come in the way, look upon them as an unconcerned witness, with detachment, and do not let your mind be affected. Teach it this witness attitude. Man has all the capabilities in him, but he is unaware of his glory; he knows only a fraction of his power, and even that faintly and falteringly. He is degrading himself by yielding to three temptations: physical, worldly and scholastic. The scholastic temptation attracts people who are learned; it prompts them into controversy and competitive exhibitionism and ruins them by bloating their ego. The worldly temptation leads man to seek cheap renown and gain fame and favor through all means available. The physical temptation insists on beautifying the body and resorts to measures which will hide the oncoming of age.

Foster divine thought; cultivate non-attachment; remember the fleeting nature of things. Then the work of resistance will be easy. Mind grows in strength every time you yield to desire. So in order to subdue it and shape it into a useful tool, reduce desire.

*   *   *

Mahashivarathri is dedicated to the disintegration of the aberrations of the mind, and so, of the mind itself—through the worship of Shiva, God. It falls on the eve of the smallest moon of the year, as the waning of the moon is the symbol for the waning of the mind.

The moon as well as the mind whose deity it is, each have sixteen phases. On Mahashivarathri, fifteen of these have disappeared, and there is just a streak of the moon in the sky. The new moon that follows will not even have a streak visible.

The pull of the mind must also be reduced, controlled and finally destroyed so delusion may be rent asunder and reality revealed. It must be mastered every day until, on the fifteenth day, fifteen phases have disintegrated and only a streak remains. Then on Mahashivarathri, a special spurt of spiritual activity is undertaken to reduce the fickle mind to nothing, in order to overcome deluding desire and attachment to the changing, tempting world of illusion — in order to win the holy vision, to achieve moksha (liberation). By undergoing the rigors of sleeplessness, by fasting, prayer and song, the devotee cries out to Shiva to destroy the obstacles in the way to inner contentment, to grant liberation from bondage to the trivial and temporary, to reveal the vision of the highest self, the basis of all this appearance.[2]

Notes

1. See *Sai Baba: The Holy Man and the Psychiatrist*, pp. 63-64.

   Repression is separating oneself from an aspect of one's own inner life, out of fear. Thus certain desires and emotions become inaccessible to conscious awareness before one learns to harness and control their energies. Detachment, on the other hand, is surrendering desires and emotions willingly as a part of our yearning to continue to evolve — after we have gained conscious awareness and a measure of self-mastery of them. The quotes in this chapter describe the process by which this is accomplished.

2. Taken from a discourse by Sathya Sai Baba delivered on Feb. 2, 1959 named "The Moon and the Mind," and printed in *Sathya Sai Speaks* Vol. 1, pp. 110-116, and Vol. 9, p. 42.

Darshan

CHAPTER EIGHTEEN

ELECTRIFYING! THE singing spoke of a love and gratitude beyond measure. The auditorium swelled to its 20,000 capacity. Oblivious to pain, thousands had been sitting for hours on hard, cold concrete, transfixed in the chanting, awaiting his appearance. Now a heightened excitement arose in the music. Light, vibrating at quivering intensity, brought all eyes to the front. There he was, standing quietly, absolutely at one with the music, orange robe softly settling over a fluid body—pure love flowing to the heart of each devotee.

All eyes were glued to the Master now, all voices in touch with his heart. He was in the music now, intoxicating our souls with the awesome grandeur of the miraculous moment—that is *Darshan*.[1]

Thousands had come from all over the world: the rich, the poor, the weak and the strong. All sat side by side in the presence of Sathya Sai. I had been in his physical presence before; this was now my eighth trip to him. Yet I was filled with an excitement and vision I could have at no other place but here. There is no way to describe the actual encounter. The mind cannot hold the vision that the heart grasps in this moment of intimate contact. Everlasting reality is revealed. I am He—I am eternal—I am divine!

He began to move slowly in the distance, like a soft breeze, to the ebb and flow of outstretching arms and waves of praying hands which swelled and receded at his approach and passing. Humanity en masse crying for liberation, praying to be lifted from the animal to the divine. Here he was amongst us in all his glory: compassion incarnate, beauty and love beyond description—here to give us peace.

I began to choke up. "Oh Baba, I am so far away. So many needy have come from afar—how can I push them aside, to get closer myself? Never again will I draw your personal smile, feel the joy of your close company, sit at your feet, part of a small family. Your family is all of humanity now. I can never be close to you again." My eyes dropped and I sat enveloped in a dark cloud of separation and sadness, and wept.

The rustling in the crowd came closer. Looking up, I saw that the people in front of me were parting. "Is this a dream—this only happens in a dream. He can't be coming to me." But he was!

Motioning for me to rise and come forward, he said, *"Sandweiss, how are you?"* Through tears of joy I replied, "Very happy, *Swami*."

Personal, familiar—absolute intimacy in a crowd of thousands—he said with innocent eyes atwinkle, *"Where are the psychiatrists?"*

"They'll be coming in about one week, *Swami*, I will go to Delhi to meet them and bring them here."

"How many will be coming?"

My mind was a jumble. I didn't know how many. Over a hundred American psychiatrists led by Dr. Masserman were scheduled to tour India, sight-seeing and meeting Indian colleagues. I had made arrangements to meet the group in Delhi to talk about Sai Baba and bring those interested to him for a meeting. But I didn't know how many would want to break their preplanned schedule to join me. How embarrassing to tell Baba just a few were expected if all 100 were to come, or to declare many when only a few would show up. I couldn't admit that I was so ill-prepared I didn't know, and this certainly wasn't the time or place to discuss the matter in detail. Opting to seem important, I replied, "Maybe as many as 100, *Swami*."

Turning to move, Baba gently needled with a knowing smile, *"No, not so many."*

For days thereafter, Baba continued to ask about the psychiatrists.

At first I was delighted with his interest, but then after a while, I began to have second thoughts. I really hadn't firmed up any specific plans and didn't know how the group would react, especially after a long plane trip and jet-lag. I could see it now—no doubt they would see me as a religious fanatic telling them the Lord has come, and would you like to join me for a visit with Him? I might look like a real scatterbrain—not only to the psychiatrists, but how about to Baba if no one came?

Now the fight with my monkey mind began. My thoughts turned to the *Nataraja* form of *Shiva*,[2] dancing on the child body of desire, burning it to ash and encouraging detachment, granting peace and equanimity. These very same sweet feet were dancing on my mind.

> *What makes you think that "doing" is so important? Be equal-minded. Then you will not be bothered about "doing" or "not do-ing," success or failure; the balance will remain unaffected by either. Let the wave of memory, the storm of desire, the fire of emotion pass through without affecting your equanimity. Be a witness of these. Commitment engenders holding, narrowing, limiting. Be willing to be nothing. Let all dualities subside in your neutrality.*
> (Sathya Sai Baba)

The day of departure finally arrived. Seven days had passed since *Mahashivarathri*, and Baba had moved from *Prasanthi Nilayam* to his *ashram* in *Brindavan* outside the city of Bangalore. The ride from the city to *Brindavan* was a meditation; my mind took on the stillness and expansiveness of the open Indian countryside in which we were traveling.

The day was freshly cleansed by an overnight rain, the morning sun sparkled everywhere. Thoughts of my recent stay at *Prasanthi Nilayam* came, bringing great peace. Sitting eight to ten hours a day in quiet meditation in his divine presence had left me feeling cleansed and with new insight. The heaviness of my active, hectic life in America seemed washed away. Gone was the impulse to overeat, over-work, or become lost in meaningless television. Stripped for the mo-ment of attachment to family and profession, of desire for luxury and materialism, I awakened to a feeling which seemed somehow familiar, yet never before experienced in this lifetime. My inner life had become so peaceful and unruffled it seemed more attractive than the outer world. I felt content in just being still; there was no need to struggle. I could stay here forever. Baba had granted me a brief glimpse into a profound inner truth: exquisite peace really does exist within.

> *Ignorant people seek joy and contentment from external objects, though there are treasures inside them. They arise from the Lord who is inherent in them, everywhere. Underground we have a stream of potable water; between us and the stream there is a thick bed of soil. By spiritual work that soil has to be removed. So too, peace and contentment exist deep within the consciousness of everyone, but they are overlaid by thick beds of evil tendencies and habits (greed, hatred, lust, desire, pride, jealousy, attachment to the outer world) and so, man has to remove these in order to benefit from the treasure.*
>
> (Sathya Sai Baba)

I knew I would go back to my home, no question about that. I loved my family and they needed me; I had duties to perform, obligations to fulfill. But in this moment of reflection, I saw more deeply into Baba's mystery. For if from my limited consciousness I had begun to see the inner life as more attractive than the outer, what must Baba's reality be? He must dwell in pure glory—in sheer ecstasy! What need, then, would he have of this world? Yet he had come to heal and teach, to give to the poor and ailing, to hear their cries of sorrow. He gave all his love—his very life—and all with a simple and innocent smile. Here was a life of sacrifice to love, *for* love, likened to Christ's life and Christ's sacrifice.

> *Life is a song—sing it.*
> *Life is a game—play it.*
> *Life is a challenge—meet it.*
> *Life is a dream—realize it.*
> *Life is a sacrifice—offer it.*
> *Life is love—enjoy it.*
> (Sathya Sai Baba)

Now, in this peaceful moment I could feel so clearly that the purpose of life, when one is made empty and without desire, is to love the Lord and to express that love in kindness to others.

The world can confer, at best, only momentary joy. Happiness, prosperity and power are but flashes amidst the dark clouds of misery, poverty and defeat. Kith and kin of whom we are proud and in whom we lay our trust succumb to death and depart without a word of farewell. But we do not learn the lesson; we cling to the belief that the outer world is the treasure chest of peace and joy.

Almost always, man is anxious to ignore the faults and failings of the objects that draw his attention. If he only recognizes these, he is certain to evaluate them correctly and behave more intelligently. When a man becomes aware that the cobra is a poisonous snake and that the leopard is a cruel beast, he avoids them with constant vigilance. Similarly, when we become aware of the transitoriness and triviality of worldly triumphs and possessions, we can easily detach ourselves from them and concentrate on inner wealth and inner vision. All things in the outer world of objects are subject to change. Impermanent objects can confer only impermanent happiness to man who is himself impermanent. How can it ever be otherwise? Only the spring of bliss can confer bliss. A fitful spring, a drying, decaying spring, can give happiness only in fits, and even that will, before long, decay and dry.

Atma[3] alone is the ever-full and ever-fresh spring of bliss. The atmic energy motivates every being in the universe—man, animal, bird, worm, tree and grass. Once man contacts it, he is blessed with universal vision, absolute delight and eternal wisdom. Everyone has the thirst to realize it and be with it, but very few take steps to reach it. Thousands proclaim the glory of the atma, but only a handful strive to attain it.

Consider for awhile the fate of the rulers of all realms, the leaders of armies and nations, the presidents and prime ministers, emerging from oblivion and merging in the same—did any one of these carry with them, when they passed away, any portion of their wealth or possessions? When one dies, another takes his place; when he dies, still another is ready to assume the role. And all are equally forgotten—except those who have heroically realized the atma and raised themselves to the divine state. So, believe that the struggle for status, for power, for fame and for wealth is not commendable at all. Having been blessed by this chance to live as human beings, have as the ideal, the realization of reality. The

Upanishads[4] exhort you to march on to this goal. They address you as "children of immortality." Try to deserve that honor, to achieve that height. Learn to use all your skills, all your intelligence, all your time for attaining that victory. You are Gods in human form, for only Gods can be immortal. You are embodiments of the divine atma. Do not degrade your life in low pursuits. Spend it in sacred thought, loving service, selfless acts and sweet words of solace.

(Sathya Sai Baba)

Baba had allowed me to experience a moment of marvelous peace. But now, back into the world for me—back into a drama with my fellow psychiatrists. Planning to leave for New Delhi on the noon plane, I was coming to Baba with hopes of receiving his blessings one last time before takeoff.

As I thought of what lay ahead, I became a bit uneasy. Why this impulse to share my experience of Baba with colleagues, I wondered. It certainly would be hard for them to swallow. Why subject myself to having to explain—perhaps to lose composure and defend or, even worse, to sell? How distasteful to become a traveling salesman for spirituality, developing a slick sales pitch for God. So why undertake such a trip?

Finish what you started, Sam, I said to myself and took solace in knowing that Baba would have mercy if somewhere in all this jumble of motives and antics there was a small genuine impulse to bring happiness and share joy. A prayer rose from my lips: "Baba, sustain me with your sweet strength; keep me close, help me remain the detached witness, protected from the coils of the drama."

The taxi stopped, awaiting the passing of a rickety, weathered red train, rushing by with a loud clanking. Shifting attention from the blur of wood and wheels, my eyes fell to the side of the road, onto the smiling face of an earthy Indian woman who was holding out garlands of freshly cut flowers for sale. I would offer flowers to Baba.

Does the key exist in the outer world or in the inner? So long as man embroils himself in the "seen," he cannot see the "see-er." So long as his attention is caught by the flowers in the garland, he cannot recognize the string that holds them together. Inquiry is essential to discover the base which upholds the garland. So too, inquiry

alone can bring into human experience the atmic base which
upholds the objective sensory world.
(Sathya Sai Baba)

On arrival at the *ashram*, I quickly found a seat next to the path
that Baba would take when he came out for *darshan*. A brief wait in
the warm sun—and then an electric hush signaled his presence.
Opening my eyes, I saw him approach, smiling and looking so fresh
and lovely this clear morning. How immediate and spontaneous was
his smile. Coming closer, he said, "Sandweiss, *why are you still here?*
Go get the psychiatrists."

"I am leaving after *darshan*, Swami. I have come for your
blessing," I replied, holding the garland up to Baba. Playfully and
with a mischievous smile, he reached out. But instead of taking the
garland, he began to play with my fingers. The more I tried to
maneuver the garland into his hand, the more he jumped from finger
to finger, playing a teasing game of tag.

"*Go get the psychiatrists,*" he said with a smile, blessing the
garland but not taking it. Then on he moved, to his devotees and into the day.

When Baba disappeared into the house, I stood and walked to
the *Krishna* statue on the grounds. Here *Krishna* was playing his
magic flute, calling his devotees to him and bathing them in his music
of love.

If you have the capacity to draw the Lord to yourself, he will
himself come to you and be with you. Be like Krishna's flute: a
hollow reed, straight, light, with no substance to hinder his breath.
Then, he will come and pick you up from the ground. He will
breathe divine music through you, playing upon you with delicate
touch. He will stick the flute into his sash. He will press his lips on
it; he will fondle it, favour it and flourish it. In his hand, the in-
finitesimal will be transmuted into the infinite; the anu (microcosm)
will be transformed into the ghana (heavens). One day Krishna
pretended to be fast asleep, with the flute carelessly thrown aside by
his side. Radha (a great devotee) approached the fortunate flute and
asked it in plaintive terms, "Oh lucky Murali (Krishna's flute), tell
me how you earned this great good fortune. What was the vow you

observed, the vigil you kept, the pilgrimage you accomplished?
What was the mantra you recited, the idol you worshipped?"
    The flute got tongue through his grace: "I rid myself of all sen-
sual desire, of envy, greed and ego—that is all. I had no feeling of
ego left to obstruct the flow of his love through me to all creation."
                    (Sathya Sai Baba)

I placed the garland around *Krishna's* neck and, kneeling at his feet, prayed to be made into a worthy flute.

Notes

1. To see the Lord.

2. See photo of *Nataraja* on p. 138.

3. The soul—see definition, Note 2, Chapter 26.

4. Hindu scriptures.

So-Hum

CHAPTER NINETEEN

SAI BABA tells us of a holy *mantra* called the *hamsa*,[1] or *so-hum mantra*.[2] It is the constant and automatic sound of each inhaled and exhaled breath, prompting us to merge into the other, by repeating, "*so-hum, so-hum*—I am He, I am He." With each inhalation, He is brought into and merges with "me," and with each exhalation, "I" am released into Him and become "We." In this way the two become one; and duality is transcended.

The same is so with the sounds themselves. The separate sound of "*so*," made with each inhalation and that of "*hum*," made with each exhalation, merge into one another and become OM,[3] the sound the Hindus call the *pranava*, the holy primordial sound—the basic vibration upon which all of creation rests.

> Each individual is born with the question, koham (Who am I?) on his lips. And the answer is given by every breath—so-hum—He am I. The inhalation whispers so (He), and the exhalation, hum (I). But the question is brushed aside by the mind, impatient to dabble in the toyland it pictures the world to be. The answer is denied admission into the understanding by the ego,

155

which derives temporary pleasure thereby. Realize that your breath is answering the question correctly and live in the consciousness that you are a wave of the He that is the infinite consciousness, that is God. Let your mind have no waves; let it be silent, level, calm—so that the hamsa (the celestial swan that is the symbol of so-hum) can sport thereon.

(Sathya Sai Baba)

For years, I have been practicing the *so-hum* meditation. It has had profound and lasting meaning for me and has been a source of great strength. At first I thought that it was just a simple exercise of observing the breath moving in and out. But then something happened; I began to experience an extension of myself. With each exhalation I could feel something inside release into some subtly perceived expanse filled with light. And with each inhalation I could feel this energy, this light, merge with and energize my sense of self.

This experience became increasingly more intense, captivating my awareness, drawing me ever deeper into its stillness and peace. I naturally and consistently awoke in the early morning between the hours of 3 and 6 a.m. to meditate and was surprised to learn that this is considered by *yogis* the most auspicious time for meditation—a time called *brahmamuhurtha*. This became a time of great rejuvenation and exhilarating communion with Sai Baba. For in this inner space of heightened awareness and peace, I was most aware of Sai Baba's glorious presence.

So-hum meditation not only led me into this inner dimension of great peace during the early morning hours, but stayed with me throughout the day. It became my constant friend and companion, surprisingly most evident and helpful during the time I spent with patients. Frequently while listening to a patient, I went into a deep inner state of meditation. In some strange way I found that my inner reaction with patients could be used to intensify the *so-hum* meditation—and the meditation in turn sharpened my insight into the patient. It seemed the source of my intuition, directing me where to focus, showing me what was important and what was not in the patient's treatment.

And beyond all that, of most importance to me was how my work itself became devotion: a time of heightened awareness of the magnificence of creation, and my love for God as I experience Him through Sai Baba. The *so-hum mantra* was showing me how to function happily and effectively here on earth while my soul soared joyfully in the heavens. As I set out on my trip, I knew it would guide and protect me, and if held to faithfully, would draw me closer to *Krishna's* flute.

The following story by Baba shows the relationship of this meditation to *Krishna's* flute, *Murali*—the power of this vehicle to lead us to the love of the Lord, and the nature of this all-encompassing love when fully developed in us. Again, *Radha* is the principal character.

Radha, the great devotee of Lord Krishna, fell ill and was dying from pangs of separation and sorrow after Krishna left. Although Krishna sent word by way of a messenger, the gopis (milk maids, Lord Krishna's closest devotees) would not listen to mere words, they wanted him in person. They said, "Will it be possible to get rid of all the darkness in the world by simply bringing a message about some brilliant light? Will the poverty of a poor man disappear merely by his listening to the might of wealth? Will a hungry man's hunger be relieved only by hearing a description of the food? Will the disease of a sick man be cured if you describe the greatness of various medicines to him?"

Uddhava, the messenger, found that, out of suffering, the physical strength of the gopis was gradually sinking because they were not eating or paying attention to their bodies. Radha, in fact, was so weakened she was preparing to die—to merge her life with Krishna.

At a lonely place, with the sacred intention of imprinting Krishna's picture in her mind, she said, "All these days I had the form of Krishna in the lake of my mind. I have been protecting it with tears of love. In the course of time this lake began to dry up. Then I kept the form in my eyes and nurtured it with my tears. Even these tears are now becoming scarce. In what other manner can I protect the lotus of Krishna? The time is fleeting away and I may soon have to leave this body. The jyothi (light) of my life has to merge in the divine.

As she was thus thinking of Krishna with great intensity of feeling, Krishna came. She had only one last wish: she wanted to

*hear the Lord sing on his Murali. While listening to the Murali,
she gave up her life. From that day, Krishna gave up his Murali
which had been with him always during his younger days.*

*It is necessary for us to recognize the close connection which
exists between Radha and the Murali. The human body and the
Murali both have nine holes. Radha was like a Murali and she
had no place in her for any worldly ideas. She was above all worldly ideas. Such a Radha came out of the Murali and she returned
and merged back into the Murali. Here Murali means the body.
The breathing in and breathing out represent God's sankalpa
(divine will). This is also termed so-hum (I am He) in the form of
the hamsa gayatri (that which saves when repeated). It also gives
us the idea, "I am that, I am that." The same idea has also been
described in "tat, twam asi"⁴ or "that art thou." While everyone
is identical with the divine, few realize it. Radha, however, was
actually experiencing and establishing this great truth in her earthly form.*

(Sathya Sai Baba)

Notes

1. *Hamsa*, the celestial swan, is the vehicle for *Brahma*, the Hindu God of creation. This legendary swan of purity, with plumage of perfectly white feathers, is said to have the power always to distinguish between right and wrong. It is capable of carrying one beyond duality; the entire creative force of the universe rests upon its shoulders. The *so-hum mantra* is *hamsa*, come to save.

2. A *mantra* is a sacred word or formula, potent with spiritual enlightenment. When meditated upon, it has the power to save.

3. The primeval cosmic OM is the vital vibration that fills the universe. OM is the original sound, the symbol of *Brahman* (the all-pervasive, vast, immanent, nameless, formless, eternal, absolute—the divine), the basis upon which the universe rests.

4. A central Hindu statement of unity.

The
Psychiatrists

CHAPTER TWENTY

HALF AN hour to go before my scheduled talk to
about a thousand Sai Baba devotees at Sohan Lal's house. I was tired,
absolutely bushed from all the hectic running around in Delhi. Sinking deep into the soft, overstuffed mattress, covered with large, bulky
comforters and two huge pillows burying my head, I felt myself
release into an immense, safe, black, womb-like void. How would I
get the strength to speak? No question: if I was to speak, it would
have to be with Baba's strength because I had none left of my own.

My mind turned to the events of the last two days. Upon arrival
in Delhi I was met by Mr. Sohan Lal, a long-time Sai devotee, president of the Sai organization in Delhi and the head of publications for
the Sathya Sai Baba organization in India. He was a short, energetic
man with a ready smile, full of life. When speaking about Baba he
became childlike, laughing frequently when describing his own short-
comings. He was kind and gracious and we became fast friends.

Accommodations were great. I was to stay in a large guest room detached from the main house. Although cool with its heavy cement construction and bare floor, it was more than comfortable—and marvelously quiet and private. A small electric heater stood at the foot of and between two large, overstuffed beds. I was happy to find fresh grapefruit, tea and toast frequently delivered to my room by pleasing housekeepers. Sohan Lal smiled broadly when talking about his favorite grapefruits, knowing that they were a real delicacy in Delhi at this time. He was a great host, genuinely happy when I was happy, especially pleased when showing me a glowing account of him and his hospitality in James Michener's book, *The Voice of Asia* (pp. 270-277). Michener had visited Sohan Lal some years back and described him as "a brilliant, darting, handsome hummingbird of a man."

The *Mahashivarathri* observance at Sai Baba's *ashram* had been glorious, although it drained me to the quick: 36 straight hours without eating or sleeping, one day after traveling 40 hours from the U.S. to India. I was exhausted and hobbling—I thought I would die on the spot. But, oh, what a marvelous way to die! The holy surroundings were especially charged and vibrant with the worship of thousands of devotees, all willing to forego eating and sleeping to keep this special vigil. And then there was Baba's extraordinary presence and his two breathtaking public miracles: the *Vibuthi Abheshekam* and the creation of the *Shiva Lingam*. I would recount these events in detail in my talk in just a few minutes. I knew that this holy event was a very special communication from God to man, direct and potent with meaning—no doubt an historic event, to be cherished and revered by countless people in the future.

The day after my arrival I called Dr. Masserman and arranged to meet him for dinner that evening at the Ashoka Hotel. Also expected were Dr. Schwab, chairman of the Department of Psychiatry at the University of Louisville in Kentucky and co-director of this trip, the chairman of the Psychiatric Society in Delhi, the tour guide, and wives.

I showed up at 8 p.m. on the dot. The Ashoka Hotel is one of Delhi's finest: long extended driveway lined with tourist buses, doormen dressed in regal red uniforms and turbans, an open reception and lobby area of wood and marble two to three stories high; fine statues, paintings, sparkling artwork—and the hustle and bustle of an international array of visitors from many lands.

I wonder what's in store, I thought, as I walked down the wide carpeted stairway toward loud music and the distant clinking of silverware on plates. I felt completely out of place in this formal dinner atmosphere, surrounded by wine, women, loud music and dancing—people getting drunk and the smell of freshly cooked meat in the air. It was a far cry from the austerity of the *ashram*. I was feeling the worst kind of culture shock. I'd better walk down these stairs slowly, I decided, or like a diver surfacing too quickly I'll get the bends and be put out of action.

And as I made my way down the stairs in slow motion, I recognized the first auspicious sign of the evening. Knowing that I was in store for an elaborate dinner, I reached for my wallet for comfort— and came up empty-handed! I had forgotten it! I couldn't believe it; what an awkward position to be in. Was I to ask for a loan? Would the restaurant allow me to work off the dinner by washing dishes? Was this a lesson in humility—or had my brain melted from all the meditation at the *ashram*? How embarrassing! I was walking right into a lion's den. "Baba, please be with me—and I'm not kidding! If ever I needed your help it's now."

Smiling and in good cheer, we met and were seated at a well-serviced table. Everyone ordered five-course dinners, and I stuck out like a sore thumb, ordering a small orange juice. "Oh, I'm really not hungry; I'm on a special diet—I eat infrequently, etc., etc. excuse, excuse." They knew I was lying.

And then the conversation started. They began talking about experiments with rats and certain case histories—and I felt a million light years away. How can I be losing so much interest in that level of reality—and so quickly? I asked myself. How in the world can I tell them anything about Baba? They're not interested in talking about spirituality—and I look completely out of it, like a spaced-out kid.

They didn't seem even remotely interested in Sai Baba. And even if by a miraculous turn of events the conversation turned in his direction—would they ever want me to address the entire group? And if so, how would the group respond to a talk about God being on earth after they had just traveled 40 hours and were sleepy and irritable. And even if everything did work out and two or three people came with me the thousand miles to Bangalore, what interest did I really have in acting as a tour guide?

Is it me or you, Baba—is it me or you? Because if it's me I'll never do it again, I promise. I know that I have a big ego—thank you for pointing it out. Okay, I promise to work on it harder than ever. But if it's you—boy, am I stymied. I don't know what to say. I'll sure gain a new respect for your mystery—and your sense of humor. If it is you, and even though I can't fathom the purpose, I'll try to do the best I can. There's only a short while left of this ordeal. I'll continue to try although to tell you the truth, I've given up hope. If you can turn things around, you are really omnipresent, omnipotent, omniscient and everything else.

All of sudden, while I was sitting dejected and defeated, someone turned to me for a comment of some sort. I half-heartedly said, "Yes, and that's what's nice about Baba." They were talking about something, I don't know just what, and I decided to try and relate it to Baba. "You know, the exciting thing about Sai Baba is that he can prove to psychiatrists that our identity is really beyond mind and emotions, that we're something eternal." And then I turned to the Indian psychiatrist, as if we were brothers, and he would understand: "You know, like *atma*." And he said something that could be roughly translated into the likes of, "Bunk—fooey." I knew I had struck out.

Then something strange happened. The tour guide spoke up: "You know, I once met a holy man and they can do things that we can't begin to understand." Everyone became interested. Can you imagine? Not a flicker of interest in me, but when he began speaking, they turned with real excitement and said, "Like what?"

So the tour guide described his experience with a *guru*—how he could predict the future and had an uncanny awareness of past events in his life. Their interest deepened. Dr. Masserman turned to me. "You mean Sai Baba can do these things?" I said, "Yes, even more." He pulled out his pen and within minutes we had composed a notice for the blackboard, announcing my talk. I would speak for about half an hour. I smiled and whispered to myself, "Baba, I don't know how you pulled that off, but it was impressive—simply fantastic. I'll remember that one for a long time."

Then Dr. Masserman said, "My wife and I want to go on a sightseeing tour tomorrow. Do you know any interesting places to see?" I began feeling my oats. After such a quick turn of events in my favor, I felt like a big deal—that everything was in hand. And speaking way out of line with only the hope of Sohan Lal's help in mind, I said, "Oh, I can arrange for a car and a personal guide." Dr. Masserman asked about the cost and I continued like an Indian diplomat: "Don't worry, I'm sure I can arrange this with my friend Sohan Lal at no expense to you. We'll pick you up at 8 a.m. And by the way, Sohan Lal also invites you, Dr. Schwab, and your wives to lunch."

It was true that Sohan Lal had invited them for lunch. He had arranged the lunch for me to meet some friends, including an Indian supreme court judge and a high financial expert in Indian affairs. Knowing that the psychiatrists would also enjoy it, he had invited them as well. But lunch was one thing; arranging a tour at this late hour, quite another.

I hurried back to Sohan Lal's, tiptoeing in at about 11:30. Not up to waking him at this late hour, I planned on stewing with the problem overnight, hoping to catch him early next morning. But as fate would have it, just as I entered the house, my host came down to meet me. Hearing about my predicament he said, "No problem—we'll take the big car (a '57 Chevy) and I know just the driver."

Sure enough, next morning, driving with pomp and splendor in a '57 Chevy, we arrived at the Ashoka Hotel at 8 on the dot. The tour was wonderful. We visited historic sites, holy Hindu temples and lovely gardens, and everything went off like clockwork. Then off to Sohan Lal's for a beautiful lunch.

This time he outdid himself. The food and company were superb. It was inspiring to hear the supreme court judge talk about his moving experiences with Baba. Seeing educated and respected Indian people talking about Baba in this way pricked the interest of the two psychiatrists. They especially enjoyed the friendly hospitality, even wanting to have their pictures taken in Sohan Lal's shrine room. A bit too much—but he was accommodating as usual and let them have the run of the house.

That evening I gave a talk about Baba to the psychiatrists gathered in a conference room at the Ashoka Hotel. The presentation came off well—considering that I was trying to explain the concept of *Avatar* and the possibility that this unique historic event was happening right here and now in India.

I was surprised to find a former teacher of mine among the psychiatrists. Respected as one of the most talented psychoanalysts in Detroit, his exciting case conferences had opened my awareness to the importance of unconscious forces at work in the personality. Dressed always in a formal suit and handling himself with a certain regal elegance, he looked so proper and so in control at these case presentations. Once he had brought a leather attache case to a teaching conference, one corner of which had been badly mauled and chewed by his new puppy. I was glad to see this sign of humanness in someone who seemed a bit remote.

Dr. S. remembered me and we met with a smile. He had been treating two Indian patients in psychoanalysis. They reported experiences in meditation that he couldn't quite understand. "There was something more there than meets the eye," he said—"either something cultural or a subtle intrapsychic phenomenon that I don't quite grasp. I hope to learn something on this trip."

"You have a great chance to do just that," I replied, "and observe something about man's inner dimensions seldom recorded in all of history—and something very profound and deep about Indian spirituality as well. This is the most fascinating area of investigation you could find. It has much relevance to psychoanalysis and our understanding of psychodynamics."

I tried to explain the meaning of an *Avatar*—and the conversation seemed to deteriorate until I looked like a babbling religious fanatic. I remembered being interviewed by Dr. S. when I was applying for psychiatric training at Sinai Hospital in Detroit. Thank God I passed those interviews then, because based on this brief exchange, I'm sure he would have flunked me now. At any rate, I left saying, "You've got to come. You can't imagine what you'd see about man's inner life—and our vast capabilities. I promise, you won't be sorry." But he didn't come.

Only four people out of about 70 wanted to see Sai Baba. Although small in number, they were big in spirit—and very talented people indeed. Realizing that even if a fraction of what I was saying was true, they knew that seeing Sai Baba was more important than going the next day on a trip to the Taj Mahal.

Dr. J. and his wife B.J. were active in the bioenergetic movement in the United States. This approach had also interested me prior to my meeting Baba, and had led me towards *yoga*. Dr. J. was beginning to experience a subtle flow of energy in his body and a peculiar sensation in his forehead between his eyes, as if something was opening. "Could this be related to the third eye described by *yogis*?" he wondered. Further, he described a sensation of cloudiness in this region and wondered if it was more than imagination.

Although they thought they understood many of the factors leading to this trip, Dr. J. and B.J. recognized the possibility of an influence from another dimension as well. Could it be that a teacher or master had been influencing them in subtle ways, and that it was now time for them to have a deeper spiritual experience?

Dr. H. was an L.A. psychiatrist who came with his friend N.S. He had worked with the poor in the community mental health system in Los Angeles and was interested in using drama as a way of developing deeper psychological insight and of promoting growth. Warm and giving, he was having some difficulty making certain professional decisions and hoped that this trip might help clarify them and give him some direction. N.S. was a friendly middle-aged woman who had an emotionally ill daughter. She hoped that Baba could help in some way. I felt that Baba had chosen these four people. Open, receptive and sensitive, they seemed hungry for spiritual insight, and he seemed to be calling them closer. We would be leaving early next morning, but first the evening program was about to begin.

As I lay in a deep trance-like state, I could hear the hustle and bustle outside my little sanctuary. I had to stir my limbs and ready myself for the *bhajans*[1] which would start in about ten minutes—and then speak to the thousand or so devotees now gathering. My four traveling mates would be in the audience. Seeing the devotion of Sai Baba's followers would deepen their understanding and help prepare them for the trip.

Notes

1. Devotional singing.

Delhi
Talk

CHAPTER TWENTY-ONE

Dear SATHYA Sai Baba, who is omnipresent and always with us; gracious host, Mr. Sohan Lal; respected guests and Sai brothers and sisters:[1]

I feel privileged to have the opportunity to speak here tonight and to take part in these lovely *bhajans*. As I sat immersed in their vibration of devotion, I thrilled to the vision that people all over the world are similarly singing to our wonderful Lord Sathya Sai.

In a world so enveloped in darkness, how exciting to experience these lovely *bhajans* transforming the darkness to light. This must be Baba's most potent expression of love—rallying people all over the world to peace. The Sai love present in the *bhajans* and nurturing the steady growth of a large world-wide Sai family is the most hopeful sign of our times. I would like to share some of my most moving experiences with this Sai love.

Five years ago I came to Baba as an egotistical psychiatrist, imagining that I understood reality and skeptical of anything so

intangible as a spiritual dimension. I thought that I knew who I was, what life was about, and had even tricked myself into thinking that I was happy. But how could I be, thinking that I was this transient, limited body—a strange accident existing briefly between life and death—alone in a meaningless abyss of emotionless physical laws governing a vast, cold, unfeeling material universe? Coming from such a dry and lifeless place, how can I now even begin to measure the gift that Baba has given me? I am *atma*—I am the infinite consciousness and boundless love that permeates and sustains everything.

That thou art—*tat twam asi*. What a glorious awakening, to realize, "*so-hum, so-hum,*" I am He; and that the consciousness, the love—the "I" and the "He"—are our Lord Sathya Sai. The only way to express gratitude for such a gift is to lay one's life down as a flower at Baba's lotus feet. I pray he grants us the strength of character and fullness of love to render our lives worthy of the offering.

This is my eighth trip to India and I am beginning to feel as if India were my home. One reason for coming this time was to witness first-hand the *Mahashivarathri* holiday with Baba. This must be just about the holiest event of the year, dedicated to our deepest yearning inside: to merge with God. And what great monumental grace, that *Shiva* himself has come to be with us during this holy time, showing us through the miraculous creation of the *lingam* that the entire cosmos was formed by an act of his divine will. Whenever, wherever, has such a holy event taken place? His gift is beyond measure. The egg-shaped *lingam* truly symbolizes his divine attributes: that which is infinite, without beginning and without end; that from which all forms come, and to which all forms must return; that in which all forms merge.

Baba tells us that *vibuthi* is the most precious object in the truly spiritual sense. *Shiva* burned the God of desire into a heap of ashes, then adorned himself with that ash and thus shone in his glory as the conqueror of desire. Through the attributes of renunciation and detachment, symbolized by *vibuthi*, desire is destroyed and thus love reigns supreme. So it is fitting that the electrifying ceremony of the *Vibuthi Abheshekam* should occur early on *Mahashivarathri* day. It is through this act that Baba shows us how to offer *Shiva* our triumph over tantalizing desire by cultivating the attitudes of renunciation and detachment.

I have seen the miracle of the *Vibuthi Abheshekam* on film, but seeing it first-hand is quite another experience. Baba first materialized a beautiful necklace which he placed around the *Shirdi Baba* statue— *Shirdi* being Baba's previous incarnation and also an incarnation of *Shiva*. As the lovely *bhajans* slowly rose in tempo and excitement, he washed the statue with milk and water. Then, placing his hand in an empty upturned urn held over the statue, he created a steady shower of *vibuthi* which poured from the urn, bathing the silver statue of *Shirdi*.[2]

This ritual washing continued for about five minutes. Sitting fairly close, I was enveloped by the cloud of sweet-smelling ash as it blew out over the crowd. Here was Baba the Father, totally in command of the elements, transcendental and other-worldly as he brought the spiritually rejuvenating ash from fathomless space. Baba's radiance and my immersion in the materialized *vibuthi* and exquisite *bhajans* created an unforgettably sublime experience.

Then the forgiving and redeeming Baba walked into the audience, blessing his devotees with the beautiful *teerth* ceremony. With the milk-and-water mixture from the washing of the *Shirdi* statue, in an act of purification, he washed his devotees. Dipping a small straw hand broom into the fluid, he walked in among his devotees, sprinkling them with this mixture and creating immense joy. All felt their souls washed clean by the Lord Himself. What grace!

Following the ceremony, I had a conversation with Professor Kasturi, who has been with Baba some thirty years. He said that when Baba places his hand in the empty urn, it immediately and completely fills with *vibuthi*. In fact, Baba leans over to warn the man holding the urn to prepare for the sudden increase in weight. He churns his hand inside the urn until it is emptied, then replaces it with his other hand and the whole process is repeated, the urn again instantaneously filling with *vibuthi*. This is repeated until five or six times the amount of *vibuthi* that the urn could normally hold has been created.

Professor Kasturi has been fortunate enough to hold the urn during many different *Mahashivarathris*. He says the moment is so spiritually intense that he completely loses contact with the crowd and is filled only with Baba's presense and the sacredness of the miracle. When asked whether he had ever inspected the urn to make sure it was empty before the miracle, he simply laughed and said, "Of course."

Professor Kasturi told me that he personally reveres Baba as *Shiva* and that he has had marvelous experiences with him that have deepened his reverence. Once when they were alone and talking about his *Shiva/Shakti* (*Shiva's* consort) aspect, Baba said, "Kasturi, look at me." Kasturi relates that as he looked up, what he saw was startling and deeply moving. Instead of Baba's familiar appearance he saw *Nandi* the bull (*Shiva's* vehicle), upon which sat *Shiva* on one side and *Shakti* on the other in a characteristic pose. The vision remained before his eyes for a few seconds and then melted back into the Baba that we all recognize. *"Now do you understand, Kasturi?"* Baba gently asked.

The enormity of this simply boggles my mind—to think that *Shiva* himself has come, allowing us to draw closer. As hard as this is to grasp, witnessing the birth of the *lingam* first-hand has immensely deepened my understanding and appreciation of the relationship between Baba and *Shiva*. This magnificent event was, for me, both moving and sad.

At about 8 o'clock *Mahashivarathri* evening, while Baba was giving a discourse in the *Poornachandra* Auditorium, suddenly he began to choke and weave back and forth as if in pain. To see our great Lord in the throes of what are, in fact, "birth" pains brought me to tears. To me this incredible act represents a sacrifice, the holiest gift of selfless love, through which the Lord personally beckons us to merge with him. Through the love that wells up in our hearts, as our hearts reach out to the supreme master, one experiences the yearning for, and the bliss of merging.

Some say the *lingam* is formed out of unconditional love in the region of Baba's spiritual heart. The birth itself is very physical as well as ethereal. The *lingam* is brought up the esophagus and delivered through the mouth in a divine paroxysm—much like the birth spasm accompanying a corporeal birth. I don't know why I should be sad, because this sacrifice is so glorious—serving to make the devotee more firmly resolved to surrender more and more of himself to God. Nevertheless, to see Baba in this state was uncomfortable for me. He rocked back and forth, then swallowed some water. Suddenly, in a convulsive burst, a glistening, crystal-clear *lingam*, perfectly spherical and almost three inches in diameter, erupted from his mouth into his hand. In this supremely holy moment, the Lord allowed his devotees to witness the mystery of the creation of the universe.

Then Sai Baba spoke and Dr. Bhagavantam translated his words:

> *The lingam which has just been generated is called the Prutree Lingam. The five elemental substances which constitute the creation of the world are present in this Prutree Lingam. In the past, lingams have been named according to the various attributes which they contained. This Prutree Lingam, signifying the entire creation, holds within it the basis of all creation.*[3]

Too much mystery for me to comprehend, I could nevertheless sense the holiness of the moment.

Grasping the exquisite *lingam* between thumb and his first two fingers and holding it high for all to see, the innocent, radiantly smiling Baba walked out to his devotees. Here was the young, ecstatic *Krishna*, a marvelously content and happy smile playing across his face and dancing in his eyes. Here was triumphant *Krishna*, displaying a ball of butter taken from the universal pot. Here was loving *Krishna*, giving the wealth of his kingdom — the priceless, spiritual insight which brings eternal peace — so happy, so happy. And in the light of this act, in the crystal clearness of this transparent *lingam*, in this moment of exquisite love, I saw *Krishna* and *Shiva* — in fact all names and forms — merge.

How lucky to have been present at this *Mahashivarathri*! To take any of Baba's activities for granted, to assume we will always be able to approach so closely, is a mistake. We mustn't miss a single opportunity. Before making this trip, I thought, "How long will Baba allow such a public observance of *Mahashivarathri*? This might be the last time." For the past year I had seen such growth of interest in Baba that I knew that he would soon have to relate to these vast numbers in an altogether different way.

And so it happened. On the morning that ended *Mahashivarathri*, Baba said that he had to deliver sad news. This would be the last time *Mahashivarathri* would be celebrated like this; the crowds were becoming too unruly — devotees were being injured in the commotion. So this forecasts an inevitable change in which Baba will not be so easily accessible on the physical level.

Another reason for this trip was to take some American psychiatrists to see Baba. Since meeting Baba, I have wanted to introduce him to my colleagues; in fact, I think his reality is so important to psychiatry that one day it may be renamed "Sai-chiatry." It so happened that a group of about a hundred American psychiatrists and spouses are touring India now, and the group leader thought that some might be interested in visiting Baba once they knew something about him. I've just met with the group, and some of the people who will be going with me tomorrow to see Baba are here in the audience. I'm happy that they've experienced the Delhi *bhajans* before seeing him, as his love is so evident here. The devotional *bhajans* convey more of Baba's meaning to the sensitive observer than could a million speeches.

I would like to say a word about the book I wrote, *Sai Baba: The Holy Man and the Psychiatrist*. I know that it's because of this book that I was invited to speak here. I've been embarrassed by the recognition, because I know that without Baba's help I would be totally unable to complete such a work by myself. I'd like to tell you about his part in this project because it's such a nice story about his mystery and his love.

All through my education, English was my worst subject. In fact one of my English teachers at the University of Michigan told me that I'd never be able to get through medical school, so poor was my ability to express myself. He shook his head as though there were no hope. Needless to say I was devastated—and perhaps that's why Baba took pity. Also, in his infinite playfulness, he must enjoy taking us at our weakest point, to show that he can bring water from a rock. But most of all he does it out of love—to help us realize more deeply that it is not we, but he, who is the doer. When he gives us such a great gift, when we understand how unlikely it really is, we are less likely to get a big head.

Baba's grace allowed me to be in the right place at the right time—to meet him just before the Western world would come to know of him. And all the feelings I had about him—the devotion, the understanding of the profound influence he would play in the world—all these were not my impressions, they were prized gifts from him. I had nothing to do with the immense energy and excitement that poured from me. It was unusual behavior, almost as if I had no choice. I was overwhelmed, overjoyed with the clear vision of Baba's immense importance, thrilled knowing that no one like him had lived for thousands of years—knowing without doubt that the entire world would soon know of him, that he would be worshipped and revered forever. How could I know such a thing without his letting me see? His grace is boundless.

Not only did he allow the vision but he helped me in very tangible and practical ways with the writing. Just at the right time he sent a talented editor and an accomplished artist. When I took the manuscript to Baba after a year of writing, although he had never read it, he showed me that he knew everything about it. Then, unexpectedly, he instructed me to publish the book myself.

Knowing almost nothing about printing or publishing, needless to say I felt uneasy. But the most trying time came when I sent the book to press—knowing that I had no money. Then, as Baba so frequently does, he made one of those marvelous, last-minute rescues. Baba's timing was exquisite. The very week of the printing, a check came in the mail for almost the exact amount required. An old investment that I had thought was dead had finally paid off.

The book came off the press just one week before my departure for India. Clutching it to my heart and with a special prayer of gratitude on my lips, I scurried off to Baba's lotus feet for the 50th birthday celebration.

At least a quarter of a million people were at *Prasanthi Nilayam* for the birthday celebration. "I'll never get close enough to give Baba the book," I thought. It seemed an utter impossibility in this swelling ocean of humanity. So many people were in greater need than I, how could I place demands on his precious time? I was perplexed. There were people from all over the world who might help with the distribution, yet I didn't want to show it to them until Baba approved. Then in his own sweet, mysterious and grand style Baba solved my problem.

One evening I was sitting in an audience of thousands, carrying the book. I always kept it with me in case, by chance, an occasion arose to present it. Baba had just completed a discourse. Rising to leave the large auditorium, I noticed a commotion on stage. Some young students were preparing to perform a dance, but I was tired and turned to leave.

To my surprise, I noticed a chair moving slowly over the crowd, carried overhead by students. Strange, it seemed headed in my direction. Yes, slowly but surely it was coming my way. And of all the unexpected "coincidences," it settled exactly right by my side. Sai Baba would sit here to watch the dance. Within seconds he was sitting right next to me!

I was stunned by this dramatic turn of events. Here was my big chance. But although able to approach him now, I hesitated — embarrassed about being in the midst of thousands while all eyes were turned to him, and uncomfortable in calling his attention from the students who were to dance in his honor.

Baba saves. He simply looked at me and smiled. "Should I present him with the book now?" I wondered. Answering my thoughts, Baba fixed his gaze on the book. What could I do but give it to him? Gently and with great love he accepted it, began to thumb through its pages, showed some of his students the pictures — told them that I was the author. He was happy with my efforts and my heart melted.

In closing, I pray that Baba makes us all instruments of his love — that he fills our lives with meaning and purpose — that he is happy with our offerings . . . and that he allows us to merge in his ocean of infinite love.

Notes

1. Talk given on February 26, 1977.

2. The miracle of the *Vibuthi Abheshekam* is pictured below.

3. The *Prutree Lingam* seen on p. 166 is being held by Sai Baba immediately after its creation.

First
Lesson

CHAPTER TWENTY-TWO

N O QUESTION that we were in store for the un-
expected. We landed in Bangalore to find that our luggage was missing. Right off the bat I showed the depth of my spirituality, the level
of my renunciation and detachment, by running all over the airport
yelling and screaming. I hadn't brought much, but my four friends
had lost everything they brought to India. I thought it would be nice
to start off at least with the material necessities. But ranting and raving didn't bring them back. We would have to wait until later that
day after airport officials had had time to check. Recovering my composure, I said, "Oh well, let's take a philosophical and spiritual look
at this. It must be an auspicious sign: preparing us to take pleasure
and pain with equanimity."

Bangalore is a beautiful city, and the ride through the countryside, dotted with multi-colored foliage, animals and people meander-
ing about in the slow-paced down-to-earth Indian village life brought
a welcome calm from the shock at the airport. We would stay at the

175

East-West Hotel, where accommodations were comfortable and the food palatable to the Westerner. As we walked through the front lobby toward the reception desk, we were startled by a tremendous crash. Turning in its direction, we saw that a large light fixture had just fallen from the 40-foot ceiling, crashing down on the very spot we had just passed seconds before. We all gave a slight shudder, and I—now getting the hang of this drama—piped up: "And that's the second auspicious sign today!" By this time, my receptive and open traveling companions had sized me up: I was a raving religious fanatic.

Still, they gave me their undivided attention and tried whatever I suggested. I asked the ladies to wear saris. Although they had no familiarity with Indian dress and didn't know how to wind themselves into the 18 feet of cloth, they willingly accompanied me to a store and bought the material, then good-naturedly allowed the lady desk receptionist to wrap them from head to toe.

It was now about noon. We planned to rest for a few hours and then take a taxi the twelve miles to *Brindavan*, the site of Sai Baba's Science and Arts College for Men, where he was residing at this time. He would be coming out for *darshan*—to walk among the people, letting them see him and taking their notes asking for his help. We were all excited about this first contact. Unfortunately, N.S. developed severe abdominal cramps and would have to stay back with hopes of feeling better the next day. Before leaving for *darshan*, we received the happy news that the luggage had been found—retrieved from its extended journey to a remote mountain town.

As we entered the grounds I saw that the crowd was larger than usual. The men and women sat separately, so we pointed B.J. in the right direction, bid her adieu, then found seats for ourselves. It wasn't long before a hush came over the crowd and all eyes turned in the direction of Baba's residence. Out he came, looking startlingly beautiful. He walked like a soft breeze, seeming to float gently over the earth, out toward the middle of the grounds, and then paused for a moment. Turning in our direction, he made his first contact with the crowd right in front of us. As he approached, his eyes caught mine and he smiled. Motioning me to rise and come closer, he said, *"How many psychiatrists?"*

I rose a bit timidly, thinking, "Oh, my, I've done it now. Last time I saw Baba I said perhaps a hundred—and only two are sitting by my side." Wanting to beef up the numbers a bit, I added the two women and said, "Four, Baba."

"*Good—and how's the patient?*"

I was perplexed. Did Baba mix me up with someone else? "What patient, *Swami?*" Then Dr. H. poked me and whispered, "You know, N.S. back at the hotel."

I was stunned. Although I had seen evidence of Baba's omniscience many times, when it happens out of the blue and you're least expecting it, it is absolutely beyond belief. He appears to be so much like you and me that when he nonchalantly reveals his obvious and breathtaking omniscience, it is overwhelming. I felt a bit unnerved, became somewhat unbalanced and started to teeter back and forth. "Oh, Baba—she had a problem."

With a broad smile and great love he said, "*Yes, I know—the stomach.*"

He materialized *vibuthi* and poured it into my hand. By this time I had lost my bearings. I said, "For me, Baba?" and began to eat it.

"*No, no,*" he said, "*for the patient. Bring them all tomorrow and I'll see them.*"

I was completely unmade—overcome by the moment. After I'd sat down, Dr. H. leaned over and said, "You know, I was watching him very closely. I hadn't told you, but I'm a magician and I understand sleight-of-hand. But he materialized that ash right in front of my eyes—and I swear, I don't believe it's a trick. I don't know how he did it."

"Yes, that's right," I mumbled.

Back at the hotel I quickly found N.S. and gave her the *vibuthi*. She was thrilled to think that Baba not only knew who she was, but had administered to her pain. She ate it immediately and the next morning she was fine.

From the start we had good luck, being admitted to the vestibule of Baba's residence, where only a few are allowed. We saw Baba come and go and meet visitors, and at times he stopped for a brief word. But for the most part it was waiting in silence—thrown back into our own inner world. I love this time of simple quiet, charged by the periodic exciting contact with Baba. But my friends weren't used to this stillness and began to feel a bit edgy.

At the end of the first day we were invited into the main house with some of Baba's college students and older devotees. Baba picked two or three students from the crowd to give impromptu talks. I've always shuddered at the prospect of being selected. Since meeting Baba I've become acutely aware of my ignorance. I wonder, "What in the world would I say?"—and marveled at these young students giving moving spiritual discourses without preparation or forewarning—simply speaking from the heart about their experiences with Baba.

Following the talks there was a period of delightful *bhajan* singing and then Baba spoke.

> *It is important for man to have confidence. A child without confidence in his mother, a husband without confidence in his wife, a pupil without confidence in his teacher, will lead a miserable life. In India there are many people who go on pilgrimages. They visit sacred centers and temples, but the question is, with how much dedication and confidence do they set out on their pilgrimage?*
>
> *The result of any action is dependent upon the amount of confidence with which it is done. We might not have confidence or faith in what we're undertaking, yet at the time, asking God for great gifts. If a person wants to benefit in what he's doing, he must have a steady mind and a vision that is not so easily shaken.*
>
> *Today, man has developed a disease in his hearing. Many people give their ears to all types of spiritual discourses, but that doesn't mean they're seeking the maximum benefit from listening. Many satisfy themselves by saying that it is enough to merely listen. This sort of confidence, this kind of approach is not proper. We listen to Swami's discourses for a long time and derive a great deal of happiness by merely listening. But the real question is—are we able to put into practice anything that we have heard? If not, then we can conclude that the sense of hearing is becoming diseased. In addition to hearing we have to develop the faculty of thinking of what we have heard, and consider what is good and useful about it— and then putting into practice the good things that we have heard. Nothing will be achieved if we merely listen and don't think about or do.*
>
> *A small example. Let's compare this to the preparation of food in the kitchen. Is our hunger satisfied by the preparation we do in*

the kitchen? That is like listening. Then we take the food to the dining table and put it on the table. But does just putting the food on the table satisfy our hunger? Preparing it in the kitchen and transferring it into the dining hall—these are the first two stages, like listening and thinking. But they do not satisfy the hunger. The eating and then the proper digestion in the body—the taking action—that's what satisfies the hunger. So if you want to derive spiritual strength you must develop all three functions: hearing, constantly thinking about the merits, and then putting into practice. Without these three aspects one can't attain spiritual strength or the spiritual bliss which follows as a result.

Take, for example, what is happening now in this hall. We are all seated and listening to Swami. But after listening, you'll leave the hall and forget. What kind of an attitude is this? What kind of confidence in Swami's teaching is this? If you immediately forget, then what a waste of time it is for all of us! What an effort has been wasted on Swami's part! Think of what you are asking of Swami, the kind of spiritual gift you wish to receive from me. Do you have the confidence—are you willing to give the kind of attention and practice needed to achieve your dream? Only when you think about what you have heard, and put it into practice—at least one or two of the items that Swami is talking about—only then will you be consecrating your life and finding some meaning in your life by coming here.

I was struck by how much time and emphasis Baba gave to this point. What a sorry state to see that even when we are with the Avatar, we've lost an appreciation of the importance of his words. Bombarded by so many "wise men," we've lost confidence in anyone really knowing answers—and what's more, we've lost confidence in ourselves and our own grand potential. Consequently, words go in one ear and out the other. But just what was the message that Baba wanted us to hear and do something about? He went on to say:

We must develop a sense of oneness and brotherliness. If we are to win the vision of our atmic reality, if we are to experience the unity and love that is the basis of all creation, we must practice brotherliness. But man has fallen into a sorry state. He says one thing but practices another. He says that we are all brothers—but then brother takes brother to court to fight over property and land—struggling one against the other. To gain the bliss that comes from realizing the atma, one has to put into practice a true sense of brotherliness.

There are four qualities which characterize a human being. They are love, mercy, compassion and forebearance. Unless a person has these four qualities he can be compared to an animal. Man must develop these qualities and express them in the outer world with an attitude of service and brotherliness.

The evening was long and tiring. We had been sitting all day and my four friends felt weakened and irritable. The ride back to the hotel in the dark of night was uncomfortable. There were long silences. The one or two comments indicated a general feeling that Baba's talk was overly simple.

But this teaching of brotherhood was far from simple—simple only in appearance. Baba was actually teaching about man's deepest spiritual insight—the way to realize union with the universal. He was teaching about the oneness of all and the way to realize it through love—as Jesus had taught in his message of brotherhood: "Do onto others as you would have others do unto you." The message sounds simple, but what a profound cosmic vision is captured by these few simple words. Centered in the awareness that the transient, changing universe is based upon and created by an unchanging and eternal consciousness, one realizes this to be a grand affirmation of the reality of God, and of our ability to merge in Him. Baba has perhaps best captured the essence of his teaching in the following "simple" phrase, repeated over and over for the benefit of his devotees:

There is only one caste,
The caste of humanity;
There is only one language,
The language of the heart;
There is only one religion,
The religion of love;
There is only one God,
And He is omnipresent.

I'm sorry to say that modern-day psychiatry is not rooted in such a penetrating vision as this. Instead of leading to selflessness, a vision of brotherliness, a dedication to sacrifice for the good of the community and the attainment of higher levels of consciousness, psychiatric values which frequently overemphasize the emotions, too often lead to a preoccupation with self-interests. We don't quite seem to understand what the saints have long known about the very special importance of morality in shaping character, and how character influences the unfolding of consciousness. It is character, the concretization of morality, which determines the heights to which one's vision soars.

How essential it is for the establishment of world peace and for the highest state of individual growth that we come to recognize and accept a morality centered in an awareness of Universal Consciousness and leading to selflessness and brotherliness. Instead of dismissing this holy vision, we should be asking, just what are these values, this morality which leads to union—and how are we to adopt and incorporate into our character this special approach to reality?

Most choices of daily life are basically moral in nature, challenging our capacity to balance our need for gratification of animal drives and impulses with higher human aspirations and our yearning for the infinite. These range from lower-level choices related to regulation and control of the senses and drives (do I need to eat so much?)—to higher-level choices (should I lie for selfish gain?)—to still higher choices regarding how best to spend time: for personal gain and self-gratification, or sacrificial service for the benefit and happiness of others, and the cultivation of our relationship with God.

Choices lead to action; action forms habits; habits solidify into character. The saints tell us that character is a concretization of our moral vision, and that it is this structure which determines the depth of our vision into reality. If choice is strongly influenced by higher values and aspirations, if character grows out of the spiritual vision of oneness and brotherliness, it will lead us to ultimate union with the infinite. Seen in this light, morality—the guideline for directing thought, action and behavior—takes on a new importance.

Psychiatrists may have a problem in seeing morality in this new light. We have too often seen overly harsh and punitive morality lead to psychological illness and bondage instead of freedom. Yet there is a need to inquire more deeply into the nature of a balanced and sensible morality—to realize its central importance in the dynamics of unfolding consciousness.

In psychiatry, we see people whose consciousness is fixated or caught by conflicts originating in early developmental stages. Frequently the object of therapy is to return with the patient to that stage of development in order to undo, resolve and relearn. Released from the bondage of fear, consciousness is free to move on in its evolution to higher levels. It is at this point that the therapist, if not grounded in awareness of the dynamics of higher levels of consciousness, may unknowingly or knowingly focus too strongly on gratification of animal needs as the way to happiness and a fuller sense of self.

But the great spiritual personalities throughout history have taught the danger in this approach, that more important than self-gratification is the establishment of a morality and character that lead to real and lasting happiness. Here we can learn from the saints the special kind of disciplined spiritual work that leads to detachment from the temporary and transient, the world of duality—the world ruled by emotions and the pleasure/pain principle—in order to achieve higher levels of consciousness and, ultimately, union with the divine.

The dynamics of this process go something like this: First, one must have faith in the reality of a Universal Consciousness, or God, that created all this that we call the cosmos. As faith in this reality deepens, so too does our appreciation of the glory and grandeur of His handiwork. With this deepening appreciation comes an awareness of the love which prompted the creation. In turn our own love and devotion are ignited and form the basis for the development of higher consciousness. One begins to perceive divine handiwork and love in everything, and thus begins our vision of the unity underlying all the apparent variety in the universe.

This vision, practiced in the outer world in the form of service to others and acts of brotherliness, and done in the spiritual attitude of selflessness without demand for personal gain or reward, leads to an even more penetrating vision and a deep and profound sense of peace and love. Detaching, in this way, from the ups and downs of a life governed by the pleasure/pain principle, we enter a realm of steadiness of emotion and mind, peace and joy.

With emotions and mind quieted, the vision of the divine is

enhanced—and our confidence and faith in this vision grow. The more deeply centered we are in this reality, the more we are moved to greater expressions of sacrifice and surrender in its behalf. It is this sacrifice out of love, this holy act of surrender, that leads to the experience of union and the final realization that He and I are one. Such is the mystery of the dynamics of transcendence in Sai Baba's simple teaching of brotherhood.

When I hear psychiatrists discount what on the surface sounds like such a simple teaching, I can only conclude that their consciousness has not opened enough to grasp the dire straits of our world condition, nor the great possibility of our human potential. Yet we must take these teachings with the utmost seriousness. Not to do so is to constrict consciousness and to be content to live in the shallow and narrow. It is a sign of great short-sightedness, an unwillingness or immense fear of facing our mortality—or immortality.

The ride to the hotel was painful. In two short days we had confronted something very central to our lives—and now we had to sit in the dark and let it settle. How sad if we were to let this chance slip by. Sitting at the feet of an *Avatar*, having the direct experience of listening to his words—what a shame if we were now to forget or dismiss his great vision of reality as easily as one would forget a journey to a common marketplace. Oh well, maybe tomorrow would be better.

Man is not just a creature with hands and feet and eyes and ears and head and trunk. He is much more than the total of all these organs and parts. They are but the crude image that came out of the mold. Later, they have to be ground and scraped, polished, perfected, smoothened, softened, through the intellect and higher impulses and pure intentions and ideals. Then man becomes the ideal candidate for divinity which is his real destiny. The impulses will be rendered pure and the intentions will be raised to the higher level if man but decides to dedicate all his deeds, words and thoughts to the Lord. For this, faith in one supreme intelligence, which conceives, conserves and consumes this universe.

(Sathya Sai Baba)

The
Meeting

CHAPTER TWENTY-THREE

ANOTHER DAY came and went—and still no
interview. Although we were allowed in the house, our brief contacts
with Baba weren't enough to soothe the frayed nerves of my friends.
They grew more and more irritable and expounded on the discomfort
in their lives in general. I was witness to the outpouring of all their
worries, fears, discouragements and hopes. They were being opened
by that old Sai Baba technique: waiting in silence for the right moment. When they began talking about leaving I told them, "Please
wait just a bit longer; I know you'll have an interview and then everything will be clearer. Just wait—have patience and wait." But by this
time they had had quite enough of my encouragement and went
ahead with their plans anyway. It was then, at the end of the second
day, that Baba said he would see them the next morning.

During the two days in Bangalore, we had had some interesting
conversations, more so when the heat was on and feelings were stirred.
Dr. J. was a homespun, practical fellow. He was athletic in build

and it was apparently his interest in the physical which had brought him to the bioenergetic movement. When I had been interested in bioenergetics eight years earlier, I had actually attended a three-day bioenergetic workshop where he was an instructor. Now we spoke about bioenergetic theory and its relationship to *yoga*.

Wilhelm Reich, the movement's founder, discovered that an individual's posture, stance and gait reflect what he called, "body armoring": defensive holding positions in the body aimed at stopping the free flow of energy so as to avoid reexperiencing uncomfortable feelings related to traumatic events of childhood. The body armoring, it was thought, by blocking the natural free flow of energy, inhibits one's full immediate contact with his own self and environment.

Psychoanalysts reach these uncomfortable, defended-against, walled-off or repressed feelings with verbal techniques; bioenergetic therapists working with the body, reach these areas by increasing the flow of energy into "deadened" areas with specific exercises or by encouraging opposing postures or movements. Bioenergetic therapists are concerned with the flow of energy from head to foot and into the ground. When energy flows freely and without obstruction, one feels "grounded." An intimate and solid contact with the ground is thought to bring with it a feeling of strength and steadiness in character.

I felt that bioenergetic theory was not as well defined or as comprehensive as that of the *yogis*.[1] Bioenergetic theory focuses on levels of energy characteristic of lower stages of physical and psychic development. It deals with some of the coarser blocks to the flow of this energy—related to disturbances early in childhood—and with the energy itself, such as drive and emotional energy. It deals only to a limited extent with the more subtle *prana* or *kundalini* energy.

Thus bioenergetic treatment can indeed lead to more sexual and aggressive freedom and potency, but if there is no accounting for how subtle *prana* and *kundalini* activate higher *chakras*, it will not lead to higher levels of consciousness. *Yogis*, on the other hand, understand the dynamics, organization, flow and function and of the more subtle *prana* and *kundalini* energies and their influence on higher *chakras*. These are the dynamics of spiritual growth and consciousness-raising.

While the bioenergetic system describes energy descending into the earth—it's very function being to "ground" one in the real world, as it were—*yogis* describe an energy system ascending upward to heaven, whose function is to enable the individual to transcend the material world of duality and separation. Both psychoanalytic and bioenergetic therapy seem to me to confine their interest to lower stages of organization of energy and personality development, whereas *yoga* describes and defines the dynamics of the individual's unfolding energy, personality and consciousness as higher centers are activated: what might be called "transpersonal" parts of the self. For a more detailed account of these dynamics please refer to Appendices III and IV.

Dr. J. had been a bioenergetic therapist for a number of years and was now experimenting with new techniques, but he questioned their validity. He was hoping for clarification and was also wondering about the unusual sensation in his brow, as if his brow *chakra* (third eye) was opening but cloudy. His wife, B.J., had no questions. She felt life was full and happy and would let happen what would happen.

On the morning of the third day when feelings were at their lowest, we met for breakfast in the East-West Hotel. By this time my friends hardly spoke to me. They had had enough of my optimism and just wanted to ventilate about their discomfort. Dr. H. spoke at length about his dissatisfaction working with the county mental health system. Hoping for new insight and direction, he was disappointed at not getting what he wanted from his visit with Baba. As he opened to the others, they responded by sharing their own concerns and difficulties. The conversation grew distant from Baba; there seemed to be no thought of the relationship of their lives to this moment, even though we were about to meet with Baba for the much-anticipated interview. I knew this would be an extremely meaningful and important meeting for them, but they had lost hope for such an outcome and their minds were elsewhere. Even though my relationship with them was strained, I thought I'd try once more.

"Excuse me, but we're about to have a real important meeting with Sai Baba. It might be wise for us to think about it and what we might want to ask of him, what we might want from this interview."

They cut me off quickly. B.J. said, "Don't you ever just let things alone—why this need to always bring up your Sai Baba?"

I was quiet during the taxi ride to *Brindavan*. The others told me their feelings plainly enough: they thought Baba looked nice, that he was glamorous at times—but they didn't feel he was in any way divine. Contact with him hadn't changed their personal lives. "We've had enough and it's time for us to get on with our trip." I thought, "Well, let's see what you're going to do with this, dear *Swami.*"

We were escorted into an interview room. I recognized a number of my friends: Mike Goldstein, a physician from Los Angeles; John Svensson, an oil tanker captain from San Pedro, California; and Dr. V.K. Gokak, a professor and past principal of Bangalore University in India. He had brought a friend, the principal of a university in northern India. There were a number of other Indian people as well. As we entered the room, Baba quickly materialized ash for B.J. and N.S. and a silver medallion in the form of the Hindu OM for N.S. N.S. broke into tears as if struck by lightning. She was stunned and began to cry in deep sobs.

Baba materialized some objects for the Indian people and sat down in his chair while we all seated ourselves on the floor around him. There were about 25 people in the room.

I was surprised to see Dr. Gokak. I had visited him just a few days earlier at his home in Bangalore. We had had a very interesting talk about the process of spiritual development. I had commented that the journey is difficult at times, demanding great discipline, perseverance and the willingness to undertake austerities and accept suffering along the way. Dr. Gokak responded that spiritual aspirants sometimes court hardship and in a poetic way described the process as more like the natural unfolding of a flower. It took patience and time, he said, but the process could be as natural and painless as the unfolding from acorn to oak tree.

After we had both given our opinions, we looked at each other like innocent children and honestly admitted that the mystery was far greater than either of us could comprehend. Here we were, a professor for many years, as distinguished as any scholar in India, and an American psychiatrist for some 14 years, being made into little children. Smiling, we made a pact: "Let's ask Baba about this point, and whoever finds out first must share it with the other."

And now as fate would have it, here I was, sitting next to my great friend and playmate in this drama, perhaps about to receive the answer this very moment. Sai Baba's devotees say those present in any particular interview are destined to have been there, the seating arrangements were made many lifetimes ago by the Lord himself. And so we sat, perhaps by chance, perhaps not; I, right in front of Baba's feet, Dr. Gokak behind me — and who was this to Baba's right but my friend from San Pedro, the oil tanker captain, John Svensson.

How interesting. I had met John on the grounds a few days before and had an unusual experience with him. I'm sorry to say, because it shows my lack of spiritual maturity, that at the time of our discussion I had felt John was a bit naive in his spiritual outlook. He was a man in his 70's who had lived a full and active life and was as sweet as he could be. But for some reason, I had this distorted feeling that I was more sophisticated in spiritual matters than he. John, with an innocent twinkle in his eye, had asked me, "How will you answer Baba if he asks you what you want?" I said that I wasn't sure, trying to brush the question aside, not wanting to get into a discussion with John.

But he continued, "Oh, I would ask him for self-realization." John was a Scandinavian and said the word "realization" with a certain intonation that only a Scandinavian would use. I smiled at the pronunciation and with a sense of superiority wondered if John understood what he was asking for. Little did I know that Baba was about to teach me a deep and profound lesson about my judgments and ego.

So here we were, the psychiatrists, Dr. Gokak and John. The drama was shaping up just fine. All eyes were on Baba, and just as John Svensson had foretold, Baba turned to him and asked, *"Sir, what do you want?"*

John looked up with those innocent eyes, and as he had said he would, answered, "Self-realization," with that same Scandinavian intonation and vibration.

Baba looked at him with great love and said, *"And what is self-realization?"*

"Your goose is cooked now, John," I thought. John began to sputter and stammer so Baba continued. *"Man is divine. But he is not aware of his own divinity. He mistakenly thinks that he is this little body. But he is not this body, and he is not the mind."* He stopped a moment and looked at the psychiatrists. *"There are some psychiatrists here. They study man's mind, unaware that this is really not who man is. Man is something infinite, immutable and eternal — beyond time, space and beyond his body. Psychiatrists make a mistake in thinking that man is his* mind. *The mind is part of the world of duality, the world of many names and forms. But you are beyond all of that. You are beyond the material universe, beyond difference, beyond duality. You are eternal and unchanging—beyond time and space."*

He turned and pointed to a number of people in the room saying, *"She says 'I', he says 'I', they say 'I'—we all experience this 'I'. What is the significance of this? It is that beyond all the separate and distinct names and forms there is an underlying reality that is the same for everyone. This inner experience of 'I' reflects an eternal, universal basis from which everything comes and to which everything must return, a reality that is beyond time and space. This is the reality that is worth man's attention. Attaining it, realizing it—that is the purpose of his existence."*

Baba paused a moment. It seemed that his train of thought took another direction and he continued with heightened excitement in his voice. *"Shirdi Baba had a ring with a large blue stone. Blue is the color of the infinite—that which cannot be measured, that which is unfathomable. See,"* he said, gesturing with his arms, *"the sky is blue and the ocean is blue. Blue is a cool color. It is peaceful. Look around; the doctors in the room are all wearing blue—it comforts and soothes."*

Sure enough, every doctor in the room was wearing a blue shirt. He continued, *"And etched in the middle of this blue stone is the symbol of OM. OM is the inner identity of this unfathomable reality. It is this inner reality, awareness of the infinite, universal self, that is what we must learn to realize."* And as he began to circle the air with his hand, everyone froze in wonderment, awaiting his creation. In a flash, he produced a large ring. *"Here is the ring that Shirdi wore at the time of his death."*[2]

Baba passed the beautiful blue stone ring around the room for everyone to see and touch. Light seemed to emanate from its center, making the OM symbol etched on its surface seem even more prominent.

Westerners won't be familiar with *Shirdi Sai Baba*, a spiritual figure whom millions in India revere as an *Avatar*. An object belonging to this sacred figure would be as treasured as any of Christ's possessions. *Shirdi* died in 1918, after telling his followers that he would be reborn eight years later. Sai Baba was born in 1926. From early adolescence he has told his followers that he was previously *Shirdi Baba*, come again to continue his teachings. He also says that he will come one more time in the form of *Prema Sai Baba* soon after he leaves this body at the age of 96. Now he was apparently bringing back a ring he had worn during his previous incarnation.

Those in the audience who knew about *Shirdi Baba* regarded this as a most sacred moment; they were stunned, as I was. The ring circled the room and all had an opportunity to touch it and marvel at its beauty. We placed it to our foreheads as a sign of our wish that its holy vibration would open our third eye of spiritual wisdom. When it had gone around full circle, Baba took it in his hand, held it a moment—and then looking softly and sweetly at John Svensson, gave it to him. *"Here, it is yours,"* he said. *"Wear it."*

Later I was to hear that Baba told John they were very close in previous lifetimes and that soon he would reveal more to him about who he was and the purpose and meaning of this lifetime. I had made a petty, discounting judgment about the depth of John's spirituality, and now I discovered that in many lifetimes he and Baba were old buddies. It served to deepen my appreciation of the great mystery that life is. We don't have the slightest notion of who we really are and why we're playing out this drama with one another. For years I had wondered what people meant when they described experiencing Baba's play: that he was the doer. The statement had always had just an intellectual meaning for me. Now I had experienced the meaning of this reality directly.

Baba looked at the psychiatrists again. *"Do you want to ask any questions?"*

Dr. J. began, "I'm having the strange feeling that my coming to India, that my finding my way here, is not just an accident or chance occurrence. There must be something deeper than I can see. Is that right?"

"Yes, that's right," Baba confirmed. *"There is something more; your higher self, your higher intelligence, is fashioning the experience because you're now ready to see more deeply into spiritual matters."*

Dr. J. thought a moment and said, "You know, I have a feeling that this is a very important moment, a very meaningful moment in my life."

And Baba, with a great gentleness replied, *"Yes, and there is even more."* He began talking directly to Dr. J. about the concerns and worries he had voiced earlier. It was as if Baba had actually been with us for breakfast, taking part in the conversation. He touched on

specifics about Dr. J.'s worries and questions about the new psycho-
therapeutic approaches he was trying. Baba told him not to continue
with these approaches but to continue along the lines he had been using previously. And then looking directly into his eyes, he said: *"I
know you're beginning to feel the opening of your third eye, but now it's a
little cloudy. Don't worry, I will help you."*

What a poignant moment—to see Baba actually in touch with
this man's deepest aspirations, talking to him like a protective father,
assuring him of his loving protection and help. A moment like this
gives one great faith and love; one takes away the sense of an intimate
personal relationship with the divine.

Baba then confronted Dr. H. *"I know you have just stopped one
job,"* he said, *"and that's good. You have been dissatisfied in your work
and I will help. I will talk to you privately."* Then he materialized a large
gold medal and neckchain in the form of *Shirdi Baba* for Dr. Goldstein and a medal for one of the Indian guests, and indicated that he
would see each of us privately in the next room.

He did just that; each of my four friends came out of the room
looking radiant and alive. Then Baba called me into the private
room. Beaming, he said, *"They're very happy."*

"Yes Baba, they're very happy—thank you, thank you. And I'm
very happy too."

He materialized some *vibuthi* for me and as I put my hand out to
receive it, said, *"No, open your mouth."* So I opened my mouth like a
baby bird as he held his hand overhead and poured the *vibuthi* into
it. I can't begin to tell you how poignant and moving was this gentle,
gentle moment.

What a change of mood on the taxi ride back to the city!
Everyone was ecstatic and thanked me profusely. The meeting with
Baba had been deeply moving and meaningful for all of them. He had
told Dr. J. to continue to practice psychiatry with the same techniques he had been using, not to investigate along new lines. He had
told Dr. H. privately that the way to practice psychiatry was to listen
patiently until he understood and felt the patient's life deeply. *"Then
when you and the patient are one, you can teach him about our reality."*
Dr. H. was moved by this very personal remark: "Our reality." As for
B.J., Baba had agreed that she was happy and needn't make any
changes.

Baba's relationship with N.S. seemed very special. It had been apparent from the start, when he knew she was unable to come to the *ashram* the first day because of her stomach problem. Now during the private interview, he had shown her his omniscience by talking knowingly about her emotionally ill daughter, knowing that Dr. H. had been the girl's psychiatrist and promising to help. He told her to return later for *"special vibuthi"* for her daughter, to be used as medicine.

That afternoon we each went our separate ways. When we met later that evening for our final farewell, N.S. approached with tears in her eyes. "I feel terrible. I don't know how I did it but I lost that beautiful little OM medal. I can't find it anywhere. I'm going to pray to Baba to find it for me and give it back."

It's not often that he'll do such a thing, but it's possible," I said. Then Dr. H. piped up, "If he can do that, I'll really be convinced."

A few weeks after my return to San Diego I received a phone call from N.S. "Listen to what happened. I felt crushed after losing the medal. I returned to Delhi, traveled with the group, and finally ended the tour in Bombay. Every night I prayed with all my heart for Baba to bring it back. In Bombay I went through the same ritual, praying to Baba for the medal. The morning after I arrived I awoke to find it right next to me in bed!

"I felt such deep contact with Baba, I wept and wept — I was exhilarated. Dr. H. was stunned. It's so difficult to share an experience like this. People wonder if it's just imagination or if I overlooked it in my searching — but I know. I know how much I searched every day of the trip. I know what lengths I went to to find that medal — and for it to show up right next to me in my bed was an absolute miracle.

"I told the group leader and he asked me to speak to the group that evening about the experience we'd had with Baba. I felt it was such an honor and privilege to be able to speak to them about Sai Baba."

Notes

1. See Appendix III *Prana* and *Kundalini* and Appendix IV for a discussion of the limitations of the humanistic-existentialist theories of energy, compared to the yogis' understanding of the dynamics of *prana*, *kundalini* and the *chakras* and their influence in promoting spiritual growth and raising consciousness.

2. Photo of the *Shirdi Baba* ring is on p. 264.

Something you have held, seeking something to hold. Hold on to it firm and fast. Something you have asked for, though asking is not needed. Well, stay on till the gift is granted. Some resolution you have entertained in your mind though you have no need to resolve. Still, knock at the door until it opens and your resolution is fulfilled. Either I must grant you the thing you crave for, unable to withstand your yearning, or you must realize the absurdity and the audacity and thus conquer the wrong yearning.
(Sathya Sai Baba)

The Making of a
New-Age Therapist

CHAPTER TWENTY-FOUR

HOW IS a therapist trained in the dynamics of unfolding consciousness? Not only must he know about the lower realms of mind dominated by desires, pleasures, pains and ego, but also the higher realms and beyond. That means having direct experience of higher spiritual dimensions—in other words, becoming no less than a spiritual aspirant himself. Much more than being in touch with animal instincts and being successful at gratifying basic needs, such a therapist must be a teacher in the highest sense of the word— that is, a truly moral and just person. And it's perhaps here where the therapist realizes the most fundamental demands of his profession— and here that the deepest resistance to spirituality arises. For the therapist as for anyone else, the path demands a deep yearning for spiritual insight, and the courage to face the challenges and fears along the way.

Sai Baba has defined four stages in the course of one's spiritual development—self-confidence, self-satisfaction, self-sacrifice and self-realization. These phases refer to the same process of transition and transcendence that Wilbur described in terms of differentiation, transcendence (dying of the old and rebirth into the new) and integration—and Hegel (1949): "To supersede is at once to negate and to preserve."

I'd like to investigate these steps along the path of a spiritual education by way of recounting how I experienced them on my journey. The journey, the incidents and lessons along the way, are really a puzzle, an intimate play between the aspirant and God Himself, filled with the unexpected, trials and tribulations, sorrows and joys, humor, excitement, and awe. Although being born into the new is exhilarating and awe-inspiring, as one dies to the old, one must have courage and faith. And always, one must be open to the unexpected, able to accept uncertainty, and be filled with constant appreciation and awareness of God's presence as teacher, guide and Lord.

(1) Self-Confidence: The development of confidence in the higher self begins with an explosive awakening. The sudden insight that a spiritual dimension higher than mind actually exists is shocking—all previous concepts of the world crumble before it, the mind is humbled. The awakening may be so profound and moving that the psyche is almost shattered; the experience is commonly described as a death. It is being "unmade," to be born into a new dimension of reality with a new organization and integration of character. This is a stage of great vulnerability as one faces the fears associated with the death of the old with the innocence and openness of a newborn babe. It requires courage to face all fears, including *mortal* fear, with a steady vision of the divine. Accompanying the process may be a period of retreat into this new inner world to gain stability in and familiarity with it. It is like building a fence around a small sapling to give it protection to grow and mature so that one day, when it is strong enough, it can face the outer elements by itself, and even provide shelter and protection for others. With growing confidence from direct experience with this higher inner self, the delusion of the old, limited self crumbles.

(2) Self-Satisfaction: The reality of higher consciousness becomes stabilized and solidified by experiencing profound "satisfaction"—the sense of peace, bliss and love that accompanies all acts directed to the higher experience, such as thoughts, contemplation, meditation, devotional practices, and the development of a

just and moral character as well as selfless service to the needy. The higher self is perceived ever more directly and strongly until it becomes the most moving and meaningful experience of life: the source of all intuition, empathy and creativity.

(3) Self-Sacrifice: The higher self is selfless, motivated by higher moral impulses, compassion and love. As one is centered more deeply in selfless love, life becomes a service to others without desires for personal reward. This selfless sacrifice without need for personal gain in turn serves to more deeply break the shackles of the pleasure/pain principle.

(4) Self-Realization: Out of the sacrifice of the small self, which has been bound by the pleasure/pain principle, one realizes the self-less, universal state of union with the divine.

SELF-CONFIDENCE & SELF-SATISFACTION

Many of us who enter the field of behavior sciences are searching for our real higher self, and our interest in our field can be seen as a spiritual quest. And in the course of our training and practice many of us feel a lack of wholeness and fullness in a field which identifies man with just his body, emotions and mind. I summarized what I consider the strengths and limitations of psychoanalytic, gestalt and bioenergetic therapies in my first book, *Sai Baba: The Holy Man and the Psychiatrist*. I had come to an impasse. Even though investigating thoughts, feelings and emotions by way of these approaches led to a greater range and depth of emotional expression with others, I also experienced my aloneness more fully. They led me to the edge of "the great void—the dark abyss" as the existentialists call it—and left me having to accept my limited, at times absurd, mortality as the ultimate reality.

And so the confusion and fear that we must face on the path to a new vision of higher self. Was my desire for transcendence of this bleak destiny a defense against fear of death? Most psychotherapists would answer yes. In *The Future of an Illusion*, *Totem and Taboo* and *Moses and Monotheism*, Freud concluded that religion was an illusion and that positing an omnipresent God was a defense against feelings of anxiety and helplessness.

So as therapists, if we seek transcendence we not only doubt our motives, we must also face the even more terrifying possibility of hav-ing to give up the basic assumptions upon which our life and profession rest. Fearing that if they break with convention they will lose the sense of community with their peers and lose their referrals and livelihood, many therapists choose to dig in and solidify their traditional position. Many become opinionated, resistant, rigid, when faced with data that challenges their assumptions. And on the other side are psychiatrists who "believe" and become renegades—defying and ridiculing the mainstream. Taking the leap, while trying to build a bridge from one system to the other, is difficult indeed.

To face these challenges and fears, one has to draw on a deep source of inner strength. This was provided me through an extraordinary and monumental experience with Sathya Sai Baba which convinced me of the reality of the divine and gave me the strength to face the fears accompanying death and rebirth.

When I first visited Sai Baba in May of 1972, he was introducing a course in Indian culture and spirituality at his highly respected science and arts college in Brindavan. I went there, a 35-year-old psychiatrist, thinking that I knew who I was and what life was all about. When you really think about it, this was absurd. All the eons that have been and will be, a timeless vastness beyond imagination, and I had the bright (certainly not exclusive) idea that I knew what it was all about. Then I met Baba, and of course he smashes such ideas very quickly: instant humility.

The school facilities are built up now, but at that time the courses were held in a makeshift auditorium made of poles and leaves, with monkeys jumping all around. There was great excitement, however, with prominent speakers and bright students from all over India and around the world converging for this inaugural event with Baba. The speakers were seated in front near the podium while the students sat on the ground. I was fortunate enough to be allowed to sit with the speakers. That was just great for my ego, as it played into my misconception that I knew something of real significance and might even be considered a teacher myself. We waited for our first lesson to begin.

There was a lull in the program and I began talking to a tall distinguished-looking American in front of me. He told me that his son, upon graduating from Harvard Business College, had gone to India on a vacation and written back that he had met God and was planning to stay. Like any concerned parent he had come to take the foolish young man back home. It was apparent from our conversation that the father was quite wealthy, from a successful business in the Midwest, and that he was intelligent and mentally strong.

"Who is this Sai Baba?" we asked overselves. "The best I can make out is that he's probably something like an Indian Billy Graham," he said. I know more than that, I thought to myself, but we'll wait and see.

Suddenly there was a hush, and there in the opening of the auditorium stood Baba. He was swaying slowly back and forth and appeared peaceful, beautiful—and very much in command. All eyes were turned to him; there was absolute silence.

He smiled and set about filling the room with love, walking among the students, stopping to talk, soon putting everyone at ease. He circled the hall slowly and began to approach us. As he passed my acquaintance, he patted him approvingly on the shoulder, and all at once this big powerful man began to cry—so heavily that I was embarrassed to look.

Shaken by this sudden turn of events, I thought, "Oh my God, what are we in for here?" Then a volunteer came over to the man, summoning him to an interview with Baba. When he returned some time later, he appeared quite changed. Bending forward, I asked in a whisper, "Can he really materialize objects?" That's what I was interested in at the time: a material sign of a higher level of consciousness than that possessed by all the rest of the hundreds of teachers we were always hearing about.

Subdued now, he replied, "Yes, he can materialize objects, but what's more moving is his joy, his friendliness—his love." From then on he stayed very quiet. I saw him on the grounds, absorbed in contemplation or reading a book by Baba. It seemed Baba had unmade and remade him in an instant.

Well, it wasn't long after that shock and after witnessing at first hand the most extraordinary materializations of objects and hearing incredible stories of Baba's power and glory (described in detail in my first book) that I began to realize how extraordinary Baba was. Speakers would get up and talk, but what did they know? Baba would appear, move through the audience with great love and seemingly complete knowledge of everyone, with remarkable energy, peace and poise—and no one could take his eyes off him. It was so clear: the speakers after all were merely mortal—but Sai Baba was something else. That's when my speech-giving phobia began.

Confidence in my old self and in what I knew crumbled. "What if he asks me to talk in front of his students?" I wondered. The realization hit me that I didn't know as much as they did. I should actually be in the back row, not sitting here with the teachers. Every one of the students knew of a reality far beyond mine; I was a babe in the woods. I began to shake: "Oh, my God, what would happen if he asked me to speak?" This was my unmaking. I realized that I knew absolutely nothing; I withdrew.

What a powerful awakening! Certain that what I was observing was absolutely real, I entered another dimension of consciousness. Stripped clean of all my preconceived concepts about reality, I began to feel that anything was possible. I became an innocent child again: all openness and vulnerability, groping for an identity. Reality changed—it was a whole new ball game, and I didn't know all the rules and regulations. How would I lead my life now, practice my profession, relate to my wife and children? Although lost, I literally, physically, felt an expansive, exhilarating inner dimension soaring beyond me into space and extending forever. Perhaps I was giving up familiar theories and practices to gain a knowledge beyond thinking—direct experience of a higher intuitive plane. Did this expansive feeling truly represent an extension of consciousness; and could it be translated in therapy into greater empathy, a more intimate knowledge of the other?

I returned home feeling exhilarated but extremely vulnerable. People were suspicious of this dramatic change in me. From their point of view, I must have looked stark raving mad. Innocently thinking that everyone would be as thrilled as I was about Sai Baba and what he seemed to represent in terms of human consciousness, my wife and I opened our home to a gathering of some 300 friends and acquaintances, many of them colleagues from the university. Reputable and prominent speakers told of their experiences with Sai Baba, attesting to his divine qualities. These were believable people, stable, decent and strong-minded, holding respectable positions in society. But lo and behold, that evening saw the parting of most of my friends and acquaintances. They still said hello in passing, but now with a rather strange look in their eyes.

I served on the abortion boards of two large San Diego hospitals, including the University Hospital. At that time, psychiatrists helped decide if a woman should be considered for a therapeutic abortion on the grounds that the pregnancy threatened her mental health. Before India, I was "liberal" minded and thought that all women who wanted an abortion should have one. My Porsche and dirt motorcycle rounded out the image. Now, resigning from the boards for spiritual reasons—"This kind of decision about life and death should be left to God and not mortals"—was an all too sudden switch to be considered altogether sane. I sold the Porsche and motorcycle and bought an old jeep.

How was I to handle the "outer" world of relationships and profession when everything inside had been so transformed? To regain my balance and bearings, I went back "inside" to the real, palpable, exquisitely felt expanse of space, peace and joy I had discovered in India. I felt a need to deepen my relationship with Sai Baba, to find solace and protection in reaffirming all that he stood for.

And he did protect—no question about it. One of his greatest miracles was keeping my practice alive. Even though referral sources dried up, in spite of all the statues and paintings of Hindu gods and goddesses and Baba's pictures adorning my office, and even though I was turning inward to meditation and devotional practices— throughout it all, my practice thrived. I'll never know why. You'd think a liberal-minded psychiatrist returning from India obsessed with God and unable to stop talking about a holy man would go broke pretty quickly.

When I went to Baba the second time, he took me aside and asked, *"How's your practice?"*

"Do you know about that, *Swami?"* I replied with a smile, "People don't understand."

Looking at me with great love, he said, *"I know, I know—in time they will. Don't worry about money—everything will be all right."*

I said, "Okay—thank you, *Swami.*" And I didn't worry (well, not too much anyway) and he kept my practice going. What a wonderful sense of his omnipresent protection at a time of great vulnerability! It cemented the relationship forever.

Immersing myself in Sai Baba, suddenly I had the urge to write about my experiences with him.

Now, writing had always been difficult for me. I almost flunked my freshman English course in college and could do no better than a "C" in others. I couldn't put two words together correctly on paper. But now, all of a sudden I couldn't stop writing.

I took over our bedroom. My wife really loved that: paper, pencils, erasers all over the place. She could hardly find a place to sleep. Words came pouring out and I couldn't think of anything else but Baba.

RETREATING INTO INNER LIFE

The awakening is glorious—but even so, the road is not easy. Being unmade leaves one vulnerable as a child. It is here in this vulnerable stage, where it is so easy to make mistakes and look foolish, that one feels Baba's protection so clearly. For without it one would surely fail. Courage to face fear, steadiness, and Baba's omnipresent protection—this is the recipe for success. Let me tell you of my mistakes and impending doom—and then being saved at the last moment, which deepened confidence in the higher self.

Soon after meeting Baba I put a meditation and devotional room in my office—right next to the waiting room. Bad judgment. A paper-thin wall separated the two rooms. One day as a patient was sitting in the waiting room, in whisked Indra Devi, one of Sai Baba's most ardent devotees, and with a joyful smile said, "Let's have *bhajans*." "Fine with me, I'm ready any time," I replied happily—and then in my best professional and respectable posture went to the door of the waiting room and said, "I'll be just a few minutes late, something has come up that needs attention and I'll be with you soon." Then into the devotional room we sprang with drum and clanker in hand, and in ecstasy sang our hearts out, clapping and yelling and singing like fervent fanatic devotees.

When I came to my senses and looked at my watch I saw that 15 minutes had elapsed. Tapping Indra Devi on the shoulder, I motioned that it was time to stop. And when I opened the door to the waiting room all I could see was an open door to the outside and the breeze gently blowing through an empty room. Completely empty: dematerialization.

A young graduate chemistry student came to see me. He had difficulty communicating with parents who were cold and aloof. As a result he became somewhat hardened and defiant of authority, tending to keep himself distant from people and hence prone to depression. Feelings about parents can easily be transferred to the therapist and such a client may become angry and defiant. It was at a time of my early developing relationship with Sai Baba and I was attempting to put into practice his teaching about the *so-hum* meditation. I had prayed to Baba that he teach me how to make my practice worship so that I would never forget him. I had picked up skills and insights from my psychiatric study, but they had been limited. Now I wanted to sacrifice all that and take Sai Baba as my only teacher—to apply his teachings in every aspect of my profession. It just wouldn't do any more to refer to other teachers—Freud, Jung, Maslow, Perls—during my professional life and Sai Baba only while at home in my devotional room. It was time to transform my work into worship so it served as part of my continuous devotion to him.

Yet it was early in my relationship with Baba, and I fumbled about and made mistakes. During this hour with the graduate student, I was feeling spacey and high from my breath-control exercises and meditation on *so-hum*, and was using the *client's* energy to heighten the inner experience of meditation. And so if he got angry, confrontive or defiant, I chose not to address those feelings directly, but tried to use the energy from these feelings to promote and intensify the meditation. I was finding a way to connect feelings with breathing and actually breathing the feelings in, to energize the meditation.

This young man began sensing my distance and got angry. And I, trying to see the outer world as delusion, and to see Baba behind every act, and seeing everything as energy to breathe in for the meditation, said to myself, "Oh how wonderful, this is not really a young man getting angry at me, but you, *Swami*, showing your love in another form. Let me use this wonderful energy to promote and intensify the meditation." I sat there smiling. My client became irate—"What are you smiling for?" Again I said inwardly, "Oh swell, you're going to test me—to see if I'll get caught in appearances and forget that all is you. But, no, I'm not going to react—I know this is just a disguised way of your expressing love—and I'm going to use this lovely energy of love to increase my meditation and my immersion in your glory." I continued smiling peacefully.

Now, as I look back, I see that I was naive and foolish—a child learning how to walk and stumbling. So engrossed with the inner world, I had lost some sense of proper relating to the outer. My client, not understanding my seeming indifference, became angrier and angrier, "You're just like my parents! Why are you taunting me like this—not answering—just smiling—Why are you acting like this?"

And then he got up and stomped out. Another miraculous dematerialization.

This early stage of transition is a vulnerable one, and without the protection of the Lord Himself, we would surely perish. And slowly, through the ups and downs, the mistakes and triumphs, confidence in the higher self is attained and satisfaction in experiencing the higher self deepens this confidence. Then we are ready for the next stage: self-sacrifice.

SELF-SACRIFICE

We have to pay attention to the outside world too. We must be careful not to turn our spiritual path into a narcissistic and self-centered act, and we must be ready to sacrifice our own desires and pleasures for a higher purpose. We must balance our inner world with the outer, and be sensible. After a certain honeymoon period, with its feelings of great closeness with the divine and in which we may be allowed to withdraw from the outer world, we are thrust back, now remade in the spirit. For only a short time in this present age, are we allowed to retreat—and then we must move back into the outside world and spiritualize our work there.

Being moral, spiritual people in the outer world may entail a sacrifice. Sai Baba says that he can transform sky into earth and earth into sky. It seems to me his greatest miracle is that he has transformed sky (superconsciousness, himself) into earth in the form of Sathya Sai Baba, in order to transform us (earth) into sky (him, superconsciousness). It is our task to transmute our vision of him (sky) into our work on earth so that it becomes sky. What a glorious transformation!

And so from the first stage where we withdraw inside ourselves to develop increasing confidence in the higher self, there comes a day when we must move back into the outer world, remade in the image of his teachings, to develop the skills to operate in the outer world and transform this outer world into sky. This moving back into the outer world, after being so satisfied with the inner, can be difficult and in the last analysis is really a sacrifice. Because being in the outer world means being subject to temptation and the pull of lower elements, and it takes a constant remembering of the higher life to escape being caught. The trick now is to be in the outer world but not affected by it. At a certain stage in my development I began getting the message that I was to be more actively involved with the outer world. One day I was walking in the hospital when a secretary approached and said, "Dr. Sandweiss, you should stop now." I should stop what? She said, "Your pants are falling off, you're too skinny." Before meeting Baba I was a stocky 205 pounds and after meeting him I became a strict vegetarian, observed periods of fasting and had lost weight to 165 pounds. So my pants were sagging, and I was getting to the point where if I turned sideways some people might have had trouble seeing me. Not even my best friend would tell me about this "spiritual anorexia," until a kind secretary told me to stop.

This is how Sai Baba helped awaken me to my responsibilities in the outer world. It was at a time when I was with Baba during Christmas 1978. I love to go to India—something special always happens. Away from the hectic life here, the emotions and mind quiet down and I move from the outer to the inner world—and into a seemingly paradoxical state combining great peace and joyful exhilaration. It's a level of consciousness and a way of life I can't express in words, though God knows I've certainly tried.

The central focal point at *Prasanthi Nilayam*, Baba's *ashram*, is the temple in which he lives. He's always going in and out so people are constantly looking that way and gathering there to see him and sing to him. And if one is extremely fortunate, as I have been once in a while, you may be allowed to sit on the veranda, just outside the temple door. The area is charged with a marvelous excitement. I sense Baba's presence strongly there, and when he appears at the door I can hardly remain in my skin, the excitement is so great. Devotees congregate around the temple twice a day for *darshan*, when he walks through the crowd. The vision of Baba in the midst of all those open hearts is so beautiful. I love to space-out on that porch and move into my inner life. I could sit there eight to ten hours a day until my legs turned to tree stumps—and still crave to stay longer.

I particularly took to the *so-hum* meditation. According to Baba, the breath itself is a very holy *mantra* or sound: *so-hum*—"I am He." With each breath we're saying, "I am He, I am He," constantly being reminded that we are one with God. Baba says that we should link our awareness to each of the 21,600 breaths we take every day in order to constantly challenge the delusion of duality. He asks us to have such determination in our spiritual lives, and this experience gave me great strength.

We were expecting a big Christmas celebration with a special play performed by Westerners. The *ashram* was filled with excitement. All the devotees' minds and hearts were filled with an exquisite sense of the love and sacrifice that Christ had come to give.

The Westerners had worked on their play for weeks. I hadn't had much to do with it and at this point kept myself quite away from most people except for those who approached occasionally with an emotional problem and needed a little Thorazine or Valium. But for the most part I tried to stay away from other people who might distract me from my focus on Sai Baba. I had heard that the play was having a little bit of difficulty getting off the ground because of some squabbling and that there was a possibility of it's not even being performed. But that was the most I knew about it. I just stayed by myself, spacing out in meditation, and every once in a while I'd open my eyes and see Baba and feel so exhilarated and excited that I never wanted to return to the earth.

I was sitting on the veranda, eyes closed in meditation, about an hour before play time. A hush came over the crowd and I heard, *"Sandweiss."* I peeked out from behind half-closed eyelids to find to my amazement that there was Baba calling for me. So I ran over to him like a little mouse saying, "Yes, *Swami.*" He said, *"Sandweiss, you're in charge of all the activities this evening, the Christmas play and all the events."* Now not only would I probably not be able to handle that responsibility now when I'm stronger in the world, but then when I was so vulnerable I was almost helpless. I said, "Me, *Swami?*" And he said, *"Yes."* So all there was for me to say was, "Thank you."

Little beads of sweat appeared on my brow. It simply isn't easy — the path isn't easy at these times. So I had to go around with the unpleasant task of telling the people who were in charge — that I was now in charge. And of course, they didn't know how to take that.

Very unpleasant. And I was overcome with the urge to go to the bathroom. So I ran off to my little apartment and was away only about 10 minutes. But by the time I came back, the play had begun — and I saw that I wasn't in charge of anything. I went to the back of the room and just sat and looked at Baba and said inwardly, "Am I doing a good job, *Swami?*" Sometimes the mill of God grinds slowly but exceedingly well. Was it time to move more actively into the world but remain unaffected by it?

STILL MORE INTO THE OUTER WORLD

One day I was sitting on the porch *so-huming*, literally spaced out, and Baba came out and said, *"Sandweiss."* I looked up and murmured, "Yes, *Swami?"* He said, *"Come along—and your brother* (who was along on this trip) *also come along."*

So we got into his car and drove with him to the village of *Anantapur* where he has a women's college. It was pure grace to be with him for that hour-long drive. He put us at ease, almost as if he were an old school chum of ours. When we stopped at a train crossing, everyone on the road would come running. They'd fall to the ground, raise their hands and arms in worship, and weep and pray for a glance or a wave. Then I would be shocked back into the strange realization that we were with the *Avatar.* Just to be in the car and witness what happened along the road was absolutely amazing. Then we'd move on and *maya* would return and we'd think we were back with our old school mate.

Riding with Baba that day, I saw the quality of detachment in a way I had never imagined. He seemed actually to be vibrating: energy seemed to be pouring from him with incredible intensity. Much of the time he appeared to be in another dimension. He would draw his gaze inside, making hand movements or sitting in a particular posture which appeared to reflect a state we weren't in touch with. Then all of a sudden he'd return his attention to the car—tell us a joke or a simple story—and be with us like old chums. Then off he'd go again.

At one point the road turned to enter a long, flat stretch of countryside. Half a mile down the road I could see a tiny speck which I guessed to be a person stirring. Baba leaned forward. *"Look, see the woman? She knows Baba is coming. This woman has been blind from birth but she is in constant joy. Her attention never got attached to the sense of sight, her gaze has always been inward. If she had first had sight and then lost it, she would be grieving for the gratification of that sense. But her attention has always been inward where she has learned to know me. She knows I'm coming. Watch her come to the road to greet me. See."* As we approached the old woman, she rose with excitement and hobbled to the roadside, bowing with reverence and a large smile.

Baba never makes it easy. My brother Donald and I shared a front bucket seat and were squished together like sardines. The driver was to our right, Baba directly behind us, and Mr. Joga Rao, a contractor who has done much building for Baba, beside him. Of course you can't just sit looking out the front window with Baba behind you; you can't take your eyes off him. So we strained our necks to the limit, looking over our shoulders nose to nose, like two big lap dogs. We couldn't sit that way for long, however. Even though Baba allows people to watch him all day long, day after day, just letting you drink him in, when you're that close and intent about it, it's downright embarrassing. But even though we'd turn our gaze aside to relax for a moment, back we'd come to our twisted, staring lap dog impersonations.

About ten minutes to arrival time, Baba looked my way and said, *"Sandweiss."*

"Yes, *Swami?"* I replied, straining my neck even further to meet his eyes.

"You'll give the girls some advice," he said with a smile. My public speaking phobia roared with a passion.

"Give the girls some advice, *Swami?"* You can't say no to Baba; So I just wanted to make absolutely sure.

"Yes."

"What should I talk about Baba?"

"Anything," he said. *"Give advice."*

"How many students?" I asked.

"A thousand," he replied.

The rest of the ride was very difficult. Beads of sweat began to form on my forehead as I strained to think of something to say. I was lost in this contemplation when we pulled up to the school. And then everything changed. The devotion of these students was overwhelming. What an event to see: the important personages in the area, all the girls neat and clean, full of devotion and discipline, sitting quietly and singing; people prostrating themselves, hands clasped in a reverential manner in front of the heart—all eyes and souls toward Baba.

It's like arriving with the greatest celebrity imaginable. What a powerful impression, to see this kind of devotion to someone whom just minutes ago you were feeling almost as comfortable with as an old schoolmate. It was shocking to be drawn back into this reality, to realize again that we were sitting in the car with the *Avatar*. Baba got out and walked among the people, administering love . . . love . . . love.

Through the crowd we walked — up the stairs to the spacious dining room where we were to eat before Baba gave his address. Leaves sewn together into mats lined the room. These were to be our plates. Before eating we all walked to an open porch bordered by a brick wall. As we stood with our hands held out over the wall, someone came by and doused them with water from a pitcher which splashed to the ground below. We then seated ourselves cross-legged on the floor and all eyes were turned to Baba who sat at one end of the room.

I tried to put some thoughts together for my talk but was roused from them by the sounds of my brother diving into his rice with a passion. Here was the same man who had been deathly afraid of catching some kind of illness in India, now driven by hunger to eat with his hands like a native Indian. Even he found it amusing, though he was too busily engaged to laugh.

After the meal, my brother and I were escorted to a waiting room on the ground floor of the school. I was happy for the time to gather my thoughts. It's hard to explain my fear of speaking in Baba's presence, but it's more than just stage fright. It has more to do with being truly speechless when trying to grasp the full meaning of Baba and the reality he represents.

In the past I had questioned the statement that divinity is beyond words and concepts. Now I began to see this as more than just an abstract concept. When one contemplates or experiences Baba, something strange happens to the mental processes. They get fuzzy and fade out, and one perceives an intense, inner vastness where words and concepts simply have no place. I have struggled to express this glorious inner experience of expansion and boundarylessness in some kind of concept or description — but what a futile task that is!

When I'm really in touch with Baba, the only natural expression is to be quiet, close my eyes and immerse myself in devotion, exhilaration, awe and gratitude. Yet he had said I was to give some advice, so advice I would try to give. Besides, I thought, this will test what I've heard other devotees describe: that when it was their turn to speak in such a situation, they would just stand and open their mouths and Baba would speak through them. Now I could test this out for myself.

After a while, Baba came into the room and lit it up with his excitement. We all filed out behind him on the way to the auditorium. Before I left, one of the teachers at the college asked for my credentials as she was to introduce me. I said that I was simply a devotee, and she smiled.

The auditorium was filled to capacity. What a lovely sight: these disciplined young ladies, sitting straight and tall with faces beaming a great light of love. Within moments it was my turn. I walked to the podium on wobbly legs, opened my mouth—and to my great disappointment, Baba did not talk through it. I was left to my own devices—bobbing and weaving like a drunken sailor on unsteady legs, stranded in the midst of my phobia. Dizzy and dazed, my mind whirling, I said my piece: Baba's teaching on the four "F's." That is, follow the father, face the devil—which in this case was my phobia, a devil that Baba had me face directly and with full force; fight to the end—which I was trying to do on my rubbery legs, all the time calling out for Baba's help; and finish the game, which I managed to do with a shaky smile on my lips. What a relief.

Then Baba gave his talk. Just to watch him is a great treat, even more so when filled with gratitude at having finished my struggle with moderate success. But to watch this great figure, who is attracting so many great personalities on earth and turning them toward light and service—to watch him deliver, with such poignancy and meaning, the most profound messages of all the scriptures, teaching us with parables and stories and, most of all, his great love and the example of his life—is to be filled with the deepest reverence. His movements, his voice, his gestures, his love, come with such spontaneity, immediacy and innocence. He melts all hearts. You must see this sometime—love literally pouring from his heart. He sang to the girls and his love enveloped us in waves of ecstasy.

He spoke in *Telugu*. I was sitting next to my brother now and was so happy, having done my part and now being treated to this divine discourse, that I was just beaming. Although I couldn't understand a word, I was so caught up in Baba's spontaneous gestures and his delight, that I was filled with love. You could see by the smiles on the faces of the young girls that they were drinking in every word and returning immense devotion. I smiled from ear to ear and with each of his gestures shook my head yes, and nudged my brother with a body language which shouted, "Isn't he great, isn't he wonderful?" Finally my brother looked over and whispered in my ear, "Sam, I've never seen anyone pick up *Telugu* so quickly."

At the end of the discourse, Baba sang a *bhajan* with such sweetness and melody that everyone melted into his music of love. And when it came time for these young ladies to sing back to him in their excited, high, chirping voices, one was treated to an intimate conversation between divinity and innocence.

Why, Baba, do you bring us out of our minds, into the depths of our devotion and then ask us to translate this great experience back into words? The *so-hum* meditation, singing *bhajans*, watching you administer to all these people—these aren't intellectual exercises; they are deeply moving and humbling spiritual experiences, way beyond concepts and words. How can we translate this great vision into words? What can one say to catch your mystery? And yet, Baba, you ask your devotees to do just that.

You ask us to face our weakest points and confront and overcome our fears. You take us out of the world, show us that it's an illusion, and then you toss us right back into its treacherous tentacles while we hold on for dear life to your love for protection. What an incredible game! You ask us to be strong in the world, not to get caught in it but to be of service—to use you as a role model. Well, I pray that you give me the strength to do my role well, so I can win a smile from you. I'll try to live up to your example. I know you don't need the world at all, not in the slightest. You are complete love, the basis of all creation; you have come to allow people to pull on your gown, to cry to you, to ask for all the many varied and crazy things that tempt us in the world. And you come with just yes, yes, yes! Oh, how can one even come close to your divine example—but I'll try.

Do you, by chance, delight when I allow you to be near me? The next moment I might cause the sorrow of separation. Do you talk among yourselves that Sai takes delight in your tears? The next moment I might make you laugh till your sides ache and continue to grant you joy again and again. Do you feel a sense of elevation because I praise you a little? That very moment I may prick the bubble by means of ridicule. Do you feel secure since I have given you the grace? Do not fear—next moment I might inflict pain and keep silent while you pray for relief. I do not allow you to go forward. I madden your mind and smother your ego. Find out how anyone can move away from this charming Sai, the embodiment of love and light. Find out the reason why He is indispensable in spite of this dual role.

(Sathya Sai Baba)

Self
Sacrifice

CHAPTER TWENTY-FIVE

ONCE I was with Baba in Bombay when he was speaking to a group of educators, lawyers, scientists and scholars. The talk was given in the auditorium of a building called the *Bhartya Vidya Bhavan*. Everyone looked disciplined and educated once they got inside the front door. But passing through that door was a different matter. It was a very small door and everyone wanted to get through it at once, especially since someone was stationed there, stopping some from entering. So the milling and shoving reminded me of some of the grim play on the front line in a San Diego Charger football game. But once everyone got through the door it was peaceful. We all waited with high expectation.

After a while Baba appeared on stage. All eyes were riveted to him as he moved slowly and gracefully to center stage and then sat on the carpet in a peaceful posture. Gently leaning to his left and resting on an extended arm, he seemed in another dimension, appearing in ecstasy and filling the room with bliss. After a short while he got up and moved softly with a smile through the audience, tapping some-one playfully on the shoulder here, stopping to give encouragement or a serious word there, materializing some *vibuthi* for a lucky one, until we all felt deep intimate contact with him. Slowly he returned to the podium and moved gently to the microphone—and sang in the sweetest and most angelic way. He was so lovely. Pure honey.

Then he got down to business. Starting slowly, his talk, trans-lated into English by an interpreter, gained in power and pitch until he came to his major points—and he made these points with such strength and authority, like a king, a ruler, a Lord. He said: *"It is so easy for the poor to stay poor, to eat with the poor and play with the poor and continue to take on the suffering and problems of the poor. And it's so easy for the rich to be with the rich and eat with the rich and play with the rich and forget about the poor. It is very uncommon and very difficult for the rich to live with the poor, to eat with the poor, to take on the problems and suffering of the poor. But this is what I'm telling you to do. Go to the poor, live with the poor; be with the poor, the helpless, the suffering, and serve them."*

I was just overwhelmed with the power and authority of this declaration. What a tremendous message to bring to us and to say it with such authority. My brother was on this trip and I said to him, "Donald, did you hear that? Did you hear what he said we should do?" I was terribly moved because I took it to heart. And my brother said, "Yeah, yeah, every religious leader talks like that."

Later, after returning to *Brindavan* from Bombay, I was standing with Baba. He must have known that I was impressed with his talk and was soul-searching as to whether I had the power to carry out his instructions. With a gentle smile he looked my way and said, *"How did you like my talk?"* I said, "Swami, you were so great." With a broad smile he replied, *"Yes, I was strong, wasn't I?"*

Are we strong enough to do what we know is right? And if we surrender our material wealth, position and comforts toward these ideals, will the Lord himself come to protect, teach and help? By this time I had so much confirmation that Sai Baba actually comes direct-ly and concretely into our lives if we turn our lives toward him, that I was ready to try a small sacrifice. What I actually wanted to do was to pick up and move to India, much to my wife's alarm. But every time I asked Baba's permission he directed me back to the U.S.

So I decided to develop the skills that I might use one day if he allowed me to live by him. I decided to get some experience working with the poor in a clinic setting and perhaps one day I could run a clinic or day treatment program at Baba's hospital. Of course, I asked myself, what does an *Avatar* need with a psychiatrist—but even so one has to have a dream and perhaps this one could come true. Baba actually does ask us to perfect our skills for the day when he might allow us to work directly with him as an instrument in the unfolding of his mission.

Back in San Diego I went to a clinic in a poor area to meet with the head of the psychosocial department. I told her that I would like to be a volunteer half a day a week and she was delighted. She told me about the operations of the clinic and then said that she had a question. "You're the first doctor that's ever come here asking to volunteer—they're all making a lot of money out there. So why are you doing this?"

Hesitantly I began, "Well, if you really want to know"—I was still naive enough to think that people would understand my experience with Baba. No matter how many times I get bopped on the nose because I open my big mouth too quickly, it seems that I can't stop talking about Baba. So again I put my foot in my mouth and said, "Because the Lord of all creation—if you can believe this—the Lord of the entire cosmos, he who has created the world by simply one thought, has come in human form and is alive in India. He is actually here, walking the earth, teaching us at this very moment—what extraordinary grace, pure unending joy! And he tells us to go to the poor and suffering and be of service."

And the miracle of this whole thing was that even though she looked a bit taken aback she said, "Well, okay, let's start next week."

And so I worked in the clinic, volunteering my time doing things that I was familiar with, and nothing new or startling happened. But it did teach me that one has to start slowly and be patient. To progress along the path takes time, perseverance and steadiness and a great deal of patience. So I worked at the clinic for about a year, even though I didn't seem to be very effective or learning very much at all—in fact, it seemed a bit boring to tell you the truth. Finally I decided to stop. Shortly thereafter I saw an advertisement in the paper for a medical director for a day treatment program. It was just

what I was looking for, a setting where I might gain experience directing a program and developing a community for mentally disabled
people who would attend up to five days a week for 7 or 8 hours a day
for a structured, enriching, educational and therapeutic experience.
And I got the job.

I wasn't going to make the same mistake twice. I said to myself,
"Sam, you don't have to talk about the Lord incarnating, you
needn't tell everyone about your experiences with Baba. If you can
just live his message, be kind and nice—do it that way. Don't rock
the boat. You've got a nice job here—now just watch yourself." So
with that resolve I started the program. They respected and liked
me—and I liked them. We were getting along just fine.

One day about a month and a half after I started, the staff and I
went to visit a board and care home—a structured living setting for
people too disabled to live independently. We wanted to offer our ser-
vices and to provide some enrichment. As we walked into the park-
ing lot someone asked, "Whose car should we use—Sam how about
using your car?"

I said, "Fine," before I realized what I was doing. I had a little
beat-up Jeep, not too bad looking from the outside—but inside it was
plastered with Sai Baba pictures—and incense sticks protruding from
everywhere. It was a wild, new-age traveling temple in there. So I
started to worry, "How about—I mean we could take somebody else's
car?"

"Come on, Sam , let's take yours," because they wanted to see
what a wealthy psychiatrist's car looked like. Little did they know
that I'm not wealthy—but when they met my car, they learned. And
when I opened the door—BOOM! I mean it was a fantastic shock.
Silence. As if nobody saw anything. Then one brave person said,
"Who's he?"

"Oh, he's a friend," I said.

Sai Baba's mystery is really something. What he puts us poor
souls through! You can, of course, say this is all a mirage; it's all a
dream and I'm not reacting and they're not reacting and they're not
really feeling uncomfortable—I'm just the "I", the eternal witness.
But you know, as long as we're in this body we react a little bit and so
I was feeling badly. One person politely tried to muster up a question:
"Do you ever take the Jeep up into the mountains?"

I said, "No, not very often." That was the extent of the conversation. I was really peaked by the time we arrived.

The board and care facility had a staff of about seven people and we added another five. I was numb during the conference. I guess we all contributed a bit, but I can't remember much of what went on. Afterwards the head of their program showed us the rooms, introduced us to some of the boarders and walked us around the grounds. As we finished the visit I began feeling uncomfortable—anticipating the ride back. We ended up at the front of the facility—the staff of our program and the head of theirs. I had never met him before and he seemed quite friendly.

Then something unusual happened. This young man, the head of their program, walked up to me with hands clasped before him in the devotional, prayerful posture that one uses to greet another in India. And with a big smile he said, "Is that *Swami's* ring you're wearing?" He pointed to a ring that Baba had materialized for me, and I broke out in a big grin. Can you imagine this turn of events? I was a zero in the eyes of the staff before—and now I was a hero. "*Swami's* my *guru*, too," he joyfully proclaimed. We both became children, smiling broadly as he told me about his trip to India, how he became deathly ill in north India and was saved by Baba.

That was delightful. You know, whether you're a hero or a zero doesn't make any difference. What does, is the faith and forbearance that develop when he graces you with a sweet and loving sign of his omnipresence. Whatever the play—and the play can be tremendously mysterious and trying—we must have faith, perseverance and patience and know that he is with us always. We may make all kinds of mistakes and feel as if we are a zero—but that doesn't really matter. If we just hold on long enough, and with steady enough faith, he will give us a deeper vision—that is his play. Just wait. He saves only at the last moment.

What matters is holding very strongly to him. Then he takes the responsibility for teaching and for saving. We just have to develop the faith that what happens, no matter how it looks from the outer material world, is really grace and that through it he is teaching the deepest spiritual insights. And these insights are not easy to come by. He teaches that to escape suffering and pain we must yearn for God with the intensity of a baby crying for its mother, as a pitiful, starving beggar cries out for a morsel of food.

This is no easy insight to attain; the ego must be humble before we gain a clear vision of the divine. But let's not be worried by this awesome task, let's not fear—only hold more strongly to the hem of his robe. And then one day, in the wink of an eye, he'll come with his full glory, showing us that he has always been with us. When we make our lives into a devotional practice, when we sacrifice all to the Lord, He Himself will come to show that he has always been with us and is here now to protect and save.

Dear Dear Loved One,[1]
  You ask, "How will you know when
                  I am near you?"
  When on a sultry night
  everything is hot and still,
  The first cool breeze
  Brushes your cheeks
  Think of me.
  When the pangs of hunger are satisfied
  And loneliness is pierced by happiness
  Think of me.
  When your mouth is parched
  And you can hardly speak,
  The first sip of cool water
  I am soothing you
  Think of me.
  When I sprinkle your face with cold rain
  and wash the earth, the dry brown leaves,
  The first smell of clear rain
  I am cleansing you
  Think of me.
  When pain dissolves
  And tears disappear
  Think of me.
  When steadfast eyes are horrified
  By the cruelties of life,
  The first glance of the silent setting sun
  I am comforting you
  Think of me.

Then you ask "How will you know when you are near me?"
    When the burning sun
    Has scorched you and the earth,
    The sand and dust fill your eyes
    Not a sliver of shade about
    And you love me.
    When loneliness is accompanied by
        hunger and not one can be satisfied
    And you love me.
    When your lips are cracked
    Your tongue feels like clay
    Your throat seals up
    There is no water about
    Not even a mirage in sight
    And you love me.
    When pain becomes unbearable, you smile
    And you love me.
    When I take from you
    Your most cherished possession,
    on the first loss of sight
    darkness envelops you
    And you love me.
For everything that you see, hear, smell, taste, or touch belongs to me.
So how can you give to me what I already own but your love. And
that, I gave to you before time began as your soul's possession. When
you return it to me then I will know you are truly mine and I will
dissolve your sorrow and happiness into me—That one being me, I
will place you in bliss forever. For I love and think of you constantly.
                                 From your most loving Father.

Notes

1. A letter poem written by Sathya Sai Baba to a devotee.

Poornachandra Auditorium, the largest pillarless auditorium in the far east. On the left front wall from right to left are pictured four major world teachers, Krishna, Jesus Christ, Buddha and Zoroaster—and on the right wall the major *Avatars* of the Hindu tradition.

PART III World Teacher

In this book I've proposed that Sai Baba may be the clearest living proof of the highest spiritual principle and of the reality of *atma*, of our soul's extension beyond space, time and the grave. I've suggested his relevance to the behavioral sciences and how insight into his reality will bring soul and substance to our field. Beyond this, I feel that it is important to consider Sai Baba's relevance to the world population and his impact on global consciousness.

In this section we will look at the possibility that Sai Baba may indeed be a world teacher of unparalleled stature. I'll offer my observations of a world conference of the Sathya Sai Service Organization held at *Prasanthi Nilayam*, in southern India, in November, 1980. Then I will present a discourse given by Sai Baba regarding the nature and meaning of his miracles. Finally, I'll present an unusually revealing interview given by Sai Baba to Mr. Karanjia, senior editor of the *Blitz* newspaper, one of the largest in India. Here Sai Baba declares and discusses some centrally important aspects regarding the meaning of his life and his world mission.

World Conference

CHAPTER TWENTY-SIX

THE THIRD World Conference of the Sri Sathya Sai Organization was held outside the small Indian village of *Puttaparthi* on November 19-21, 1980. Sai Baba called members of his service groups from around the world to this meeting. What a joy to attend a happening that proved to be both a message and a vision— revealing signs and wonders of a spiritual truth, and the dawning of a new world order centered in that truth. R.N. Goenka, in an article appearing in the November 16, 1980, edition of the Indian newspaper *Sunday Standard Magazine*, wrote:

> It is estimated now that Sai Baba has over 30 million followers, and that the Sathya Sai Organization today has more than 15 thousand units in 64 countries. This movement appears to be spearheading a revolution that is more powerful and persuasive than any that Man has known so far. It is neither political nor economic nor scientific nor technological. It is deeper and more

basic. It is a spiritual revolution with love and compassion both as its means and end. It is the hope for humanity at large.

THE PLACE

Arriving in the mountain city of Bangalore, some 450 miles southeast of Bombay with a population of about 1 million, we were met with large welcoming signs draping the airport entrance. Similar banners canopied the road on our 120-mile journey to the village of *Puttaparthi*. The three-and-a-half-hour ride was punctuated by rest stops where Sai volunteers served coffee, tea and biscuits.

Prasanthi Nilayam, Sai Baba's *ashram* (the name meaning "abode of the highest peace") is the place of pilgrimage for hundreds of thousands of people the world over. Its location, just outside the village of *Puttaparthi*, Sai Baba's birthplace, tells much about his values.

Although Sai Baba is now famous throughout India and could choose almost any location for his *ashram*, he remains close to the village of his birth—still serving, supporting and protecting his family, early friends and fellow villagers. He tells his devotees that friendship should deepen and mellow with age—that "old is gold."

Devotees around the world have asked Sai Baba to visit their countries. *"First a person must have enough strength to care for himself,"* he says, *"and if he has strength beyond this he must serve his family, then his community, his city, state, and then country."* Only when one can serve people in this fashion does he have the right to go outside his country and give advice, he says.

Sai Baba seems to have universal appeal, drawing all colors, creeds, nationalities, religions and languages—people from every station in education, culture and life—people usually separated by a myriad of boundaries and distinctions, all gathering now, as one unified family—an estimated 200,000 in all coming to this event.

Seated in this vast gathering, experiencing the intensity of the power, energy and excitement moving in the crowd, one wonders what must be held in the soul of this being who so attracts and inspires. An Indian child born in an obscure, remote Indian village, literally a cow pasture, is now surrounded by an enormously impressive array of bricks and mortar, hearts and souls.

The physical plant housing this gathering was immense and still growing. Hundreds of acres of once untended land are now occupied by buildings of all shapes and sizes. These, and the large statues of Hindu gods and goddesses adorning them, sparkle with light pastel pinks, yellows and blues in a shimmering surrealistic dream scene. Dormitories bordering the periphery of the *ashram* house thousands of devotees. Inside stands the holy *Mandir* Temple where Baba lives, and the *Poornachandra* Auditorium—now swelling to its 20,000 capacity—the largest pillarless auditorium in the Far East.

Outside the walls of the *ashram*, spread out over a square half mile in area, four massive two- and three-story buildings form an educational complex consisting of an elementary and high school, and a men's science and arts college, housing courtyards, classrooms, auditoriums and work centers. So well respected is this Sri Sathya Sai Institute of Higher Learning that it is the first university to be accredited by the Indian Government since Indian independence in 1947! These are the manifestations in brick and mortar of Sai Baba's central interest in the education of the young.

The success of his program is measured in the excellence of his students and their already apparent contributions and accomplishments in Indian society. The Indian government is so impressed with the outcome of the spiritually-oriented curriculum that it has established an aspect of it in *all* Indian elementary schools. Reflecting Sai Baba's orientation that "the end of education is character," and called "Education in Human Values," the program teaches the central values shared by all religions. The lives of saints and great souls from every religion are studied, with the primary emphasis on developing moral strength and good character.

PEOPLE AND EVENTS

Arriving at *Prasanthi Nilayam*, my wife Sharon, twin 13-year-old daughters Ruth and Rachel, and I were housed in a newly constructed six-story circular building. Our neighbors were highly accomplished and respected men from around the world. Ravi Shankar, the world-renowned Indian sitar player; successful businessmen from Sweden, Italy, Central America, India and the U.S.—some having given up everything to live close to Sai Baba; doctors, scientists, lawyers, newsmen, politicians, generals—all forming a truly international family.

Westernized food was served to the guests by students and professors from Sai Baba's colleges—all dressed in white, immaculately clean, well-mannered, always courteous, pleasant, humble and happy. Every effort was made toward our comfort—from running errands to serving seconds to washing dishes and cleaning the grounds. How startling to find these very same helpers delivering profound and moving discourses in front of thousands in the large *Poornachandra* Auditorium during the course of the conference! Once finished, they quickly and without fanfare left the podium and hurried to their areas of duty—never once needing to show that they were anything but servants. What a lesson for my daughters—what a lesson in humility for me.

The intoxicating sights and sounds, activities and people were all being caught by many film crews, photographers and newsmen. *Sai Gita*, Baba's pet elephant, dressed in full parade regalia, led parades and processions. Monkeys, donkeys, dogs, crows, water buffalo, lizards and roosters formed the varied animal contingent. Bagpipes and bands, drums, bugles and horns, provided a frenzy of musical sounds. Ceremonies, rituals, ribbon-cuttings, garlandings, fireworks, plays, dedications and discourses—songs, dances and performances by some of India's foremost musicians filled the days with excitement.

Talks by a variety of distinguished men and women from different backgrounds and countries provided insight into the extent and significance of this international movement. Dr. V.K. Gokak— eminent writer, poet, professor and educator, past Vice-Chancellor of Bangalore University and past director of the Indian Institute of Advanced Study, Simla, and author of over thirty books in English and Kannada—gave the opening address. He spoke of an emerging new world order in which we were all taking part—centered in a sense of brotherhood, unity and love.

Books from every corner of the world—foreign translations of Baba's teachings as well as biographies of him—were presented. *Golden Age 1980*,[1] a compilation of articles from distinguished writers and educators produced by The Kingdom of Sathya Sai, a group of graduates from Sai Baba's colleges, showed the Sai influence already present in every dimension and aspect of world society, as well as the great esteem in which he is held in his own country! He is now considered India's most widely-respected and followed living holy man.

THE MESSAGE

During this conference Baba delivered a number of moving discourses. Always beginning by chanting a central theme or message, he talks for about an hour and a half without notes, always at ease, spontaneous, completely flowing and graceful. He seems directed by some inner vision, difficult for us mortals to fully understand. When he looks at us he must not see separate bodies as we do, but one glorious effulgent light — or oceanic waves of light that bind one heart to another, uniting us in one glorious body of light and love. It must be so because he is always speaking of this reality — and says that Christ spoke of it also when saying "You are all one my son — be alike to everyone." It was about this unity, this oneness, this *atmic*[2] reality that he spoke most poignantly — teaching us, with a smile full of love and compassion, to be servants to all, for God is in all.

At times Baba would make sudden changes in the direction of his talk, as if responding to a devotee's need — or sensing the time right for a certain teaching. During an especially memorable discourse, he made such a sudden change to reveal some interesting historical and spiritual information. Perhaps it was because several groups of Russians and Chinese were present for the first time. At any rate Baba suddenly began:

At about the year 1917 Stalin was coming into power in Russia. There was a great change in the social order. A man by the name of Wolf Messing came to Stalin to tell him of the reality of the atma, the unseen basis, the real self, the infinite divine aspect of man. Stalin could not understand Wolf Messing and his message, and what followed was hardship and suffering in Russia. Wolf Messing went to Vienna. He met with Freud who seemed interested and wanted to study him but Messing was not interested and moved on. In 1937, when this body was 11 years old, I was walking near a train station. On the platform was a lone man awaiting a train. He had come to India to see the great saints and to find further evidence of his vision of the atma. When I came closer, his eyes looked into mine and filled with tears. He became excited and joyful beyond bounds and began rushing toward me. Reaching out to me he cried, "I love you, I love you, I love you, I love you."

And as Baba said this he welled up in exquisite joy himself, sending waves of excitement and love into the audience. We sat electrified as Baba continued.

This man rushed to me and took my hand. He was filled with joy—with ecstasy. My friends were frightened, thinking that he would take me away. They grabbed me and began pulling me from his grip. They took me from the train platform. Although this man lost hold of this body, his eyes never left sight of me until I was out of range. This was Wolf Messing. He had seen the atma.

Notes

1. Titles and authors from this book include:

   "God Fulfills Himself" by Honorable Justice Sri V.R. Krishna Iyer, distinguished senior judge of the Supreme Court of India.

   "The Sathya Sai Era: Glimpses of a Spiritual Revolution" by Dr. Duane Robinson, college professor, sociologist and social worker.

   "What Sri Sathya Sai Baba Means to Me" by Sri V.K. Narshimhan, internationally-known journalist. He was Deputy Editor of *The Hindu*, and Editor of the *Indian Express*, largest newspaper in India, as well as the *Financial Express* and *Deccan Herald*.

   "The Second Coming Has Come!" by Ron Laing, British writer on supernormal phenomena.

   "The Finger of God" by Howard Murphet, teacher, journalist and writer from Australia. Author of *Sai Baba Man of Miracles*, considered the first major Western book about Sai Baba, he has also written his second, *Sai Baba Avatar*.

   "Grains of Grace" by Sri Govind Narain, Governor of Karnataka.

   "At His Blue Lotus Feet" by Charles Penn, advertising manager of a publishing house in Los Angeles and editor-publisher of technical journals in Australia and Canada.

   "An Avatar's Reality, His Powers and His Mission", by Sri Maharajakrishna Rasgotra, currently India's Ambassador to France, and earlier serving as India's Ambassador to Morocco and Tunisia, Acting High Commissioner in London.

   "The Oneness of Jesus Christ and Sathya Sai Baba" by Rev. Robert E. Pipes, an ordained Baptist minister in the U.S.

   "Reflections" by R.R. Diwakar, presently Chairman of the Gandhi Peace Foundation.

   "Brighter Than a Thousand Suns" by C.C. Chang, who has been professor of mathematics at the University of California.

   "Preparation for the Boon" by Dr. William M. Harvey, Director of the Narcotics Service Council of St. Louis, Missouri. He is a professor at Washington University in St. Louis.

   "Baba and His Materializations" by Dr. Man Mohan Varma—scientist who has taught at Oklahoma University, Tuft University and Harvard University.

   "All the World's a Stage" by Christopher St. John, film producer, director, writer and actor.

"The Priest and the Avatar" by The Rev. Canon John Rossner—Anglican priest and professor of comparative religion at Concordia University in Montreal, Canada.

"The Avatar's Time-Clock" by the Hon. Justice Sr. V. Balakrishna Eradi, presently Chief Justice of the Kerala High Court.

"Coming Home" by Peggy Mason, gifted British writer.

"Singular and Plural" by Professor N. Kasturi, Sai Baba's biographer and noted humorist and professor of history.

"My Beacon" by Dr. V.K. Pillay, orthopedic surgeon and Master, Academy of Medicine, Singapore.

"Communicating Divinity" by Richard Bock, noted Western Sai Baba film maker.

"A Tribute to Baba" by Pandit Ravi Shankar, internationally know sitarist, composer and music director.

"Sri Sathya Sai Baba: The World Phenomenon" by Sri J. Jegathesan, Director, Investment Promotion, Malaysian Industrial Development Authority, Kuala Lumpur.

"My Spiritual Journey to Sathya Sai Baba" by Victor Kanu, former High Commissioner to Sierra Leone in Great Britain, Norway and Sweden.

"The International Problem" by Dr. John S. Hislop, distinguished academician, businessman, administrator, philosopher and president of the Sathya Sai organization in the U.S.

"The Sathya Sai Theory of Education" by Dr. V.K. Gokak, eminent writer, poet, professor and educator.

"One Flower Does Not Make a Garland" by Dr. Somnath Saraf, presently Senior Consultant at the UNESCO International Institute for Educational Planning, Paris.

"The Battle of Love" by Nityananda Menon, President, Kingdom of Sathya Sai, and one of the first students to graduate from Sai Baba's college at Brindavan.

"True to His Nation" by Dr. Erlendur Haraldsson, Associate Professor of Psychology at the University of Iceland.

"Parapsychology and Sathya Sai Baba" by Er. Karlis Osis, internationally known parapsychologist and Fellow of the American Society for Psychical Research.

2. *"The atma is the unseen basis, the substance of all the objective world, the reality behind the appearance, universal and immanent in every being. It is inherently devoid of attachment, is imperishable and does not die. It is the witness, unaffected by all this change in time and space, the immanent spirit in the body, the motivating force of its impulses and intentions. It is one's own innermost reality, one's divinity, the real self—the soul.*

"The atma cannot be grasped through metaphors and examples. No form can contain it; no name can denote it. How can the limited comprehend the unlimited, the now, measure the ever, the wayward understand the stable? The atma persists unchanged, however many changes the thing motivated by it might undergo. It contacts the senses of perception and affects the mind; it awakens the intellect to discriminate and decide upon the lines of action. It activates the instruments of thought, speech and action, of expression and communication. The eyes see; but, what force prompts them? You may have ears but who endows them with the power of hearing? Words emanate from the mouth; but what urges us and frames the manner and content of the speech? That force acts like the cells in

a torch which provide the bulb with the current to illuminate it. Doctors know that the body consists of cells, billions of them alive and alert, busy and active. Each cell is motivated by the atma; it is immanent, all over. The atma is in each of them, as well as in every spot of space. When we realize it as such, it is experienced as effulgent, total, splendorous light: endless, incomparable, unique light."
(Sathya Sai Baba)

God represents the concretized divine principle that is immanent in the universe—that moves the dew to drop, the lotus to bloom, the butterfly to flit and the sun to rise. That is all the power, all the wisdom, all the love, all the miracle that ever was, is and will be.
(Sathya Sai Baba)

Signs
and Wonders

CHAPTER TWENTY-SEVEN

THE MATERIALIZATIONS of *vibuthi* (sacred ash), of religious objects, talismans and gifts, of fish and loaves for the poor—the raising of the dead—what is the meaning of these signs and wonders, for what purpose, toward what end? Are these indeed signs of a higher, perhaps Universal Consciousness? If so, can man's individual consciousness expand—and literally merge with this Universal Consciousness? How does consciousness evolve to this dimension?

Sai Baba addresses these questions in a spiritual discourse delivered on his birthday, November 23, 1976. Entitled "Signs and Wonders," he speaks of spiritual concepts not clearly understood by Western psychology. Let us try to grasp the meaning.

SIGNS AND WONDERS

The conflict between persons who accept God and deny God and those who declare that God is to be found in this place and those who affirm that God can be found nowhere is never ending;

it has continued throughout the ages. While considering this situation, one has to remember that while it is unnecessary to awaken a person already awake and easy to awaken a person who is asleep, we cannot awaken, however much we try, a person pretending to be asleep! Those who know can be taught, by means of simple illustrations, what they do not know. But, those afflicted with half-knowledge and proud of that acquisition are beyond any further education.

The two eyes give a picture of a vast expanse of space; but they cannot see the face to which they belong! They are important instruments of the body; but they cannot see the entire body; the back is beyond their view. When you wish to see your face and back, you have to keep a mirror in front and another mirror behind, and through the front mirror you can see the reflection of your back. So too when you desire to know your reality (face) and your future (back), you have to adjust the mirror of "self-confidence" (confidence that you are the self) in front and the mirror of divine grace behind. Without these two, to affirm that you are aware of your truth or of your destiny is sheer fantasy.

The divine is now denoted by various words that are common currency in limited human vocabularies. These words describe and propose a meaning to the divine — "miracles," "magic," "wonders," etc. Of course, men cannot contain in their minds more than they can hold. They cannot express in words the inexpressible. Only those who have dived deep and contacted the underlying principle of love can picture divinity with some clarity. The divinity that is me has not been acquired or earned, nor has it been added to or evinced after the lapse of some years, in the middle of this career.

The divine has to reveal itself through these manifestations, largely shaped and modified by the nature of the times, the region, and the cultural environment. The signs and wonders that I manifest are given names that do not connote the purpose or effect. They can be classed as chamathkar, leading to samskar, which urges one on to paropakar resulting in sakshatkar. Chamathkar is any act which attracts on account of its inexplicability. This aspect of attraction is inherent in the Avatar. The very name Rama means "he who pleases or causes delight." Krishna means "he *who attracts or draws toward himself" (Karshathithi-Krishna). This attribute of attraction is a characteristic of divinity.*

Why does the divine attract? Is it to deceive or mislead? No. It is to transform, reconstruct, reform—a process called samskar. What is the purpose of the reconstruction? To make the person useful and serviceable for society, to efface his ego, and to affirm in him the unity of all beings in God. The person who has undergone samskar becomes a humble, humane servant of those who need help. This is the stage of paropakar. Service of this kind, done with reverence and selflessness, prepares man to realize the one that pervades the many. The last stage is sakshatkar. The Vedas proclaim that immortality (the stage when one is merged in the birthless, deathless, universal entity) is feasible through renunciation and detachment only, and not through rituals, progeny or wealth. When one renounces selfish desire, his love expands unto the farthest regions of the universe, until he becomes aware of the cosmic love that feeds all the four processes mentioned above. It is important that you know this underlying urge in all that I do.

Let us consider the chamathkar: acts that attract and cause wonder. You see a flower. You long to hold it in your hand only when its color or fragrance is attractive. You enter the market and see heaps of fruits. If the fruits are not attractive, you have no urge to possess them and benefit by them. Attraction is the very nature of the divine.

When the person is drawn near, the process of samskar starts. Without this, man remains fallow and feeble. He has no dignity or personality. Two annas worth of stainless steel is transformed by skillful manipulation and reconstruction into nuts, screws and springs, into a watch that is worth two or three hundred rupees. This is the result of samskar, which turned it into a useful tool for indicating time. So too, man can be transformed into a noble, efficient, happy and disciplined member of society by the implanting of good thoughts, good feelings, good deeds and good emotions. Man can be transformed into a mahatma (great soul). Such transformed persons will spontaneously engage themselves in the task of promoting human welfare. They will be promoters of the ideals of the brotherhood of man and the Fatherhood of God.

Now, persons who have no experience or knowledge of

spiritual science or no conception of the divine make pronounce-
ments on subjects into which they stray. The eye can see, but it
cannot hear; the tongue can talk but cannot hear. The ear can hear
but can neither see nor talk. Each has to accept its limitations and
be content. The divine can be grasped only through love, through
faith and sadhana (spiritual work) surcharged with universal love.
Reason is too feeble an instrument to measure it. Denial of the
divine cannot negate it. Logic cannot reveal it. All the tirades now
being made on the divine are from atheists who are opportunists.
So, your duty is to preserve your equanimity. Be true to yourselves
and do not waver. I am unaffected by praise or blame. My love
and compassion envelop all; my grace can be shared by all. I am
declaring this so that you may face all this with fortitude. The
more you dig, the deeper the derision; the higher the mound, the
taller the praise. People with a disease in the nose cannot appreciate the fragrance of a flower. Those who cannot appreciate or
recognize the divine are suffering from illness which handicaps
them.

(Sathya Sai Baba)

Questions
and Answers

CHAPTER TWENTY-EIGHT

FOLLOWING IS an extended interview given by
Sri Sathya Sai Baba to the Senior Editor, Mr. R.K. Karanjia of Blitz
news magazine in September of 1976.[1]

Q: At the outset, *Swamiji*, we would like to know something
about your triple incarnation—past, present and future—that is,
from *Shirdi Sai Baba* to *Sathya Sai Baba* and the *Prema Sai Baba* to
come, according to your prophecy.

Baba: *First of all, you must grasp the complete oneness of the three
incarnations of contemporary times with those of the past like Rama and
Krishna. This is a difficult task. When people cannot understand the present, how can they comprehend the past? Every incarnation is full and complete in relation to the time, the environment and the task. There is no distinction between the various appearances of God as Rama, Krishna or Sai.*

*Rama came to feed the roots of truth and righteousness, Krishna fol-
lowed to foster the plant of peace and love. Now these sacred principles
are in danger of wholesale destruction by reason of human weakness under*

the onslaught of evil forces. They are overcoming the good, the spiritual and the divine in man. That is why the present Avatar has come invested with the totality of cosmic power to save dharma (righteousness) from anti-dharma.

WHY GOD TAKES HUMAN FORM

Q: By the present *Avatar*, you mean Sai Baba?

Baba: *Yes, I incarnate from age to age, time to time, to save dharma from anti-dharma. Whenever strife, discord and disharmony overwhelm the world, God incarnates in human form to show mankind the way to love, harmony and peace.*

Q: That is understandable. But skeptics wonder why God should assume human form?

Baba: *Because that is the only way to incarnate the God within man. The Avatar takes the human form and behaves in a human way so that humanity can feel kinship with divinity. At the same time he rises to godly heights so that mankind also can aspire to reach God. The realization of the indwelling God as the motivator of life is the task for which Avatars come in human form.*

Previous Avatars like Rama and Krishna had to destroy a few individuals who could be identified as enemies of the godly way of life and thus restore the dharmic path. Today, however, wickedness has tainted so many that humanity itself stands under the threat of destruction. Therefore, in my present Avatar, I have come armed with the fullness of the power of formless God to correct mankind, raise human consciousness and put people back on the right path of truth, righteousness, peace and love to divinity.

MESSAGE OF TRIPLE INCARNATION

Q: Why had this task to be divided into three separate incarnations of the *Shirdi, Sathya* and *Prema Babas?*

Baba: *They are not separate. I have already mentioned the complete oneness of the three in the final objective of the mission. I will give you an example. Take a kilo of gur (a sweet substance). The whole of it tastes sweet. Next break it into small pieces. Each of them is sweet. Finally break them further into small grains. You find the same sweetness in them. So the difference is one of quantity and not quality. It is the same with the Avatars. Their tasks and powers requisite to them differ according to the* time, the situation and the environment. But they belong to, and derive from one and the same dharma swarup or divine body.

Let us take the example of fruit. It begins with the seed which grows into the tree and from it comes the fruit. Work can be compared to the seed, worship to the tree and wisdom to the fruit.

The previous Avatar, Shirdi Baba, laid the base for secular integration and gave mankind the message of duty is work. The mission of the present Avatar is to make everybody realize that the same God or divinity resides in everyone. People should respect, love and help each other irrespective of color or creed. Thus all work can become a way of worship. Finally, Prema Sai, the third Avatar, will promote the evangel news that not only does God reside in everybody, but everybody is God. That will be the final wisdom which will enable every man and woman to go to God.

The three Avatars carry the triple message of work, worship and wisdom.

MAN MUST DEVELOP INTO MANKIND

Q: So that is the holy mission and divine purpose of this triple incarnation?

Baba: To unite all mankind into one caste or family in the establishment of the unity—that is, atmic realization—in every man or woman, which is the basis on which the entire cosmic design rests. Once this is realized, the common divine heritage that binds man to man and man to God will become apparent and love shall prevail as the guiding light of the universe.

In the first place, man has to develop into mankind in the fullness of its integrated potential. At present mankind as such is absent in the world. There is no synthesis between thought, word and deed. Man today thinks one thing, says something different, and acts quite the contrary. So what we have is the individual man, confused, confounded and bombarded with contradictory thoughts. What we do not see is mankind in him motivated by good thoughts, good words and good deeds. We have to make him realize God within him to develop a synthesis correlating thought, word and deed.

EVANGEL OF LOVE AND DEVOTION

Once this primary lesson is taught in the family, the school, the college, the society, the cities, the states, the nations of the world, then man will become conscious of the fact that all mankind belongs to one family. As Christ preached, all are one, be alike to everyone. The vital issue is the oneness: one caste, one class, one creed of humanity: and this can be humanity: and this can be achieved only by the surrender of one's self or ego to pure, selfless, universal love and devotion. Love is the basis, the common denominator, and devotion the divine spark, the cementing, unifying, integrating factor between man and man, and man and God.

Let me give you an illustration. (Baba spreads his handkerchief on the ground between us). Here is a piece of cloth. As you see, it is all made of threads. Pull out the threads separately and the cloth becomes weak. Put them together and it is firm and strong. It is the same with mankind. Love binds it like the million, billion threads in cloth and devotion reunites it with God. I, therefore, embody love and use it as my instrument to regenerate man and create the brotherhood of mankind with the help of the latter's devotion. I always say: Start the day with love. Fill the day with love. End the day with love. This is the quickest way, the surest path to God.

> Life is love, enjoy it;
> Life is a challenge, meet it;
> Life is a song, sing it;
> Life is a dream, realize it;
> Life is a game, play it.

SHIRDI BABA INCARNATE

Q: Did Shirdi Baba actually claim that he would be born eight years after his death in 1918?

Baba: Yes, he did. This has been recorded by Kaka Dikshit as well as a number of other devotees who were with Shirdi Baba.

Q: What makes you so sure that you are Shirdi Baba incarnate:

Baba: The knowledge of my own authentic experience, of course. Since no one who knew Shirdi Baba is alive today, there is no evidence except my own knowledge and experience.

The very fact that I announced that I am Shirdi Baba 40 years ago, when I was only 10 and when nobody in this part of the South had known or even heard of Shirdi Baba, proves this fact.

DHARMA (RIGHTEOUSNESS) ALONE CAN SAVE THE WORLD

Q: The existing situation driven by evil forces to destruction as you have correctly analyzed it, appears to suggest the inevitability of another Mahabharata-type (an epic relating to the battle of Kukuke-shethra) war. Does this mean that the salvation for which you are working can be consummated only after a destructive war?

Statue of *Shirdi Sai Baba* in the *mandir* (temple) at *Prasanthi Nilayam*

Baba: *The evil must and shall be removed before such a catastrophe takes place. There will be minor wars and skirmishes, of course: these cannot be helped in the existing state of affairs. The Mahabharata war was a different issue altogether. Lord Krishna decreed it and, in fact, led Arjuna to the battlefield in order to rid the world of evil men and ungodly forces.*

Today, as I told you, the evil is so widespread that humanity itself would be destroyed in a nuclear holocaust in the event of a world war. It is to prevent such a catastrophe that this Avatar has come to raise human consciousness above the existing syndrome of anger, hate, violence and war and save the world from disaster. This can be achieved only by the reestablishment of the brotherhood of mankind through the Vedas, Shastras and all religions with their evangel of dharma to liberate the human race from the chains of karma (the cycle of birth and death).

I always say: Let the different faiths exist, let them flourish, let the glory of God be sung in all the languages in a variety of tunes. That should be the ideal. Respect the differences between the faiths and recognize them as valid so far as they do not extinguish the flame of unity.

GOD IS MAN MINUS DESIRE

Q: From what Baba has said, it seems there is not much difference or dichotomy between God and man. Am I right?

Baba: *Quite right, God is man and man is God. All of us have something of God, the divine spark, within us. All men are divine like myself, but with the spirit embodied in human flesh and bone. The only difference is that they are unaware of this Godhood. They have come into this karmic prison through the mistakes of many lives. I have taken this mortal form out of my own free will. They are bound to the body, while I am free of this bondage. The main difference is that they are shoved hither and thither by desire but I have no desire except the supreme one to make them desireless.*

Take paddy or rice by way of an illustration. Every grain of rice is enclosed in a husk. You have to remove the husk to get the grain of rice. Now husk and rice, both come from the same seed. Rice is the equivalent of God in man, while the husk can be compared to desire which reduces God to man. Therefore, my formula is:

$$LIFE + DESIRE = MAN$$
$$LIFE - DESIRE = GOD$$

THE WAY TO SELF-REALIZATION

Q: In what way can life without desire make Gods of men?

Baba: *Life without desire means the realization of the pure, genuine self that is atma. Bound to desire, the self degenerates into selfishness. Atma turns into ego. The way of self-realization is to cleanse the self of this ego of selfishness. Then you reach a state of consciousness beyond the mind or intellect, revealing the true self that is God. The mind is like a cloth that covers and stifles consciousness, the threads of which are desires. If we give up the desires, the threads fall and the cloth disappears, revealing our true nature. This is what the Vedanta (epic of ancient wisdom and knowledge) means when it enjoins that one must get rid of the ego to realize oneself.*

Q: You mean that the mind of man as such creates the block between man and God?

Baba: *Yes. One must make a distinction between the mind that is the ego, and the real self that is consciousness. The latter helps us to cross the frontiers of the ego-mind and become aware of oneself as the witness of truth. Normally the scientist of the mind looks outside to what can be perceived by the senses existing in the world of the mind to ask: What is this? The scientist of consciousness, on the other hand, always looks inside to that which is beyond the senses or the grasp of the mind to ask: What is that?*

One has, therefore, to rise beyond the mind to consciousness to achieve self-realization. To gain the infinite, universal atma, the embodied self must break out of the puny, finite little prison of individuality. Desire belongs to the senses, the brain, the mind; once you become free of it, you realize the self, atma, consciousness, enlightenment, and become one with the cosmic power. Self-realization is God-realization. Thus man reaches God.

Q: What is the significance of the *vibuthi* (holy ash) and the trinkets that you materialize and give to people? Is there any need for a Godman to demonstrate such miracles which any magician can conjure?

Baba: *So far as I am concerned this is evidence of my divinity. It is not by any means an exhibition of divinity. All performances of magic, as you know, are done for the sake of income. These are tricks of the magician's trade. They constitute a kind of legalized cheating, the transfer of an object from one place to another by a trick of the hand which goes unnoticed. They involve no siddhi (occult power) or miraculous power.*

What I do is quite a different act of creation. It is neither magic, nor is it siddhi power either. For one thing, I seek no return. For another, I do not cheat people by transferring objects, but I create them. Again, I do so not because of any need or desire of exhibition of my powers. For me this is a kind of calling card to convince people of my love for them and secure their devotion in return. Since love is formless, I do materialization as evidence of my love. It is merely a symbol.

Q: Still I do not understand why you should materialize rings, bracelets, watches and those kinds of trinkets.

TALISMAN OF PROTECTION

Baba: *Most people desire talismans symbolic of my protection. So I provide them. When they are in trouble they feel the grip of the ring, bracelet or watch to remember me and call me to their rescue so that I can help them. On the other hand, if I give them something that they cannot wear, they are likely to store it and forget about it.*

The main thing is that these trinkets or talismans, by whatever name you call them, give people a sense of security and protection they need in time of trouble or crisis and create a symbolic link covering the long distances between them and myself. When the devotees need me, these objects flash the message as if by wireless and I instantly come to their rescue.

Q: I am sorry to be so persistent, *Swamiji*, but isn't the gift of an Omega or HMT watch an act of cheating the company or breach of its patent?

Baba: *I assure you there is no such thing. It would be cheating the company or breaching the patent if it were a case of transfer of the watch from one place or the other. But I do not transfer; I totally create. Whatever I will, instantly materializes. I know of no company that has complained about any breach of patent.*

SIGNIFICANCE OF *VIBUTHI* (HOLY ASH)

Q: What about *vibuthi* materialized by you? We would like to know its relevance because your critics are trying to discredit you by sending around magicians who produce exact replicas of *vibuthi*.

Baba: *What I materialize is a manifestation of divinity with a potent significance as well as symbolism. It is symbolic of the cosmic, immortal and infinite nature of all forms of God, atma or the spirit — that is, what is*

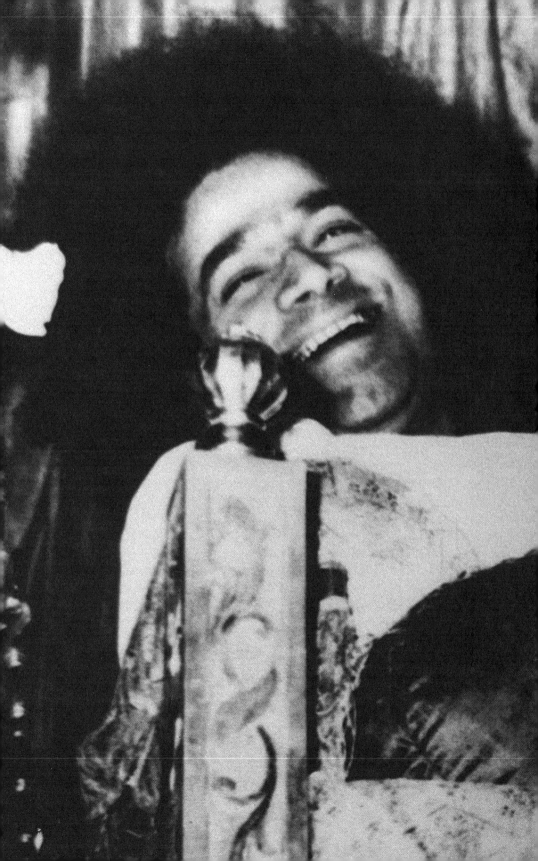

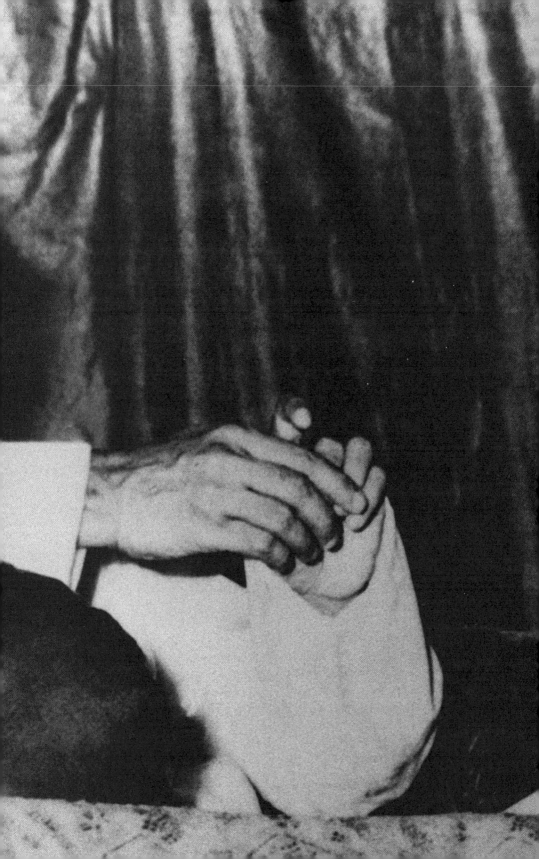

left when everything worldly, transient and changeable has burnt away.

I have spoken to you of the imperative of a desireless life. After Shiva had burnt the God of desire, Kama, into a heap of ashes, he adorned himself with the ash to shine as the conqueror of desire. When Kama was destroyed, Prema reigned as the Goddess of love. Such is the significance of ash.

In the first place, it is symbolic of the life-death cycle in which everything ultimately reduces itself to ash. "For dust thou art, and unto dust shalt thou returnest." Ash or dust is the final condition of things. It cannot undergo any further change. In the spiritual context, it constitutes a warning to the receiver to give up desire, to burn all passions, attachments and temptations, and makes one pure in thought, word and deed.

It is in order to press home this lesson that I materialize ash for those who come to me with love and devotion. Like the other materializations, it also acts as a talisman, healing the sick and giving protection to those who need it. It is the symbol of divinity, quite different from the magician's trickery mentioned by you.

MIRACLES OF HEALING

Q: You are believed to have performed miraculous cures to the extent of resurrecting the dead. There are cases where you reportedly have saved people from drowning and other accidents in distant places. Medical experts have attested to remote controlled surgical operations performed by you. How do you manage these?

Baba: *By my own sankalpa—that is, divine will and power. As an Avatar, this power is intrinsic, inherent, total and natural to my will and decision. I need no mantra (mystical formula), no sadhana (spiritual practice), no tantra (sacred writings) and no yantra (pilgrimage) to perform the so-called miracles which are natural to my state. My powers are simply the expression or assertion of the reality of godliness which merges me with everything, everywhere, at all times and places. The miracles belong to the boundless power of God.*

Now coming to the main points of your question, this healing phenomenon has a dual aspect. I can cure, save, even resurrect people provided they are in a spiritually receptive condition. It is like the positive and negative currents of electricity. My capacity to heal can be compared to the positive current. Your devotion to me is the negative current. Once the two come together, the devotion provides what is called the miracle of healing.

It is man's mind that is really responsible for his illness or health. He himself is the cause or motivator of either. So when it comes to healing or curing, the necessary faith has to be created within his mind for the purpose. All I do is to invest him with the confidence, will and power to cure himself. It is my abounding love reciprocated by the intensity of the devotee's faith in me that produce the desired result.

NOT *SIDDHIS*, NOR MAGICAL TRICKS

Q: So these are not *siddhic* powers or magical tricks, as your critics suggest?

Baba: *They are neither magical tricks nor siddhic (occult) powers, which can come to everybody with the appropriate discipline and yoga exercises, but my powers to protect, heal and save people and materialize objects originate in God and can be used only by an Avatar. They are in no way designed, disciplined or developed, but flow from cosmic power.*

Q: Some say that you command invisible spirits which can transfer objects from one place to another on your orders.

Baba: *There is no need for me to command invisible spirits since my own divine will materializes the objects. I am everything, everywhere, omniscient, omnipotent and omnipresent; and so whatever I will, instantly happens. Like the qualities of truth, love and peace, these are things that generate the atmic (godly) or cosmic forces behind the universe.*

Q: Your followers at home as well as abroad claim positive evidence of the presence of Baba in their innermost hearts. Some have written of you as their in-dwelling God. What is the explanation of this phenomenon?

THE IN-DWELLING GOD

Baba: *This is the grace begotten of my love for them reciprocated by their devotion. After all, as I repeatedly say, we all belong to the same divine principle. The godliness which is present in everybody in the form of a little spark exists in me as the full flame, and it is my mission to develop every little spark of God in everyone to the fullness of the divine flame.*

The first imperative of this development is that the receiver of the grace also provides from his or her side the devotion necessary to the consummation. Those who carry the presence of Baba in their hearts like an in-dwelling God belong to these kinds of devotees. They come to me, see me and hear me, experience my love for them and receive it with devotion. Thus, they become part of me and my divinity.

To the doubting or confused ones, I give this illustration. Those who want to secure pearls from the sea have to dive deep to fetch them. It does not help them to dabble among the shallow waves near the shore and say that the sea has no pearls and all stories about them are false. Likewise, if a person wants to secure the love and grace of this Avatar, he must also dive deep and get submerged in Sai Baba. Then, only, will he become one with me and carry me in his innermost heart.

THE IN-DWELLING GOD

Q: The critics of *Swamiji* ask why Sai Baba does not help people in distress by bringing rains in times of drought or creating food where there is famine by means of his *sankalpa shakti* (divine power, universal energy). Cannot an *Avatar* help humanity to control the natural forces and prevent calamities like earthquakes, floods, droughts, famine and epidemics?

Baba: *This is precisely what I am doing by incarnating the in-dwelling God in man to overcome such calamities. There are two ways in which an Avatar can help people: an instant solution as against a long-term one.*

Any instant solution would go against the fundamental quality of nature itself as well as the karmic law of cause and effect. Most people live in the material world of their desires and egos, which is governed by this law. They reap the fruits of their actions. This brings about their evolution or devolution. If the Avatar intervenes to instantly solve their problems, it would stop all action, development, even evolution. This solution can be ruled out because it totally negates the natural laws.

The other and more effective alternative presents a long-term solution whereby the Avatar leads the people themselves to a higher level of consciousness to enable them to understand the truth of spiritual laws so that they may turn towards righteousness and steadfastly work for better conditions. This will relate them back to nature and the karmic law of causation. They would then transcend the cycle of cause and effect in which today they are involved as victims and thereby command and control the natural forces to be able to avert the calamities you mention.

RAISING MAN TO GOD

Q: You mean that you are presently raising the consciousness of mankind to a godlike condition to enable them to command their own destiny?

Baba: *Exactly. They would become shareholders of my sankalpa shakti (divine power, universal energy). I have to work through them, rouse the in-dwelling God in them and evolve them to a higher reality in order to enable them to master the natural laws and forces. If I cure everything instantly, leaving the people at their present level of consciousness, they would soon mess up things and be at one another's throats again with the result that the same chaotic situation would develop in the world.*

Suffering and misery are the inescapable acts of the cosmic drama. God does not decree these calamities but man invites them by way of retribution for his own evil deeds. This is corrective punishment which induces mankind to give up the wrong path and return to the right path so that he may experience the godlike condition of sat-chit-ananda—that is, an existence of wisdom and bliss. All this is part of the grand synthesis in which the negatives serve to glorify the positives. Thus death glorifies immortality, ignorance glorifies wisdom, misery glorifies bliss, night glorifies dawn.

So, finally, if the Avatar brings the calamities mentioned by you to an immediate end, which I can, and do, when there is a great need, the whole drama of creation with its karmic (universal, inescapable duty) law will collapse. Remember, these calamities occur not because of what God has made of man but really because of what man has made of man. Therefore, man has to be unmade and remade with his ego destroyed and replaced by a transcendent consciousness, so that he may rise above the karmic to command.

Q: Have you succeeded in bringing about this synthesis, *Swami-ji*, particularly with the wealthy and powerful classes?

FUSION OF RICH WITH POOR

Baba: *I have not reached them all as a class, but to the extent that I am able to contact them individually, the results are encouraging. The wealthy and powerful, of course, present a difficult problem in the matter of transformation. They need a special approach. The poorer people, on the other hand, are very cooperative. They understand, appreciate and help my plans and ideas.*

Q: What is your solution to this escalating conflict between wealth and power on one side, and poverty and weakness on the other?

Baba: *The transformation of both into a single cooperative brotherhood on terms of equality without competition or conflict. This can result only from truth and love. The main issue is to fuse the two classes into one single class. The problem, however, is one of bringing them together on a common base or platform. Wealthy people live isolated in a certain state or condition. The poor also are similarly isolated in another state or condition. How do we bring them together?*

I do so in many subtle ways by breaking the barriers of wealth and poverty and creating a feeling of equality and oneness between the poor and the rich. In this ashram (spiritual community) you find them living and working together, even performing menial labor on terms of complete equality. Here there are no distinctions whatever, nor any special facilities for the rich. They live, eat, work, worship and sleep like the poor. All live like a community of workers to share the common austerities of the ashram.

PEACE OF MIND BEYOND WEALTH

Despite our rigorous discipline, industrialists and businessmen want to come here. Why? Because they secure peace of mind beyond physical comfort which no wealth or power on earth can purchase or provide.

Thus we open to them a wonderful new world of spiritual treasures and they must sacrifice material wants and comforts. My mission is to show them the way to the peace of mind which everybody, poor and rich alike, desires. In that process of spiritual evolution, the seeker learns that this blissful state cannot be purchased for money in a shop or gifted to one by anybody but oneself. It can come only from the universal source of divinity, the in-dwelling God that embraces poor and rich alike.

This concept creates a common fellowship, a brotherhood of give and take between the wealthy and the poor. Those who have too much are obliged to give up their unnecessary wants, while those who have too little get their needs fulfilled.

After all, in spiritual terms, all mankind belongs to one and the same class, caste or religion. The divine principles in each and all of them derive from one and the same God. This fundamental oneness has to be made manifest to them through direct contact with spiritual realities and the persuasive expanding power of love, till they become part of the universal religion of work, worship and wisdom.

MATERIAL WEALTH IS SPIRITUAL POVERTY

Q: All this would be simple and welcome evangel for the poor since they lose nothing and gain everything from your philosophy, but what about the rich who would have to lose all if they followed it?

Baba: *That is the crux of the problem. They simply have to lose, surrender, submerge their false values if they want my grace. So long as people continue to be slaves of materialistic definitions of wealth and poverty, there can be no solution. I therefore, try to convert their minds and hearts to spiritual values and truths.*

After all, who is the richest man? One who has the largest wants and, therefore, troubles and worries? Or one who is satisfied with the barest necessities of life and, therefore, is more or less desireless and comparatively happy? Judged from this criterion of happiness, the poor are spiritually rich while the rich are spiritually poor. It is not material but spiritual satisfaction that ultimately makes life worth living.

As I have said before, life without desire brings divinity to man; and those who seek my grace must shed desire and greed. Riches provide a fatal temptation. They are the source and cause of human bondage. The desire to raise the standard of life can never be satisfied. It leads to multiplication of wants and consequent troubles and frustrations.

NO GRACE WITHOUT SACRIFICE

The solution lies in our emphasis on the quality as against the standard of life, on high thinking and lowly living. The mind is the horse, the body the cart: to achieve mental peace, you must put the horse of high thinking before the cart of physical comfort.

Q: This is sound philosophy but how do you implement it in action?

Baba: *The rich as well as the poor come to Sai Baba to seek love, peace and liberation from their problems or troubles. My prescription to them is absolute selflessness and desirelessness. To the poor, this is a natural state or condition. So my love flows to them to embrace their devotion. Thus they obtain my grace.*

MONKEY-MIND BONDAGE

The rich, on the other hand, cannot secure this grace without surrendering their materialistic outlook and selfish attachments. So it becomes obligatory for them to sacrifice material greed to receive spiritual grace. I tell them:

> *Ego lives by getting and forgetting,*
> *Love lives by giving and forgiving.*

In this way, I change their mental attitude. I transform their monkey-minds into loving, giving and forgiving minds.

Q: Monkey-minds, Baba—what do you mean?

Baba: *It is a kind of mentality that is used by the peasants to trap and destroy monkeys. When the peasant wants to catch a monkey, he uses a big pot with a narrow mouth as a trap. Inside the pot he puts edibles which the monkey loves. The monkey finds the pot and puts its paws inside it to grasp as much of the stuff as he can hold. Once it does so, it is unable to pull out its paws from the small mouth of the pot. It imagines that someone inside the pot is holding its paws, so it struggles and attempts to run away with the pot, only to fail and get trapped. No one is holding the monkey; it has trapped itself because of its greed. If only it lets the stuff in its paws go, it will be free of the bondage.*

In the same way I tell the rich people, man is tempted by the wealth, pleasures and desires of the world. When he gets lost in such attachment and suffers the consequences of greed, he thinks that something is binding him down, capturing him, destroying him. He does not realize that he himself is responsible for this bondage. The moment he gives up material wealth and desires, he will be free. I make him realize his bondage to the monkey-mind and liberate himself.

BABA'S SPIRITUAL SOCIALISM

Q: Baba seems to be prescribing a kind of spiritual socialism based on the conversion of wealth into a trusteeship for the removal of poverty.

Baba: *Yes, a trusteeship based on love, cooperation and brotherhood. What else can one do? The change must evolve from the heart; it cannot be imposed from outside. All materialist doctrines have failed to bring about any real transformation. There is no equality anywhere. Only spiritual transformation to a desireless mentality can put through the imperative revolution in human consciousness from which alone the desired changes can accrue.*

We need to transform society from false to real values. We have to convince people that the ideal of a high standard of life is wrong. It must be replaced with a high level of living and thinking on the basis of humility, morality, compassion and detachment, as against the existing greed for competitive luxury and conspicuous consumption. People have to be convinced that the only way to rouse the latent divinity in them is to master desires and conquer greed for pleasure and luxury instead of being a slave to these false materialistic values.

SAI PATH TO *DHARMA* (RIGHTEOUSNESS)

Q: Then I take it that the various educational and social service organizations run by Baba—some 3,000 in all—are designed to create the cadres necessary for bringing about the desired socioeconomic change by means of love and persuasion?

Baba: *They are designed to put the new generation on the Sai path of truth, righteousness, peace, love and nonviolence. Their motto—work is worship and duty is God—seeks to bring in the new social order related to Sathya—that is, truth, and dharma—namely, right action.*

Q: India has been described as a rich country of poor people. We have the wealth of the whole world locked up in the bosom of our good earth. And yet the people remain economically poor and backward. Have you any solution to rehabilitate our economy?

SOCIO-ECONOMIC SYNTHESIS

Baba: *Your analysis is correct. The solution to the problem you have posed lies in hard work and increased production on a cooperative basis. To achieve this, one has to rid the people of the disease of individuality, greed and selfishness. Every individual must be taught to think and work in the broader concept of society and its needs. Once that is done, there will be less talk, more work.*

Here again, it is the spiritual path that can save this country and the world from the wrongs of a materialistic order. What we need is a synthesis of the spiritual and material aspects of life. That will provide man with the social conscience and cooperative spirit imperative to the creation of national wealth and prosperity through selfless, cooperative labor.

Q: Very good counsel, *Swamiji*—but the trouble is that all the wealth created by labor appears to find its way into the pockets of a rich and powerful minority. Have you a spiritual prescription for this inequality?

DESIRE MUST BE EQUALIZED

Baba: *There is no doubt that the distribution is not taking place properly. The existing doctrines of equality, socialism, etc., have not succeeded in achieving equality in distribution of wealth and property. The difficulty is that you can equalize wealth, land and property by legalization, but can the law bring about equality in the desires of the people? This requires the healing touch of spiritualism.*

To begin with, one has to cure desire and its evil consequences. We must persuade the rich that desire and its fulfillment in materialistic wants is an aspect of the monkey-mind which can only harm them and put them under bondage. That alone will solve the problem of inequality and maldistribution.

The rich will give up their extravagant wants, the poor will get what they need and a little more; and this process will bring about more equitable distribution.

Q: To conclude this section, *Swamiji*, would you sum up the main causes of India's social and economic backwardness?

Baba: *From a purely material viewpoint, it is a question of supply and demand. Because of the overpowering material values of our society, the demand is growing larger and larger, while the supply remains the same or decreases. The solution, obviously, is to increase the supply or decrease the demand. Then, of course, there is the problem of growing population. This triangular issue of economic imbalance needs to be spiritualized if an effective solution is to be found.*

LESSER LUGGAGE: BETTER JOURNEY

It is here that our insistence on a desireless life, in which human wants are reduced to the minimum needs, comes to the rescue as the only possible way of restoring the social and economic balance. Curb your desires, reduce your wants, live in spiritual austerity, and the available material will be sufficient for all humanity. More than that, the tensions of a competitive socioeconomic system will be dissolved and peace of mind will be restored.

Life is like a journey in a vehicle between birth and death. The body is the vehicle in which you are motoring to death. The less luggage you carry the better. Why encumber yourself with worldly riches and material comforts, when you may have to change your course or even meet with some dislocation or accident and, in any case, at the end of the journey you will have to leave behind all your possessions except your atma? Would it not be better to attend to the immortal spirit rather than waste time which is running out on gaining wealth and securing comforts?

This is the logic of spiritualism with which I seek to change the attitude of people.

WHY NO PUMPKINS OR CUCUMBERS

Q: Baba has already clarified most of the issues raised by Dr. Narasimhiah and other critics. Some, however, remain unanswered. Narasimhiah asks why you do not materialize a pumpkin or cucumber or a watch with a distinct mark to prove that it is your creation and not a transfer of somebody else's manufacture?

Baba: *Pumpkins and cucumbers can be materialized as easily as rings or objects. But these are perishable objects and the whole point of materialization as I have already explained, lies in their permanence. That is why rings or watches become more serviceable as talismans or means of contact and communication, between the Avatar and his devotees.*

The point they are trying to make is that big objects like pumpkins cannot be transferred while small ones like rings can be. But as I have repeatedly said, I do not transfer things by a sleight-of-hand. I create them to be talismans.

Now coming to your question about a ring or watch with a distinct mark to prove that it is my own creation, would you like me to materialize something for you?

MIRACLE OF OM RING

Q: Yes, *Swamiji*, I certainly would.

Baba waved his hand in the air to produce a silver ring bearing the inscription OM in the centre with *Sai Ram* marks on the sides and held my right hand to gently put it on the third finger. It was an exact fit and it was precisely what I wanted from Baba.

Q: Thank you, Baba, you have answered the question beautifully. Now to Narasimhiah's unanswered point regarding the bogus Sai Krishna or Pandavapura exposed by his committee as a fraud and a cheat. He alleges that the boy had your patronage.

NO CONTACT WITH FAKE BOY

Baba: *I can assure you there is absolutely no connection between him and myself. His people have several times attempted to arrange a meeting between us, but we have refused their requests. Of course, thousands of people, as you saw this morning, come here for darshan. There are others also who masquerade as my disciples or make money using my name. As this happens not only here but in other states and even abroad, we cannot do anything about it. They expose themselves sooner or later, as did this boy. I have absolutely no connection or relationship with such people.*

Q: The Narasimhiah Committee wanted to investigate your miracles scientifically under controlled conditions, as they put it. You rejected the proposal. Would you like to comment on this controversy?

Baba: *How can science which is bound to a physical and materialist outlook investigate transcendental phenomena beyond its scope, reach or comprehension? This is a fallacy on the face of it. One belongs to the material and the other to a spiritual plane. Science must confine its inquiry only to things belonging to the human senses, while spiritualism transcends the senses. If you want to understand the nature of spiritual power you can do so only through the path of spirituality and not science. What science has been able to unravel is merely a fraction of the cosmic phenomena; it tends, however, to exaggerate its contribution.*

Q: That is true, *Swamiji,* but science is developing all the time so that the metaphysics of yesterday becomes the physics of today.

GLOW-WORM IN SUNLIGHT

Baba: *Quite right, but it is still blind to the vast and invisible world of consciousness. The very fact that science is changing all the time proves its incapacity to investigate the ultimate and absolute truth. Some time ago, scientists maintained that the atom cannot be broken, but recently they succeeded in breaking it. They are still ignorant about the realities of the pranic force behind the atom, which is the least of its components.*

Science is a mere glow-worm in the light and splendor of the sun. It is true that it can research, discover and gather a lot of information about nature and its material functions and use it for the development of worldly things. Spiritualism, on the other hand, reigns over the cosmic field where science has no place. That is why some discoveries of science are useful while others can be disastrous.

As I have said before, Dr. Narasimhiah and his group are like the Telugu men who go to the cinema to see a Tamil film. They will see only the dancing, the fighting and violence, the heroes and villains, the star with a beautiful face and these kinds of superficial things, but they will lose the subtler aspects such as the music and the poetry, the plot, the dialogue, the jokes and the like.

WRONG SPIRIT AND APPROACH

However, as I have said again and again, those who want to understand me are welcome here. It is the spirit of the investigation that is important. Foreign parapsychologists have come here and examined me in such a positive and constructive spirit. You have seen their reports. They do not write letters or make public demands.

Narasimhiah's approach was improper; that is why I rejected it. If it were not so, he would have been welcome. I do not call people here so that they may bow to a God. I want them to come, see, hear, study, observe, experience and realize Baba. Then only, they will understand me and appreciate the Avatar.

Q: Dr. Narasimhiah maintains that according to science, "Nothing can be created out of nothing." You have evidently negated this law of science with a transcendental formula for controlling cosmic energy and producing paranormal power. Can you explain this mystery?

"WHAT I WILL, HAPPENS"

Baba: *The formula that nothing can be created out of nothing is appropriate to the limited field and dimensions of science. It does not at all apply to the transcendental field and dimensions of spirituality. In the latter field, anything can be created by the supreme will. All that exists can be made to disappear and what does not exist can be made to appear.*

Our history and tradition, scripture as well as literature, are full of such incidents which they call miracles. The material laws and formulas simply do not apply to divinity. For me this is not a matter of any mystery or mystique. What I will, happens: what I order, materializes.

Q: The Vice-Chancellor appears to ridicule your statement that "There is God in us all." He asks: "Is this not pure escapism? How can God be so unsure of Himself?" Your rejoinder, please.

GOD EXISTS IN EVERYBODY

Baba: *His questions contradict the very basis of Indian philosophy as well as that of most religions. All our scriptures assert that God is present in everyone. According to Vivekananda, "God is present in all." The only thing that is manifest and common to the whole world and, in fact, governs and directs the entire universe, is divinity. Nothing else really exists except divinity.*

Mine is no escapism but the fundamental and eternal truth. I say so not because I am unsure of my own divinity. It is my confidence in its absolute and total authenticity that makes me affirm this fact. It is the scientists who are so unsure of themselves that they indulge in escapist theories.

For example, they say that the moon is lifeless. Simultaneously, they maintain that all matter consists of moving atoms. Now isn't the moon also a conglomerate of the same moving atoms? Then how can it be lifeless? There is no matter which does not consist of atoms, electrons, neutrons and protons, which are all constantly moving. This energy, too, is God.

So also there is no human being in whom there is no divinity. To say that there is no God in man is like saying that there is no atom in the moon or any large lump of matter. The omnipresence of God has been described in our ancient texts as: "ano baniyam mahatoo maniyam" (God is a small particle in the smallest of particles and a large mass in the largest of masses). In this context, how can one say that God is not in man?

NO PREFERENCE FOR WEALTH AND POWER

Q: Another pertinent issue raised by your critics is that you show a perference for wealthy and powerful people as opposed to the poor and the weak in the matter of divine gifts, miracle cures and individual darshans. Is this true? If so, why?

Baba: *This is wrong. I never see or make any distinction between the rich and the poor. I only look at them from the viewpoint of their devotion, their desires, the sacrifice they are willing to make and their troubles. You were here this morning and saw hundreds of people, a few rich, the majority poor. Did you find me making any distinction? All those I brought with me here to this room were poor and weak, sick or troubled.*

In my view, those who appear to the world as wealthy or powerful persons, really bring to me their troubled hearts and sick minds. I cure them by asking them to surrender material wealth and power to spiritual peace and grace.

(End of first part of interview)

THE GODWARD PATH

(Comments by Mr. Karanjia)

What finally is the sum of Sathya Sai Baba's mission? *God-realization through self-realization*, he answered. In this series of interviews, Baba has shown the godward path to the realization of *sat-chit-ananda* — that is, existence, knowledge and bliss absolute.

According to Baba, this highest state of consciousness or enlightenment is possible for every man or woman to achieve once he or she is liberated from the ego-bondage of body and mind to realize the true self — that is, *jivatma*. *Jivatma* is the abode of the in-dwelling God in man. It is the embodied essence of *paramatma*, the cosmic spirit.

The *Avatar's* mission, according to Baba, is to help mankind dissolve the barrier of the ego and the mind with it, so that the embodied *jivatma* can merge and fuse with the universal *paramatma* — *the mighty ocean of nectar divine* — as he describes it, to raise mankind to a race of Godmen and Godwomen.

Baba seeks to resolve the universal problem of man's alienation from man, God and nature with the Sai philosophy of pure spiritual love.

ESCAPE FROM TERROR OF EXISTENCE

Ruth Nanda Anshen, publisher of the well-known "Religious Perspectives" books, notes this as the most serious crisis of our apocalyptic era: "The crisis of man's separation from man and of man's separation from God, the failure of love," and holds it responsible for the "darkness and cold, the frozen spiritual misery of recent times." She evokes the image of *homo cum Deo* (man with God) to call for "a new formula for man's collaboration with the creative process and the only one which is able to protect man from the terror of existence."

Sathya Sai Baba provides the desired formula: *Only evolution to a higher plane of consciousness can save man from this terror, this darkness and cold, this frozen spiritual misery.*

The formula arises from Baba's expertise in the science of consciousness and his knowledge of the cosmic dimensions of the nature of reality. Scientists, of course, scoff at Baba's emphasis on spirituality. Yet, the noblest of them, like Dr. S. Bhagavantam and Dr. U. J. Rao, authenticate the latter's supremacy.

Dr. Rao is a noted geologist who heads the Geology Department of Osmania University. He was witness to the transmutation of a rock into God. Baba picked up a rough piece of granite to ask Rao what it contained. The geologist mentioned some minerals. Baba insisted: *"I don't mean those, but something deeper!"* Rao answered: "Well, molecules, atoms, electrons, protons . . ." Baba wasn't satisfied, *"No, no, no, go deeper still!"* Rao professed his ignorance.

IF ROCK CAN TURN INTO GOD . . .

Then Baba took the rock from the geologists, blew on it, and gave it back to Rao. The geologist was flabbergasted, for the rock had been transformed into a statue of *Krishna* playing the divine flute. Baba admonished him: *"You see, beyond your atoms and all, God was in the rock. And God is sweetness and joy. Break off Krishna's foot and taste it."*

Rao found no difficulty in breaking off the granite statue and tasting the foot. It was candy with a sweetness all its own. No wonder Rao confessed to Baba's biographer, Howard Murphet: "Science gives but the first word; the last word is known only to the great spiritual scientists like Sai Baba."

. . . THEN WHY NOT MAN?

If Baba can transform rock into God—and we have Dr. Rao's word for this miracle—then why not the human being already charged with divine afflatus or divinely imparted knowledge? Apart from his own prodigious spiritual image which encompasses millions of devotees, Baba uses the 3,000 and more Sai spiritual, educational and social service institutions throughout the country to spread his evangel with the object of transforming the common people into a race of enlightened Godmen.

However controversial some of Baba's claims may be, the integrated system of education and social service evolved by him constitutes a model of its kind. It helps to understand and evolve man's total nature. Here the Sai philosophy with its five pillars of truth, righteousness, peace, love and nonviolence is not only being taught but realized through the transmission of knowledge, skill, balance and vision to thousands of students and workers. Thus Baba plans to draw the whole community as well as the nation into his spiritual empire of love and cooperation. There is no expectation of any return for himself. *Come to me with empty hands and I will fill them with my love and grace.*

SELF-REALIZATION IS GOD-REALIZATION

This suffices to introduce the last installment of the interview to the reader. Let Baba continue to speak for himself.

Q: From what Baba has hitherto said, it appears that your mission is to enable mankind to rediscover and incarnate its lost godliness. Am I right?

Baba: *You are right. When man turns inward to realize his true self, then God will become manifest to him. Self-realization is God-realization. In simple words, it is the realization that you are not just a body and mind with the physical organs, but there is within you a self—the atma that is God—distinct from these perishable things. This self is omnipotent omnipresent, omniscient. The comprehension of this truth puts you on the correct path to God-realization.*

ATMA AS SOCIAL INTEGER

(A summary by Mr. Karanjia)

Baba, You have got it right. This is the function of the individual as well as of society. Every member must be enabled to realize this *atmic* truth which embraces and integrates the whole world. It is not castes, classes, groups, families and communities which bind humanity together, but the fact that all mankind belongs to one and the same *atma* that is God.

This single factor puts "mankind" back into man to make him a socially conscious human being. As the *Sastras* say, *vasudhaika kutumbakam:* The whole world is one family. This unity which derives from God can be experienced by everyone through recognition of the supremacy of the common denominator of the self or *atma* in every single individual.

TERROR OF NUCLEAR WAR

Q: So your objective can be summed up as a brotherhood of humanity to be achieved through the doctrine of love?

Baba: *Yes, what else can save the world from thermonuclear fires? Everything points to the terror of that conflagration coming; and my mission* is to preempt the fires by reestablishing *dharma and the spiritual law of one God, one religion, one language embracing one humanity.*

I preach only one religion of love for all, which alone can integrate the human race into a brotherhood of man under the fatherhood of God. I know only one language of the heart beyond the mind or intellect which relates man to man and mankind to God, thereby creating mutual understanding, cooperation and community life in peace and harmony. On this basis I want to build one humanity without any religious, caste or other barriers in a universal empire of love which could enable my devotees to feel the whole world as their own family.

Q: Well said, Baba — but wouldn't this *dharma* with its Hindu orientation conflict with the established religions?

Baba: *No, it will not do anything of the kind because my objective is the establishment of sanathana dharma, which believes in one God as propitiated by the founders of all religions. So none has to give up his religion or deity, but through them worship the one God in all. I have come not to disturb or destroy but to confirm and vindicate everyone in his own faith.*

DHARMIC WAY TO PEACE

Q: But how will that prevent a nuclear holocaust?

Baba: *By removing all causes, sources, barriers and provocations of class, caste, creed, color and race, and replacing the existing hate and violence with love and nonviolence. I expect to provide humanity with an evangel of peaceful cooperation to replace the present escalation to death by co-destruction.*

R.K. Karanjia: Thank you, *Swamiji.* I am all the more grateful to you because I really did not expect you to answer the whole long list of my questions.

Notes

1. Reprinted courtesy of Mr. R.K. Karanjia.

An
Offering

CHAPTER TWENTY-NINE

EVERYONE WAS in the large *Poornachandra*
Auditorium and I was alone on the temple veranda. A few dedicated
ladies were preparing the grounds in front of the temple. Sprinkling
multi-colored designs of powder, punctuated with flickering lights
from scores of small oil lamps, they made the earth's crust around the
temple an exciting birthday cake frosting—with the pastel-colored
temple its crowning topping. The sun was quickly setting.

The world conference now finished, it was the eve of Sai Baba's
fifty-fifth birthday. For days I had patiently waited, hoping to present
him with books which our Birth Day Publishing Company had produced over the past year in his honor. Time and again he seemed to
avert his gaze from mine. Making one last valiant attempt to catch
him, and sacrificing my chance to get a seat in the auditorium, I stationed myself on the temple veranda close to the door he would exit
on his way to the auditorium.

But I failed. Dressed in a white birthday robe and surrounded by

a few close students, he had gone to his devotees in the large auditorium without giving me a glance. Seated in a large silver *juela*
(swing), surrounded by pillows and flowers, he would swing to the
celestial sounds of India's foremost musicians — a vision fit for angels
and gods.

But too late for me to see. The auditorium was packed to its twenty
thousand capacity and I was some distance away, alone in a quiet and
darkening night. Only from afar could I hear the happy sounds of
celebration.

Standing on the edge of the veranda, looking out over the carefully
groomed grounds and into the dark night, all I could see was my aloneness. No more last gentle moment in his presence before departing.

Memories of the past few days lightened my spirits. Along with
about 200,000 others, my wife, twin daughters and I had witnessed a
multi-dimensional unfolding of grandeur rarely seen in a lifetime.
Besides the large events involving the vast crowds, there were also
touching and cherished personal moments with Baba as when he first
made contact with my innocent young 13-year-old daughters. Having
waited patiently for days, sitting in the sun with the large throng,
hoping for just a glimpse or a smile, how thrilling when he finally approached. While passing, Sai Baba unexpectedly turned to them,
charging them with delight when he materialized rock candy and
threw it gently in their laps.

Then the time when we sat with him as a family, discussing the
education of our daughters and the work we were to do in the future.
Suddenly he turned to me, eyes atwinkle, and reached for my ring
which he had materialized four years earlier. Holding it out for my
family to see, he asked softly, *"Do you want gold?"* Surprised and
hesitatingly, I answered, "Not necessarily, *Swami* — just your love."
"No, no, gold," he replied, and with that held the silver ring to his
lips. With three slow deliberate breaths, in a miraculous and dazzling
instant, it was transformed into a bright glittering gold ring with his
picture on the surface.[1] It was an entirely new ring. To my surprise he
did not return it to my left finger where the other had been, but
instead to my right, where it was a perfect fit. Later I found it too
large for my left ring finger. For some unknown reason he made the
ring specifically for the right.

Yes, I had many marvelous memories — as when he gave three

lovely saris to my wife and two children. His encouragement, love, personal attention—the awareness that he was an intimate part of our family, all this filled me with joy. But now I grieved over the limitation of my personal consciousness that would not allow me to be fully in the *Poornachandra* Auditorium with dear Baba, but kept me bound to my personal body here on the veranda, surrounded by what I considered the solitude of my personal reality. Nighttime had come and I was alone in the dark emptiness—in the quiet stillness— separate and apart—all alone.

From nowhere a teacher from the college appeared. "Leave the books here and come quickly," he whispered. Hurriedly I followed him across fifty yards of soft sand and into the back door of the *Poornachandra* Auditorium. In a moment he sat me with some thirty others backstage looking at the back of the silver *juela* (swing), a sizzling shock of black hair bursting over the back of the *juela* pinpointing Baba's location. In a moment, quiet silence and aloneness was transformed into the exhilarating celebration of the divine birth— and I was at its center.

Musicians played and sang about the life of Lord *Rama*. A few lucky ones were seated in back of the *juela*, slowly swinging Baba to and fro to the tune of the *Rama* melody. And the throngs drank in the glorious vision of the king of kings recognized—and receiving the pure sweet nectar of humanity's devotion.

Again my unexpected friend approached, motioning me to move up to the *juela* and take part in the pushing. Yet closer I moved. Slowly, reaching toward the silver swing—I felt its slight resistance release me into the marvelous dance of motion and music. Back and forth, back and forth—we were all swinging now with Sathya Sai— to the celestial song of the *Rama* story and to his exquisite inner ecstasy. No silence and darkness now—but grace—pure bliss—wonderment— and love.

Shortly I withdrew to allow others the blessing of touching the silver swing. I closed my eyes and melted into the ethers. The program soon drew to a close. Baba stood and was quickly surrounded by musicians and well-wishers. He would soon leave through the back door of the *Poornachandra* and there was a scramble to catch a last glimpse of him as he left.

Once again my guardian angel appeared. "Come quickly! He'll

leave through this door."
Holding onto his shirttail, I was
swiftly guided to the rear entrance. Mounting excitement
and a surge from the crowd
pushed me one way and an-
other. Yes, Baba was moving
toward this door. In a moment
he was standing before me.

The sparkle and radiance in
his smile filled the room with
light. Held in the soft magne-
tism of this smile, I began to
lose contact with the crowd.
The moment lost its frenzy and
turned into something soft, intimate and holy. "May I touch
your feet, *Swami?*" I whispered.
He smiled approval and as I
knelt to the floor, as my lips
touched his feet, the moment
dissolved into jasmine and
sweet honey. Gone was the
darkness of the night and
aloneness—gone the past and
future—the sense of separation.
Now only an expanse of white
robe—a melting into an eternity of light—of vast space—of
oneness. Nothing had become
everything. And with the memory of that eternal moment
fixed firmly in my heart, I offer
this book to Him . . .

Notes

1. Photo of gold ring is on p. 264.

Receiving books written about him from around the world

(Above) The symbol of the
Sathya Sai Baba organization,
representing unity —
the fundamental oneness

of all religions

of East and West

of spirituality and science

(Turn page) Inside the *mandir*
(temple) at *Prasanthi Nilayam*

(Page after) Outside the *mandir*
(temple) at night

This next section is directed to the serious student of psychology and may be a bit too theoretical and technical for the average reader.

Appendix I is a glossary of terms related to consciousness. Appendix II summarizes some of the history and current work in the field of consciousness, including findings and observations in physics and some current spiritually-oriented trends in psychology. Appendices III and IV compare Western scientific concepts about mind and consciousness with Eastern spiritual concepts in a way which I hope adds to—and deepens—our understanding of both.

PART IV   Appendices

First ring materialized for me by Sathya Sai
Baba in 1974. Story on page 6.

Second ring, transformed from the first by Sai
Baba's breath in 1978. Story on page 6.

Gold ring, transformed from the second by Sai
Baba's breath in 1980. Story on page 260.

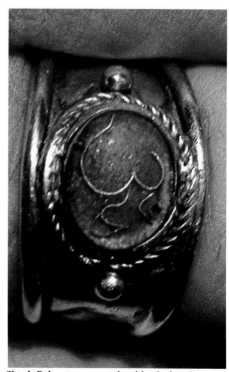

Shirdi Baba ring materialized by Sathya Sai
Baba in 1977. Story on page 190.

Appendix I

GLOSSARY OF TERMS ON CONSCIOUSNESS

Mainstream Western psychology has assumed that consciousness is a function or product of mind originating in the physical brain. Terms and definitions relating to different aspects of our consciousness reflect this attitude. For instance, the glossary of the *Comprehensive Textbook of Psychiatry/III* (1980, p. 3318), for the term "consciousness" says "see sensorium" and then defines sensorium:

> Hypothetical sensory center in the *brain* that is involved with a person's clarity of awareness about himself and his surroundings, including the ability to perceive and process ongoing events in light of past experiences, future options, and current circumstances. It is sometimes used interchangeably with consciousness.

However, many new findings in the behavioral sciences challenge the assumption that consciousness is a function of the mind linked to the brain. As Dr. Kenneth Pelletier states in *Toward a Science of Consciousness*, consciousness may not "be adequately attributed to an epiphenomenon of neurophysiological and biochemical processes unique to the human brain . . . ."[1] Consciousness is being recognized as more fundamental than mind and, in fact, may have created mind and the entire cosmos as well.

Confusion regarding the definitions and qualities of consciousness is widespread.

> After a behavioristic hiatus of over half a century, American psychologists in the 1960's began, at first tentatively, to return consciousness to its former central position of concern. Because of this long period during which the use of the term was not allowed, we lost contact with the historical roots of the several different, but legitimate, definitions of consciousness. Today, we find psychologists of a wide variety of orientations using this word and assuming that its meaning is the same for others as it is for them.[2]

So arises the need for new terms reflecting our new awareness. I'm proposing the following.

1) *Consciousness* — in its broadest sense, our capacity for awareness. In its most fundamental and pure state, consciousness is infinite, absolute, eternal and universal (see #12, Universal Consciousness). Hinduism defines consciousness as one of three fundamental attributes of divinity, the other two being absolute truth and bliss.[3]

If consciousness is more fundamental than mind it cannot be fully grasped by mind. Therefore, from the start we have to accept a fundamental ambiguity which reflects the mind's inability to fully grasp profound spiritual reality. To be specific about type, aspect, orientation and quality of a state of limited consciousness, a preceeding qualifier is needed, as in the terms below.

2) *Conscious consciousness* — immediate awareness: perceptions and impressions which engage immediate attention.

3) *Unconscious consciousness* — in psychoanalysis, a term which refers to a dimension of the psyche or *mind* in which all mental material is not readily accessible to conscious awareness by ordinary means. If we assume there is a realm beyond mind we would add, "all mental and *supramental* (beyond mind) material" which is not readily accessible to conscious awareness by ordinary means. Having consciousness of the unconscious is inferred by its appearance in dreams, slips of the tongue and in symptom formation.

4) *Witness consciousness* — the awareness of being aware, that aspect which separates man from the rest of the animal kingdom. The witness who is aware, the "observer" who is conscious of being con-

scious, lies outside the mind and represents supramental (beyond mind) consciousness.

This commonly experienced "I" aspect of the supramental has great significance. Becoming centered in and identified with this witness through a serious and dedicated inquiry into the question "Who am I?" may lead one to total conscious consciousness without limitation (see Universal Consciousness).

5) *Lower mental (psyche) consciousness*—consciousness predominantly oriented along one of the psychosexual stages of development as described by Freud (see Ch. 2). This is characteristic of certain personality types which are "fixated" or attached to thoughts, fantasies, feelings, desires, impulses, fears, motivations and behaviors of lower developmental stages (oral, anal, phallic, genital). Behavior is motivated by desire for self-gratification and is predominantly self-centered and selfish.

6) *Psychic (ESP) consciousness*—the perceptions of psychic consciousness may be divided into three general classes. Although psi researchers realize there may be significant overlapping, these include "telepathy, which is mind-to-mind communication; clairvoyance, the perception of current events, objects or people that are hidden from the known five senses; and precognition, the knowledge of future events that cannot be perceived by any known means."[4] These impressions may be beyond time and/or place and are expressions of lower mind (such as feeling the pain of another at a distance) or higher mind (such as "knowing" a cure which brings health and happiness).

Spiritual texts warn about being too attracted by this dimension of consciousness as it may lead to a glorified sense of self-importance and power and distract one from the primary spiritual goal of achieving complete freedom or Universal Consciousness.

Sai Baba's miracles are of a different nature, being a manifestation of Universal Consciousness (see #12 in this section and Discourse in Part III). Regarding his ability to materialize objects and other powers, Sai Baba has said:

Some objects Swami creates in just the same way that he created the material universe. Other objects, such as watches, are brought from existing supplies. There are no invisible beings help-

ing Swami to bring things. His sankalpa, his divine will, brings the object in a moment. Swami is everywhere. His creations belong to the natural unlimited power of God and are in no sense the product of yogic powers as with yogis or of magic as with magicians. The creative power is in no way contrived or developed but is completely natural. . . . Remember there is nothing that divine power cannot accomplish. It can transmute earth into sky and sky into earth. To doubt this is to prove that you are too weak to grasp great things — the grandeur of the universe.

7) *Higher mental (psyche) consciousness* — consciousness predominantly oriented toward expressing man's higher needs as defined by Maslow (see Ch. 2). Behavior is more selfless and motivated by empathy, compassion and love.

8) *Intelligent (buddhi) consciousness* — higher reasoning and abstract thinking characteristic of more highly evolved intelligence. Judgment and perceptive choice are employed.

9) *Wisdom (vijnana) consciousness* — higher knowledge: the capacity to envision spiritual goals and the ultimate purpose and meaning of life, the capacity for higher-order discernment between right and wrong, good and bad, real and unreal, eternal and temporal. This aspect of higher mind directs one's intelligence and thoughts in the proper way of inquiry and determines the focus of an individual's life. It is the comprehensive spiritual perception which envisions things in their essence and totality.

10) *Conscience* — an aspect of wisdom: the capacity to know right from wrong and the higher-order promptings by supramental consciousness toward righteousness. It is the capacity to experience the absolute goodness of creation and to choose to be in harmony with it even at the expense of sacrificing lower desires.

11) *Supramental (transcendental) consciousness* — impressions, intuitions and visions of a higher order, beyond words and concepts, representing awareness of dimensions beyond mind. These perceptions can be frightening as with the *mortal* fear that comes with sensing our mortality, the humbling mystery of death and the possibility of non-existence. Or, they can be exhilarating, such as when *really* seeing the awesome grandeur of creation; being shaken with the humbling sense of God's presence; feeling the miraculousness and

holiness of existence; sensing the reality of absolute truth; experiencing profound reverence, compassion and selfless love for all people; or realizing a profound, unshakable, eternal peace and bliss. It may include a unitive experience of a boundless relationship with all that is. It has been spoken of as a peak experience, samadhi, satori, an oceanic oneness with all.

12) *Universal Consciousness* — conscious consciousness without limitation. "The subject-object dichotomy is transcended and an omnidirectional experience of oneness comes into being that unifies all of the other forms of consciousness."[5] It is omnipresence, omnipotence, omniscience — boundless love, infinite, eternal, absolute consciousness.

Notes

1. Kenneth R. Pelletier, Ph.D., *Toward a Science of Consciousness* (New York: Dell Publishing Company, 1978), p. 241.

2. Jack R. Strange, "A Search for the Sources of the Stream of Consciousness," *The Stream of Consciousness*, ed. Kenneth S. Pope and Jerome L. Singer (New York: Plenum Press, 1978), p. 9.

3. Reflecting the growing respect in modern scientific thought for the importance of the Eastern view of consciousness, a formidable report originally issued by Stanford Research Institute proposes a melding of Eastern and Western approaches. Produced by the staff of and consultants to The Center for the Study of Social Policy, *Changing Images of Man** was authored by such notable thinkers as renowned mythologist, Joseph Campbell, and Willis Harman, senior social scientist at SRI International and President of the Institute of Noetic Sciences, among others. The report states:

    > The time is clearly ripe for a new vision, and it is natural to wonder if it . . . will be found in an "epistemology of the self," such as held sway in the East . . . . This is not to suggest that modern science would or should adopt totally all the Eastern notions of consciousness, but rather that they might be fruitfully adopted and synthesized with traditional Western scientific methods to produce the next stage in man's evolutionary advance.

    *O.W. Markley, ed., et al., *Changing Images of Man*, Systems Science and World Order Library — Pergamon International Library (Oxford, England: Pergamon Press, 1982), p. 105.

4. Russell Targ and Keith Harary, *The Mind Race* (New York: Villard Books, 1984), p. 53.

5. John R. Battista, "The Science of Consciousness," *The Stream of Consciousness*, ed. Kenneth S. Pope and Jerome L. Singer (New York: Plenum Press, 1978), p. 61.

Appendix II

PAST AND CURRENT INSIGHTS ABOUT CONSCIOUSNESS

Accumulated data from both the hard sciences like physics and the soft, like psychology, challenge commonly held concepts about matter, consciousness and man's fundamental identity. These findings imply that our human identity may extend beyond time, space and the physical body detected by our senses. They have done much to stimulate the growing general revival of interest in spirituality in Western society, mainstream psychiatry's resistance aside. Following is a summary of some of these findings.

In the early 1900's, Carl Jung introduced the concept of the collective unconscious, and the idea that we may well extend beyond space and time and ultimately be a part of a higher dimension of reality than that represented by the physical world. He believed that our consciousness could tap into this higher reality—drawing from it intuitive and creative insight, wisdom and direction. This collective unconscious, which more recently has been termed the objective psyche, was the deepest layer of the unconscious, Jung felt, and was ordinarily inaccessible to conscious awareness. It constituted by far the largest area of the mind, and its content was not derived from the life experiences of the person but from the entire human race—the whole history of psychic functioning.

Jung believed that the collective unconscious represented the wisdom of the ages, a knowing far superior to that of a single individual. Its contents—or archetypes—and its symbolic representation—

archetypal images—were expressed in the basic images and themes of all religions, mythologies, legends and fairy tales of all ages. The archetypes also emerged through dreams and visions, in cases of deep psychological analysis, in profound, subjective experience, and in major mental disorder.

Jung's work with archetypes greatly broadened our vision of self as he found stratas of awareness that transcended space and time, and were common to all men—an inner memory of our entire existence as a people. These archetypal images are so various and numerous, that they defy comprehensive listing, but four broad categories have been described and are briefly summarized here. They are—the archetype of the great mother, the spiritual father, the archetype of transformation (pertaining to the psychic process of growth, change and transition) and the central archetype, the Self (expressing a psychic wholeness or totality). The emerging central archetype, representing deepening spiritual awareness, may manifest in the form of a special geometric figure, called a mandala. In its simplest form, a mandala is a quadrated circle, combining the elements of a circle with a square, a cross or some other expression of four-foldness. It represents a basic unifying and integrating principle lying at the very root of the psyche. It is felt in Jungian analysis that a fully developed mandala usually emerges in an individual's dreams after a long process of psychological development. It may be accompanied by a feeling of release from an otherwise irreconcilable conflict and may convey an expanded awareness of the oneness of all creation.[1]

Developments within the past twenty years in psychology, first loosely combined under the general heading "The New Psychology" and more recently, "Humanistic Psychology," have explored the possibility of expanding awareness to enhance creativity and reveal a deeper meaning and purpose in life.

Fathered by Abraham Maslow, humanistic psychology ushered in the human potential movement and in 1973 was accepted by the American Psychologic Association as its newest branch. Maslow was the first major American psychologist to postulate that man is an evolutionary creature whose higher nature seeks actualization just as surely as does his lower nature, and that sickness arises when this upward evolution, this need for self-actualization, is blocked. "The higher nature," Maslow said, "includes the need for meaningful work, for responsibility, for creativeness, for being fair and just, for doing what is worthwhile, and for preferring to do it well." This is in contrast to man's lower nature, which seeks selfish gratification of the animal drives and instincts.

Terms of this new psychology, such as "peak" and ecstatic experiences, self-transcendence and self-actualization, energy flow and energy fields, love, consciousness, the spiritual dimension—create a language similar to that of mystics and spiritual aspirants. Investigators believe that worthwhile data can be gained by experiencing altered states of consciousness, as are found in meditation, hypnosis and sensory deprivation.

As mentioned in Chapter 2, Maslow described a powerful transcendental state he called "peak experience," in which the person experienced a sense of heightened noetic clarity and understanding, intense euphoria, and an appreciation of the holistic, unitive and integrated nature of the universe and one's unity with it. He hoped that studies of peak experiences would help bridge the gap between the relative and the absolute and establish a scientific basis for experiences of unity and eternity.

More recently, investigators have shown growing interest in studying psychic phenomena. Stanley Krippner writes: "It is likely that the apogee of the publication of books on parapsychology was reached in the years 1974-1976 . . . ."[2] In his bibliography he lists ninety-three books under fourteen subject headings, some of which include: "Medicine, Psychiatry and Parapsychology," "Parapsychology and Other Sciences," "Philosophy and Parapsychology" and "Religion and Parapsychology."

Questions about the nature of consciousness, and the relationship of brain to consciousness, are centuries old. The nineteenth century Prussian professor of logic and metaphysics, Immanuel Kant, declared, "No experience tells me that I'm shut up someplace in my brain." Charles Darwin, on the other hand, stated, "Why is thought, being a secretion of the brain more wonderful than gravity, a property of matter?" Some, confused by the issue, might have taken the point of a satirist's insight, "What is mind? No matter. What is matter? Never mind." Schopenhauer termed the impasse between mind and matter, this "world knot."

In the field of physics and the neurosciences, the question of the relationship of brain to consciousness has been posed in terms of mind and brain, or mind and matter. In this book, I take the position that consciousness is more fundamental than mind and brain, and that mind is like a bubble in magnitude to the ocean of consciousness— consciousness actually creating mind and brain. As earlier observers were unclear in differentiating between consciousness and mind, perhaps we may more profitably substitute the word "consciousness" for "mind" in their statements. In my opinion it is the properties of consciousness, and not mind, that early onlookers concluded weren't attributable to brain.

Dr. Wilder Penfield, a leading brain researcher and neurosurgeon, worked for over fifty years to prove that brain accounted for mind (consciousness). The problems involved in the attempt to account for consciousness at last brought him to this perspective: "In the end I conclude that there is no good evidence, in spite of new methods, such as the employment of stimulating electrodes, the study of conscious patients and the analysis of epileptic attacks, that the brain alone can carry out the work that the mind does. I conclude that it is easier to rationalize man's being on the basis of two elements than on the basis of one."[3]

Dr. Candace Pert, of the Biological Psychiatry Branch of the National Institute of Mental Health, believes that one day soon neuroscience will be capable of making a color-coded map of the brain. However, she denies that such a diagram could account for consciousness. "Just as a person could totally understand a television set—could take it apart and put it together again—but understand nothing about electromagnetic radiation, we could study the brain as input-output: sensory input, behavior output. We make maps, but we should never confuse the map with the territory. I've stopped seeing the brain as the end of the line. It's a receiver, an amplifier, a little, wet mini-receiver for collective reality." And what of consciousness? "Consciousness," Pert asserts, "is before the brain, I think. A lot of people believe in life after death, and the brain may not be necessary to consciousness. Consciousness may be projected to different places. It's like trying to describe what happens when three people have an incredible conversation together. It's almost as if there were a fourth or fifth person there; the whole is greater than the sum of its parts."[4]

At long last consciousness research is coming to be held in high regard in the West. In the 1981 *Annual Review of Neurosciences*, Nobel laureate Roger Sperry, renowned for his work in the hemispheric functioning of the brain, states:

> Current concepts of the mind-brain relation involve a direct break with the long-established materialist and behaviorist doctrine that has dominated neuroscience for many decades. Instead of renouncing or ignoring consciousness, the new interpretation gives full recognition to the primacy of inner conscious awareness as a casual reality . . . . Once science modifies its traditional materialist-behaviorist stance and begins to accept in theory and to encompass in practice within its casual domain the whole world of inner, conscious, subjective experience (the world of the humanities), then the very nature of science itself is changed . . . . Recent conceptual developments in the mind-brain sciences rejecting reductionism and mechanistic determinism on the one side, and dualisms on the other, clear the way for a rational approach to the theory and prescription of values and a natural fusion of science and religion.[5]

Direct awareness leads us to the one indisputable fact we maintain about the universe we inhabit—that of human consciousness. Western science now seeks to understand more about this consciousness which has for so long formed the basis of speculative systems. Many physicists like Eugene Wigner[6] hold the inclusion of consciousness research essential to further expansion in scientific understanding. And, as the physicist Sir Arthur Eddington concludes: "Recognizing that the physical world is entirely abstract and without 'actuality' apart from its linkage to consciousness, we restore consciousness to the fundamental position instead of representing it as an inessential complication occasionally found in the midst of inorganic nature at a late stage of evolutionary history."[7]

In the Australian magazine *Gazette* (December, 1984, p. 14), Professor Brian McCusker, professor of nuclear physics at the University of Sydney (Australia), noted researcher in cosmic radiation, states that quantum mechanics, proven by experiment to be the most accurate description of the physical universe yet available, demands that the universe be considered one, whole, indivisible and *conscious* entity of which the observer is an essential part. The logical implication of this, he argues, is that to properly study the universe, a scientist must study his own consciousness.

Although his own research produced evidence of a free "quark"—a supposedly fundamental building block of physical matter—he now claims in a new book, *The Quest for Quarks*, published by Cambridge University Press, that the materialist view of the universe simply does not fit with the facts as demonstrated by experiment, and that a search for fundamental building blocks is fruitless. "It is clear that no such things exist: after quarks, there would be yet another proliferation of particles . . . Materialism is like playing with toy trains—its the best fun in the world when you're six or seven years of age—but when you're forty?"

Professor McCusker reports that, "Tests of Bell's theorem[8] completed in Paris two years ago have shown that the universe is not a set of separate things with empty space between them—it's one interconnected thing, and the way things will influence one another depends on their past history, irrespective of what you think their distance apart is." He concludes that levitation, ESP, Tarot cards and many other psychic phenomena are scientifically valid.

The field of research in human consciousness has burgeoned in the area of psi research. In 1969 the American Association for the Advancement of Science admitted the Parapsychology Association to membership in its ranks. For more than ten years the U.S. government has funded a multimillion-dollar program at SRI International in Menlo Park, California. The program involves the exploration of techniques of a perceptual ability termed *remote viewing*. Remote viewing, one type of psi or psychic functioning, happens quite naturally in the course of daily events to many people. It refers to the awareness of locations, events and objects unable to be perceived by the known senses, typically due to distance. As the Committee on Science and Technology reported to Congress: "Recent experiments in remote viewing and other studies in parapsychology suggest that there is an 'interconnectedness' of the human mind with other minds and with matter . . . . The implication of these experiments is that the human mind may be able to obtain information independent of geography and time . . . ."[9]

Although Freud initially rejected psi phenomena, he reversed his opinion in his later years. He was a member of both the British and the American Society for Psychical Research. Convinced of telepathic communication between analyst and patient, Freud postulated that this was an archaic mode of contact later replaced by sensory communication. In 1924 he wrote to Ernest Jones regarding his intention "to lend the support of psychoanalysis to the matter of telepathy." Apparently Jones, fearing the disparagement of psychoanalysis, dissuaded him from public declaration. Jones had also deterred Freud from presenting a paper titled "Psychoanalysis and Telepathy" at the International Psychoanalytic Congress in 1922. The essay at last appeared after Freud's death.[10]

Stanley R. Dean, M.D., a clinical professor of psychiatry at the Universities of Miami and Florida, founder of the Research in Schizophrenia Endowment and the American Metapsychiatric Association, and author of nearly 100 papers, advocates the extension of medical horizons by exploring psychic phenomena. Metapsychiatry, a term first proposed by him in 1971, is now included in the official glossary of the American Psychiatric Association and *The International Encyclopedia of Neurology, Psychiatry, Psychoanalysis, and Psychology.* He states in an article in the professional journal *M.D.*, December, 1978, entitled "Metapsychiatry and Psychosocial Futurology":[11] Metapsychiatry is a semantically congruent term born of necessity to designate the important, but hitherto unclassified interface between psychiatry and mysticism . . . . It is not synonymous with parapsychology, for it includes the entire alphabet of psychic phenomena from aura to zen . . . . It may be conceptualized as the base of a pyramid whose other sides are psychiatry, technology, parapsychology, and mysticism." (Mysticism may be defined as "any belief in the existence of realities beyond perceptual or intellectual apprehension, but central to being and accessible to consciousness.")

"In my opinion," Dr. Dean writes, "psychic research is a legitimate concern of psychiatry, the medical specialty best qualified to investigate phenomena, assess validity, and expose fallacy in matters of the mind. There can be little doubt that a high degree of reciprocal enlightenment would result if psychiatry would lend its academic and taxonomic expertise to the religious and philosophical speculations that have preempted the field."

Dr. Dean implies that psychiatry comes naturally to this field, reminding us that "a psychiatrist, Dr. Maurice Bucke, in a remarkable book *Cosmic Consciousness*, published in 1898, developed a theory that a seemingly miraculous higher consciousness, appearing sporadically throughout the ages, was a natural rather than occult phenomenon, that it was latent in all of us and was in fact an evolutionary process that would eventually result in a higher level of existence for mankind."

In his article Dr. Dean states, "Thus far most of the attention in the literature has been focused upon descriptions of psychic phenomena, but not enough upon their purpose; therefore, I intend to ask not only, 'What are psychic phenomena?' but also 'What good are they?'" He goes on to describe a number of possible purposes, including a life-preserving function of ESP similar to the flight or fight mechanism and the self-repairative mechanism of trauma and disease. He refers to Dr. William Tiller, "a scrupulous researcher at Stanford University, who is optimistic about the future usefulness of Kirlian photography as a life-energy monitoring system. (Kirlian photography is a photographic technique which allegedly reveals pulsating energy fields emitted by all forms of life, and which is presumably capable of interacting with other energy fields past, present, and future). It should then be possible to develop a reliable monitoring system for revealing the physical, emotional, and mental tone of human beings; develop systems for determining the peak conditions of participants in critical team activities; and develop a sorely needed objective standard for psychiatric research and therapy."

Notes

1. C. G. Jung, "Concerning Mandala Symbolism" in "The Archetypes and the Collective Unconscious," *Collected Works*, Volume 9, (1), Bollingen Series xx. (New York: Pantheon, 1959), pp. 355-384.

2. *Advances in Parapsychological Research.* 1. Psychokinesis (New York and London: Plenum Press, 1977), p. 191.

3. Wilder Penfield, *The Mystery of the Mind* (New Jersey: Princeton University Press, 1975), p. 114.

   Dr. Wilder Penfield (1891-1976), one of this century's greatest brain researchers and neurosurgeons, was founder of Montreal (Canada) Neurological Institute. He located several functional areas of the human cerebral cortex in the development of a surgical treatment for epilepsy. Penfield discovered that stimulation of the interpretive cortex activated the neuronal record of past experience; he consequently developed the centro-cephalic hypothesis of memory control.

4. Interview, "Candace Pert," *Omni*, February, 1982, pp. 64 & 112.

5. As quoted in Russell Targ and Keith Harary, *The Mind Race* (New York: Villard Books, 1984), p. xv.

6. Eugene Wigner, an eminent physicist known for his work on the philosophical implications of quantum mechanics, has been honored with the Atoms for Peace Award in 1960, the Nobel Prize in Physics in 1963, and the Albert Einstein Award in 1972.

7. Arthur S. Eddington, *The Nature of the Physical World* (Cambridge: Cambridge University Press, 1931), p. 332.

8. These tests, which relate to an aspect of the Einstein Podolsky Rosen paradox, seem to confirm a phenomenon predicted by Bell's math—that the *way* one measures one of a pair of particles that have once interacted, *instantaneously* affects the behavior of the other, even when they are separated by great distance, in a way not understood by present laws of physics. This suggests a degree of interconnectedness between objects much more intimate than previously imagined in the field of physics.

   Einstein was perplexed by this possibility, as this instantaneous reaction refuted his belief that an object cannot transmit information to another separate object at a speed greater than the speed of light in a vacuum. Some physicists are suggesting that this phenomenon as well as mystical and psi phenomena are aspects of a subatomic but universal intelligence system that receives, integrates and transmits information at a level much deeper than the sensory appearances of what we call space, time and separateness. And so, now in physics there arises serious question as to whether the universe is constructed of separate and distinct objects, or is fundamentally one unified whole—an expression of an underlying infinite consciousness.

9. Committee on Science and Technology, (U.S. House of Representatives) *Survey of Science and Technology Issues Present and Future*, June, 1981.

10. Arthur Koestler, *The Roots of Coincidence* (New York: Random House, 1972), p.101.

11. Stanley R. Dean, M.D., "Metapsychiatry and Psychosocial Futurology," *M.D.* 22(12): pp. 11-13.

Statue at *Prasanthi Nilayam* of the ancient symbol of *kundalini* energy

Appendix III

PSYCHOLOGY AND SPIRITUALITY

We can best understand the relationship between psychology and spirituality by seeing these fields as different approaches to the study of evolving consciousness. Joseph Campbell,[1] Ken Wilber,[2] writers in the field of Transpersonal Psychology, and myself[3] have pointed out how Freud's psychosexual developmental stages correspond closely to the lower stages of consciousness described by *yogis*. And Wilber has demonstrated the efficacy of looking at all levels of psychological development in terms of the evolution of consciousness. He draws parallels between Western psychology's developmental stages of mind and levels of consciousness defined by philosophers, theologians, mystics and masters from many spiritual traditions, as well as the subtle states of consciousness studied by *yogis*.

Each of these levels is defined by a whole constellation of affects, styles, forms and content of thought, behavioral and motivational patterns and their relationship to early environmental determinants, and the kinds of experiences — both interpersonal and intrapsychic — necessary to promote evolution from one level to the next (more about this later). In addition, some of the spiritual techniques used in helping people advance from lower to higher stages are similar to psychological techniques and vice versa.

Let's review some basic psychological and spiritual concepts to see if we can find some interrelationships upon which to base the practice of a spiritual psychology. And as we develop the theoretical

281

groundwork let's keep in mind a very important empirical observation which points out the complex relationship between spirituality and psychiatry.

People at higher levels of psychological development do not necessarily show higher degrees of spiritual insight, and people with severe emotional problems may have a very high degree of spiritual insight. The high-powered bank executive may have very little interest in spiritual issues and show very few spiritual qualities such as compassion, detachment and devotion. On the other hand, the severely disabled alcoholic may have authentic spiritual insight and even deep mystical experiences. He may interpret spiritual themes and feelings in a distorted manner, being overly attentive to spirituality as a defense and a way of avoiding psychological issues, but he may nevertheless have authentic experiences.

William James, in fact, wrote that the psychologically ill have authentic mystical experiences more frequently than the normal population. And Christ of course said: "The meek shall inherit the earth," and, "It's easier for a camel to pass through the eye of a needle than for a rich man to reach the kingdom of God."

It's been my continuing observation, when speaking to people about my experiences with Sai Baba, that I can never predict, on the basis of psychological strength and success in the outer world, who will respond with tears and awe and who will remain completely unaffected—who seems to understand at a deeper level and who does not. Are these two dimensions unrelated, then? Contemporary debate between those who believe man developed through an evolutionary process without the intervention of a higher power, and those who believe that God participated in some way, shows the difficulty we have in accepting the possibility of an interrelationship between the material and spiritual dimensions.

PSYCHOLOGICAL CONCEPTS
STAGE THEORIES IN PSYCHIATRY

Concepts about evolution are common to both psychology and spirituality. Basically they say that each progressive developmental stage in plant and animal life is based upon, and is an outgrowth of, the preceding developmental stage. It can be hypothesized that certain genetically determined human functions develop irrespective of what happened at preceding stages and are little influenced by environment or psychological factors, but for the most part it appears that the adjustment at lower levels of development significantly and profoundly influences the way an organism unfolds, develops and evolves.

In the animal kingdom, for instance, the embryo in its individual development reenacts the evolutionary process by moving through stages of lower life forms until reaching the characteristic body configuration of its phylum and species: ontogeny recapitulates phylogeny. This same scheme of evolution from the primitive and less differentiated to the more complex and higher-functioning is seen in our psychological development. The development of mind and the particular ways in which the organism relates its inborn needs to environmental demands and conditions is described in psychoanalysis in terms of stages of development. For instance, the development of object relationships is broken down into five stages:

FREUDIAN PSYCHOANALYSIS

(1) Autoerotic, from birth until about three years of age; (2) narcissistic, from three to six years of age; (3) homoerotic, from six years until puberty; (4) heteroerotic, during adolescence; and (5) alloerotic, the stage of maturity.

The development of the vicissitudes, or changes of the innate impulses and drives in relation to reality, are described as occurring in three stages:

(1) Pre-superego sexuality, from birth until about six years of age, including: (a) oral phase from birth until two years, (b) anal phase from two until about four, and (c) phallic, from two until about six; (2) latency, from six years until puberty; and (3) genitality.

ERIKSON

Erik H. Erikson defined "Eight Stages of Man" or of man's psycho-social development. Again, from the more primitive stages to the more developed they are:

(1) Trust versus Mistrust, which extends through the first year of life and corresponds to Freud's oral stage;

(2) Autonomy versus Doubt, second and third years (Freud's anal stage);

(3) Initiative versus Guilt, fourth and fifth years (Freud's phallic stage);

(4) Industry versus Inferiority, 6 to 11 years (Freud's latency period, the time when the child learns to reason deductively);

(5) Identity versus Role Confusion, adolescence: roughly from 12 to 18 years, a time when there is a pronounced change in mental activity, with the appearance of more abstract thinking and a deepening appreciation of the complexity of life. The individual becomes more self-conscious, wondering what other people think of him and developing a sense of who he is, where he has been and where he is going. He may also compare his own family in society with what he conceptualizes as an ideal family or society.

(6) Intimacy versus Isolation, from adolescence to early middle age;

(7) Generativity versus Self-Absorption, middle-age. In this stage the individual becomes concerned with others beyond his immediate family and with the nature of society and the world in which future generations will live.

(8) Integrity versus Despair, old age.

PIAGET

Piaget describes four major stages of cognitive development:

(1) Sensorimotor stage from birth to 18 months, in which the child begins to develop the capabilities of reasoning as mental trial and error replace trial and error in action. By eight or nine months the child begins to retain in memory a mental image of an object.

(2) A preoperational stage from 18 months to seven years; symbolic thought develops but the child is still unable to reason logically or deductively. Thinking is characterized by egocentrism (selfishness), and juxtaposition and transductive reasoning—in which events and objects are associated by primitive logical linkages such as being present side by side—rather than in hierarchical and logical classes. Responses are made to what is most striking in the environment rather than through understanding. Symbolic play, graphic imagery, mental imagery and language are usually consolidated between 2 and 4 years.

(3) A stage of concrete operations from 7 to 11 years when the child is no longer bound by his or her perceptions at a given moment and can apply reasoning.

(4) A stage of formal operations from 11 years onwards in which the young adolescent can now use hypotheses, experiment, make deductions and manipulate ideas.

FAITH AND MORALITY

Educators and psychologists have also been turning their attention to the stages of development of man's higher aspects, such as the development of his values, morality and faith. Lawrence Kohlberg, for example, who has recently established a Center for Moral Development in the School of Graduate Education at Harvard University, has defined six stages of man's developing sense of morality—relating them to his deepening social consciousness and his capacity for intuitive, abstract, logical and insightful thinking. And James W. Fowler, Ph.D., Harvard Divinity School, defines six stages of faith development which correlate with Piaget's cognitive, Kohlberg's moral and Erikson's psycho-social stages.

Each one of these developmental stages can be defined by a number of parameters, including age of occurrence; association with a certain location in the body; characteristic developmental issues such as dependency, trust and autonomy; specific drives, needs and desires; critical tasks such as walking, bowel control and socialization; particular constellations of feelings and emotions; characteristic styles and patterns of thought; types of behavior; motivations, fears and aspirations and their relationship to environmental (familial, societal, cultural and economic) influences; level of maturity of regulatory mechanisms like ego, superego and ego defenses; strengths and potential for evolution; characteristic conflicts and obstacles; and specific techniques and approaches for transcendence.

The proper and full establishment of each developmental stage presupposes a healthy and complete development of the preceding stage, with resolution of its developmental challenges, issues and conflicts. If there is unfinished business from a preceding stage, it continues into the next as an unresolved conflict still demanding attention. Therefore, an individual may exhibit at any one time conflicts, emotions and motivations characteristic of a number of different developmental stages. He or she may exhibit varying levels of maturity and immaturity corresponding to the developmental successes and failures experienced.

LIMITATIONS

Contemporary psychological theories are unable to show the relationships among many of our therapeutic practices. What is the relationship of the mentally oriented talk therapies of modern psychology, for example, to the physical postures and breathing practices of *yoga*, or to the subtle energy flows of acupuncture or bio-energetics, or to the non-clinical but nonetheless therapeutic devotional practices of spiritual systems?

Spiritual systems assert that the dynamics of the mind—the aspect of consciousness with which psychology deals—do not entirely apply to the vaster and more fundamental spirit from which mind arises. Very well, then adopting a spiritual perspective doesn't necessarily mean giving up psychology's theories and techniques, but in fact offers the possibility of making them more effective—by relating them within a more comprehensive system for understanding human behavior.

Let's look at such a spiritual system. Following is an overview of Hinduism's insights into the dynamics of consciousness. At first the words and ideas may seem a bit foreign—the material perhaps hard to believe. But I encourage you to approach it with an open mind, as we will soon find some interesting and important connections.

SPIRITUAL CONCEPTS
THE *KOSAS*

The *Vedantic*[4] concept of *kosas* (a layering of man's consciousness) takes into account both Western and Eastern observations about man's psychology and spirituality. Man lives in a body and has feelings and thoughts, but his essential identity is seen as timeless, Universal Consciousness called *atma*.

In this system there are five levels of consciousness to be traversed in order to reach the ocean of the true self, the state of total oneness. Each level is considered a sheath covering a more subtle level beneath it. By a constant contemplation of these *kosas* or sheaths, the spiritual aspirant attains the discrimination to advance from one to the next toward an increasingly more profound awareness of reality. Step by step he abandons one sheath after another until finally being able to dissolve all of them, to achieve the knowledge of his unity with the divine.

From outermost to most subtle, they are:

(1) *Annamayakosa*—the physical body made from food: the level of chemistry and physiology, the main focus of modern Western medicine.

(2) *Pranamayakosa*—the sphere of the five senses, the emotions and the subtle energy called *prana* (more about this shortly).

(3) *Manomayakosa*—the lower mental body composed of thought. This is called the causal sheath with its pattern of desires, motives, resolutions and wishes, which form the complex called mind. Thought is more subtle than emotions or *prana*, and with the development of our ability to manipulate ideas and gain greater mastery over the outside world—with greater potential for gratifying our desires for fame, power and sex—we also inherit the increased potential to become seduced and remain encased in this sheath.

This is the great challenge of modern man: to see beyond this stage of development and, with the help of the more penetrating insight afforded by the next stage, to transcend it. Later we will look at the nature of the struggle to escape the bondage of this level in order to reach those beyond.

(4) *Vijnanamayakosa*—the higher mental body composed of intelligence, discrimination, intuition and the ability to choose according to higher ideals. This is the ruling aspect of the mind, charged with governing the mind's wayward tendencies, its desiring after the momentary and transient. This is the aspect that can discern higher moral principles, that can see beyond the separate individual to the universal and contemplate the eternal.

(5) *Anandamayakosa*—the stage of constant bliss beyond feelings, thoughts and mind.

And beyond this 5th sheath is *atma*—described by Sai Baba as:

> *The unseen basis, the real self, one's divinity—the soul which is the reality within the five sheaths, the outer of which is the body. It is the spark of God within, one's innermost reality. It is the sub-*

stance of all the objective world, the reality behind the appearance, the universal and immanent in every being. It is inherently devoid of attachment. It has no awareness of agency or its own needs or nature or possessions. It has no I (I or mine). Memory is a function of the intellect, not the atma. The atma is imperishable. It does not die like the body and mind. It is the essential reality of the individual, the witness—unaffected by all this change in time and space, the immanent spirit and the body, complex abode; the mystery that is beyond that complex, the motivating force of the impulses and tensions and the intentions of that complex.

PRANA

C.W. Leadbeater, in his fascinating book *The Chakras*, defines three principal forces which *yogis* have described as energizing man's "gross" and "subtle" bodies. The first of these he calls the "primary" or "life force," described as a stream of divine life which pours into our body from without to combine with *kundalini* energy which originates within. To this mixture is added a third force called *prana* or vitality, which *yogis* claim comes from the sun like light and heat and is absorbed by a certain energy portal in the body which Leadbeater calls the spleen *chakra*. This energy may actually be visible as the tiny points of light dancing about in all directions when one looks into a blue sky. When *prana* is drawn into the force center of the spleen *chakra*, it is supposedly broken down into streams of different colored energy which Leadbeater claims can be seen by clairvoyants.

A violet-blue ray moves upward to the throat where the blue aspect energizes the throat center and the violet enters up into the brain. A yellow ray is directed to the heart—a green ray to the abdomen centering in the solar plexus and vivifying the liver, kidneys, intestines and digestive apparatus. A rose-colored ray runs all over the body along the nerves and is clearly the life of the nervous system. This is the specialized vitality which one man may readily pour into another in whom it is deficient. If the nerves are not fully supplied with this rose light, they become sensitive and intensely irritable. A man in robust health usually absorbs and specializes so much more of this vitality than is actually needed by his own body that he is constantly radiating a torrent of rose-colored atoms and so unconsciously pours strength upon his weaker fellows without losing anything himself. This vitality is the food of the etheric double and is just as necessary to it as is material sustenance to the growth of the physical body. An orange ray flows to the base of the spine and then to generative organs with which one part of its function is closely connected. This ray energizes the desires of the flesh and also seems to enter the blood and help to keep up the heat of the body. If man refuses to yield to his lowest nature, this ray can by long and determined effort be deflected upward to the brain, producing intensification of the powers of the intellect and greatly increasing the quality of unselfish affection, while also quickening the spiritual part of man's nature.[5]

Prana can supposedly be regulated by mental concentration and by "right thoughts and right feelings" so that the physical body can increase its power to assimilate it and use it for enhancing its physical, emotional, mental and spiritual vitality and strength. And when focused in a certain way, it can awaken another powerful but latent energy force, *kundalini*, which is said to play a crucial role in the development of man's spiritual nature. Here we see, then, a whole new possible energy system, regulated by body postures and breathing exercises, which has not yet been integrated into mainstream Western psychological theory—although it does seem related to acupuncture and bioenergetics. In fact, Wilhelm Reich, the originator of bioenergetics, described a similar energy, which he called Orgone energy. In Appendix IV, I'll discuss in more detail how a deeper appreciation of the dynamics of *prana* will not only lead to greater therapeutic effectiveness, but will also bring us closer to understanding the connection between psychology and spirituality.

Now according to the theory of *kosas*, each sheath has its own dynamics and mode of operation. For instance, theories and practices related to the body are of a different dimension from those relating to mind—as different, say, as the language of chemistry and hypnosis. Increased mastery of one level brings better control of others—that is, healing in the body brings strength to the mind, and vice-versa. But total control and mastery over our earthly existence does not occur until man realizes his identity as God, with all the accompanying power of omniscience, omnipresence and omnipotence.

Since this seldom happens, the therapeutic approach connected with this model of consciousness would normally involve working on a number of different levels at the same time—such as nutrition, medication, exercise and relaxation (body level); acupuncture, Rolfing, bioenergetics and breathing exercises (*pranic* level); interpersonal relationships, cognitive learning and hypnosis (psychological/ mental); devotional practices, selfless service, moral observances and meditation (spiritual)—using different techniques for each level, while working toward a common goal such as increasing strength in the body or developing control of emotions and mind.

KUNDALINI

The dynamics of evolving consciousness, the way one moves from one level of consciousness to another, may be best understood through *yoga's* concepts about the evolution of *kundalini*[6] energy—an energy system in man which is little known in the West though studied by *yogis* of the East for thousands of years. Relating to man's spiritual development, it includes penetrating insights into man's psychological development as well and can help us see the relationship of the developmental stages of Freud, Erikson and Piaget to man's spiritual nature.

The dynamics of *kundalini* are recognized by all schools of *yoga* in India: *raja, karma, jnana, hatha,* and *bhakti yoga*. The theories of this energy system take into account the developmental stages and personality configurations described in Western psychology and then proceed to define others beyond. They agree with Western psychology that the personality is initially undifferentiated and primitive in its organization and becomes more highly organized with normal personal growth. More highly evolved personalities are seen as representative of higher stages of consciousness, growing from the successful maturation and evolution of lower stages, and allowing for freer, more versatile and creative interaction between inner and outer reality and representing a broadening of consciousness.

But whereas psychology focuses on those qualities in the personality that allow for successful adaptation to the outer world which we perceive through the senses, the *yogi's* system of *kundalini* describes, in addition, the development of those necessary for mastery of the inner world of the spirit and the ultimate transcendence of the material and psychological realms.

I'll describe the system of *kundalini* in moderate detail here, so that we can begin to appreciate elements of our personality and human potential which we usually do not deal with in the West, yet which may have profound impact on the evolution of our consciousness.

It is theorized that *kundalini* is latent within the body at the base of the spine. Within the spine, *yogis* say, is a central canal called *sushumna* with two other canals—*ida* on the left and *pingala*, the right—entwined around the spine like the snakes encircling the staff in the familiar symbol of medicine, the caduceus. In fact, the caduceus of Mercury, prior to Greek mythology, may have originally been the symbol of *kundalini* or "serpent fire," representing the ancient secret of achieving transcendence of the body and ego.[7]

As *kundalini* awakens, it flows into the three canals. In the well-developed *yogi*, the main flow is through the central *sushumna* canal. *Yogis* believe that will and desire are the higher and lower aspects of the same attribute; for the powerful *kundalini* force to be directed properly the will must be cultivated. At first desire directs the flow of energy, but as the individual's consciousness develops and higher spiritual centers are activated, when his character becomes strengthened and his intuition far-reaching, the energy is directed and controlled from "above" rather than "below," by will rather than desire. If such higher attributes do not develop and the individual is a servant of desire, his intention can be easily distracted and he can lose control of this powerful energy. The literature on *kundalini* always includes a warning about premature awakening of this awesome power before the moral control needed to direct it along the right path has been attained.

> If *kundalini* is prematurely awakened before moral control is attained, there is a danger of stimulating the negative aspects. It is said that it is indeed far better for *kundalini* to remain dormant at the base of the spine until the individual has made definite moral development—until his will is strong enough to control the energy and his thoughts pure enough to face the awakening without injury. Because if the *kundalini* is aroused prematurely and without proper inner controls and moral fortitude, the energy may pass uncontrolled to excite the most undesirable passions—exciting them and intensifying their effects to such a degree that it becomes impossible for man to resist them. It may intensify everything in (one's) nature, and it reaches the lower and evil qualities more read-

ily than the good. In the mental body, for example, ambition is very quickly aroused and soon swells to an incredibly inordinate degree. It would be likely to bring with it a great intensification of the power of the intellect, but at the same time, it would produce abnormal and satanic pride, such as is quite inconceivable to the ordinary man. It is said in *The Hathayoga Pradipika*: "It gives liberation to *yogis* and bondage to fools."[8]

PATANJALI

Patanjali, in his *Yoga Sutras*, or *Aphorisms of Yoga*, written in about the 4th Century A.D. and first translated into English in 1852, defined eight steps necessary to travel the spiritual path safely:

1. Moral observance, restraint (*yama*). Five basic moral rules are considered minimal requirements: truthfulness, non-violence, non-covetousness, chastity, and non-acceptance of others' possessions.

2. Personal virtue, discipline (*niyama*). Five essential habits are purity (in thought, speech and action), contentment, self-denial, study of scriptures, devotion to God.

3. Attitudes and positions of the body (*asanas*). The body is trained in proper sitting, which facilitates the flow of energy so it doesn't interfere with but promotes meditation.

4. Breath control (*pranayama*). Proper breathing purifies the nervous system, regulates the flow of energy and quiets the mind for meditation.

5. Withdrawal of the senses from the outside world (*pratyahara*). Awareness is turned inward, away from the distraction of the senses and toward higher inner spiritual states of consciousness.

6. Concentration (*dharana*). Awareness is focused on an object used as a vehicle for meditation. This may be part of the body, such as the heart or the area between the eyebrows, a sound such as OM or one's chosen name of God, a visual form, or a light such as a candle flame.

7. Meditation (*dhyana*). Meditation is described as an unbroken, constant flow of the mind—like the flow of oil poured from one container to another—toward the object of meditation. It requires exclusion of all other thought currents.

8. Merger and transcendence (*samadhi*). The unitive state beyond mind.

It is important to note that basic to this approach is the establishment of a strong moral structure and code of conduct. Again we see the relationship of morality, postures, breathing, control of the senses and control of the mind in achieving higher spiritual states of consciousness.

KARMA

And to these concepts let's add another, that of *karma*: simply stated, we reap what we sow. In order to fully integrate spiritual and psychiatric theories we must be open to the possibility that our particular life situations, challenges, obstacles, failures and successes are influenced by forces other than those limited to this present life. There is the possibility that our consciousness has existed prior to this earthly life and will go on after it, and that this life is in large measure determined by previous ones.

The law of *karma*, of cause and effect, states that we are born to work out certain unfinished business from the past. The strengths and weaknesses with which we are born and which assure success or lead to failure are related to the way we led previous lives—to the choices we made and to our accomplishments and mistakes, our rights and wrongs. Our specific genetics and the environment into which we are born are the set of conditions we have earned, established now to provide us with a framework in which to overcome failures of the past as well as to profit from merits earned, as we journey toward transcendence of our earthly existence.

From our earthly level of consciousness, we may not be able to tell whether a life condition is in fact related to good or bad *karma*. For instance, being born into a wealthy family and endowed with physical strength may not offer the same chances for growth and learning as being born physically weak into a poor family—although most of us would certainly choose the former.

It is interesting to note here that Sai Baba tells us it is only on the earth plane that consciousness has the chance to evolve to the point of merging with the Godhead. He says there are an infinite number of dimensions of reality, but that only on earth can consciousness make such an evolutionary leap: from lower levels dominated by animal needs to higher consciousness in which the individual can merge with the universal. It is for this reason that *yogis* place great emphasis on the purification of character and mastering of desire, by restraining consciousness from being attracted to the sensory and material world. The development of high moral character is the essential ingredient in *yoga's* way of raising consciousness.

THE CHAKRAS

It is thought that by disciplined moral observances, physical postures and exercises, breath-control exercises, or *pranayam* (the breath of life), focusing inward, chanting *mantras* or holy sounds, meditation on spiritual symbols and inner experiences, and devotional practices, an individual can liberate his *kundalini*. As it ascends, certain areas along the spine, called *chakras*, are in turn awakened by it and become centers of organized energy systems. These centers serve as contact points between inner and outer energies (Stanford physicist William Tiller calls them transducers) and determine the quality of consciousness by regulating the individual's development on all levels, including biological, emotional, mental, moral and spiritual.

While the *chakras* have been written about by Hindu *yogis* for thousands of years, more recently mystics and clairvoyants in the West have claimed to be able to see these energy force fields—located not in the physical, but the etheric body, thought to exist coincident with its physical counterpart. This energy system has also been receiving attention from noted scientists like Dr. Tiller. He includes the *chakras* in his scientific model of how the human body evolves in response to the radiation of energy and information from the environment. He refers to the etheric body as the "negative space time frame body" and sees each of the bodies acting as a "tuned circuit" in which one may tap energy from the cosmos or communicate with another aspect of self. In *Breakthrough to Creativity*, Dr. Shafica Karagulla, Los Angeles neuropsychiatrist, describes in fascinating detail the *chakras* as seen by "sensitives" with whom she has worked— people with highly developed sensory or extrasensory powers.

As mentioned above, *kundalini* is an energy distinct from either primary life force or *prana* (vitality). Leadbeater likens the difference between *prana* and *kundalini* as follows:

Kundalini is a terrific burning fire of the underworld. This fiery power, as it is called in *The Voice of the Silence*, is in very truth like liquid fire that rushes through the body when it has been aroused by the will. While vitality belongs to air and light and the great open spaces, the fire coming from below is likened to the power and energy found at the center of the earth, which is a concentration of heat and force of tremendous intensity. It is said to be the force, power and energy of the divine that created the material universe and which is constantly evolving and developing new elements and forms. It is described as a terrific glowing fire of the underworld, much more material than vitality — like the fire of red hot iron of glowing metal. If it spontaneously awakens or is accidentally aroused, it usually tries to pass up the interior of the spine and may cause great pain as the passages are not prepared for it, and it would have to clear its way by burning up a great deal of etheric dross. If this upward movement cannot be arrested by the will, *kundalini* will probably flash out through the head and escape into the surrounding atmosphere, and most likely no harm will result beyond a slight weakening or a temporary loss of consciousness. There is a rather terrible side to this tremendous force, however. The really appalling dangers are connected not with its upward rush, but with the possibility of its turning downward and inward. It gives the impression of descending deeper and deeper into matter, of moving slowly, but irresistibly onward with relentless certainty.[9]

Each *chakra* is associated with a number of esoteric symbols, colors and sounds which define and describe its particular dynamics and its influence on the many different levels of the individual. For instance, each *chakra* is associated with a certain location of the body, an endocrine gland, a nerve plexus, an element (earth, water, fire, air, ether), a geometric symbol that has special meaning, a color, a sound, and a lotus flower with a certain number of petals. The number and color of petals correspond to the actual color of the *chakras* as seen by clairvoyants, and although the descriptions of color or number of petals may vary among different schools of *yoga* and individual observers, Leadbeater states: "It is not surprising that such differences as these should be on record, as there are unquestionably variances in the *chakras* of different people and races as well as in the faculty of observers."

Drawings of *chakras* made by Hindu *yogis* include a geometrical form, a letter of the Sanskrit alphabet, an animal and two deities, one

male and the other female. They represent a shorthand way of understanding the spiritual teachings, the devotional practices and the rites
and ceremonies that awaken each *chakra*. In addition, they are associated with the levels of man's psychological maturity such as the predominant emotional reaction, psychological issues and concerns,
style and content of thought, level of abstract thinking, appreciation
of moral principles, and the potential for spiritual insight. Each
chakra holds within it strengths and potentials for evolution as well as
characteristic conflicts and obstacles; each requires specific techniques and approaches for transcendence.

Seven *chakras* have been defined and described. They can be
divided into three groups—lower, middle and higher—and might be
referred to, respectively, as the physiological, personal and spiritual.

The first and second *chakras*—supposedly related to the adrenal
glands and gonads, respectively, of the endocrine gland system—are
located at the base of the spine near the coccyx and in the lower
pelvis at the level of the genitals. They seem to correspond to Freud's
observation that the anal and genital areas of the body are very much
related to the development of early personality. In addition, Leadbeater states that these first two *chakras* are principally concerned
with receiving two forces which enter the body at their levels—*kundalini* from the earth, through the first *chakra*, and vitality from the
sun, through the second or splenic *chakra*. (It should be noted that
Leadbeater's splenic *chakra*, located near the spleen in the lower left
quadrant of the abdomen, does not correspond to the second *chakra*
of the *yogis*, which is located in the area of the genitals and whose
function appears more related to the development of sexual energy.)

The first two *chakras*, then, regulate biological and physical
development and the early aspects of personality. At this stage, man's
mental capacity is quite primitive, perhaps best described by Piaget's
first sensorimotor stage of cognitive development. The first *chakra* is
called *muladhara*—the root, support or basic *chakra*. The second
chakra, called by the *yogis*, *swadhisthana*, meaning "your own dwelling
or origin," and located in the area of the generative organs, is described
by the Hindus as being the source of our creative potential.

The psychological mechanisms, dynamics and aspects related to
the development of these two *chakras* can be related to Freud's oral,
anal and phallic stages and Erikson's stages of basic trust versus mis-

trust (1), autonomy vs. shame and doubt (2), and initiative vs. guilt (3). Developmental issues center around the child's acquiring a basic sense of security, developed through consistent loving care by the mother, and a sense of autonomy and strength, which is developed through the child's struggle with the parents as he or she becomes more mobile and willful. This sense of autonomy is influenced by the attitude and behavior of the parents in this challenging stage.

The way these two *chakras* develop supposedly affects the structure, dynamics and mechanisms of the psyche and the functioning of the regulatory mechanisms of the ego.[10] If the *chakras* are functioning abnormally, there might be a corresponding marked instability in personality, manifested by a lack of cohesiveness and steadiness, ease of regression and disorganization of personality, or a poor tolerance of frustration and predisposition to anxiety and guilt.

Chakras three, four and five are associated with the development of the distinctively human personality: in relationship to the *kosas*, the development of higher emotions and mental capacity. Parallels can be drawn between these three *chakras* and the higher developmental stages defined by Erikson and Piaget, as well as Maslow's hierarchy of needs, in which he defines such higher human needs as the need for meaningful work, for responsibility, for creativeness, for being fair and just, and for doing what is worthwhile and doing it well. This is in contrast to man's lower nature, so well defined by Freud, which seeks gratification of the animal drives and instincts.

The third *chakra* is supposedly located in the abdominal area just below the navel and is called *manipura*, meaning "the city of the shining jewel." It is associated with the psychological quality of expansiveness, power and self-expression. It may be likened to Adler's will to power. The interest in power at this level is different from that found at the anal stage, where the struggle for dominance and control is in reaction to a feeling of weakness and vulnerability and is primarily a defense against being manipulated, controlled and humiliated.

The power established at this point has to do with the drive to express the real power within, such as found in great generals and kings. It is the source of power on which the masters of the martial arts focus their consciousness in order to gain the sixth sense they possess in combat.

The psychological aspects of the first three *chakras* constitute man's lower emotional make-up then, and are the area of focus of modern psychology. It is not until the level of the fourth *chakra* that the specifically higher human qualities of personality are awakened. This is the level to which religious themes speak and which gives rise to religious symbols and archetypes.

Chakra number four is called *anahata*, meaning "that which is ever new." This energy center, whose symbol is the circle, is located at the level of the heart, and the chief psychological quality associated with it is love. The behavior, motivations, personality characteristics and thought patterns related to this *chakra* are those seen in the saints, who are dedicated to selfless service and acts of compassion—a level of consciousness manifested perhaps in its purest form in the life of Christ. This is an extremely important developmental stage, the dynamics of which seem to be the focus of contemporary psychology's humanistic approach.

Following will be a deeper look into the symbols associated with this *chakra*, to help us appreciate the depth of inquiry given by the *yogis* to each of these centers. It will also give us an idea of the number of different approaches and techniques that might influence their development. In the future when the deepest mysteries of these symbols are known, they may direct us to new approaches in research and treatment and bring a more profound understanding of human development. The source of most of this material is Leadbeater's *The Chakras*. (A diagram of the 4th *chakra* is on the next page.)[11]

The lotus of the fourth center has 12 petals of an orange-crimson hue. It has been suggested that each of the different petals of this lotus represents a moral quality, and that the development of that quality brings the center into activity. For example in the *Dhyana-bindu Upanishad*, the petals of the heart *chakra* are associated with such apparently dissimilar qualities as devotion, laziness, anger and charity.

The *mantra* or holy sound of this center is *so-hum*. It is associated with the eighth cervical vertebra and the cardiac sympathetic plexus and is related to the thymus gland. Its outstanding psychological quality is a pure love which vibrates outward like the ever-expanding circle which is the symbol of this center.

Diagram of 4th chakra

Leadbeater claims that there are discrepancies as to the number of petals in the lotus, although he states that this is not important. For example, he indicates that in *The Yoga Kundalini Upanishad* 16 petals are described instead of the usual 12. The *Dhyanabindu Upanishad* says that the lotus of the heart has 8 petals, but according to Leadbeater, this work is probably referring to a secondary heart *chakra*.

There is one more important point Leadbeater makes about this *chakra*:

> In the center of the heart lotus a *trikona* or inverted triangle is figured. This is not a feature of all the centers, but only of the root, heart and brow *chakras*. There are in these three, special *granthis* or knots, through which *kundalini* has to break in the course of her journey. The first is sometimes called the knot of *Brahma*; the second that of *Vishnu*; the third that of *Shiva*. The idea which this symbolism seems to imply is that the piercing of these *chakras* in some way involves a special change of state.[12]

The *granthi* or knot associated with the heart center represents a major challenge to contemporary psychology. It obstructs the evolution of consciousness to the next level, and to pass through it requires a whole new orientation to inner and outer reality. As a matter of fact, the nature of this obstruction—the ignorance and fears that hold us to duality—and the dynamics of its transcendence, leading to a marvelous leap in consciousness and our capacity for intuition, creativity and empathy, is the subject of this book.

In short, one must awaken to the reality that man is divine and that duality is a delusion—and turn from a basically self-centered selfish existence revolving around self-gratification of the senses, desires and ego, to an existence of selfless service and love without desire for rewards. And as described in Part I of this book, in order to see divinity or non-duality, one must have the courage to face *mortal* fear—to face physical death and the realization that our own ego is insignificant.

Although mainstream psychology is little aware of the dynamics of this kind of transcendence, there are contemporary writers and therapists who are. Let's turn our attention to the field of transpersonal psychology[13] and the work of Ken Wilber.

Notes

1. Joseph Campbell, *Myths To Live By* (New York: Bantam Books, 1978), pp. 108-116.

2. Ken Wilber, *Journal of Humanistic Psychology*, Vol. 22, No. 1, Winter, 1982, pp. 57-90.

3. Samuel H. Sandweiss, *Sai Baba: The Holy Man and the Psychiatrist* (San Diego: Birth Day Publishing Company, 1975).

4. *Vedanta*—A system of Hindu philosophy founded on the *Vedas*, the holy scriptures of Hinduism.

5. Edited and summarized from: C. W. Leadbeater, *The Chakras* (London: The Theosophical Publishing House, 1969).

6. Works available in English about *kundalini* include *The Serpent Power* translated by Arthur Avalone; *The Shatchatkara Nirupana* and *Thirty Minor Upanishads* translated by K. Narayana Swami Ayrar; and *V. Shiva Samahita* translated by Sri Chandra Vidyarnava.

7. See symbol of *kundalini* on p. 280.

8. Edited and summarized from: C. W. Leadbeater, *The Chakras* (London: The Theosophical Publishing House, 1969).

9. Ibid.

10. The ego of Freudian psychology.

11. This diagram of the 4th *chakra* is from Leadbeater's *The Chakras*, p. 70.

12. Ibid., p. 79.

13. Anthony Sutich, in the first issue of the Journal of Transpersonal Psychology (Spring, 1969) defines transpersonal psychology as:
    "The title given to an emerging force in the psychology field by a group of psychologists and professional men and women from other fields who are interested in those 'ultimate' human capacities and potentialities that have no systematic place in positivistic or behavioristic theory ('first force'), classical psychoanalytic theory ('second force'), or humanistic psychology ('third force'). The emerging transpersonal psychology ('fourth force') is concerned specifically with the 'empirical', scientific study, and responsible implementation, of the findings relevant to becoming, individual and species-wide meta-needs, ultimate values, unitive consciousness, peak experiences, B values, ecstasy, mystical experience, awe, being, self-actualization, essence, bliss, wonder, ultimate meaning, transcendence of the self, spirit, oneness, cosmic awareness, individual and species-wide synergy, maximal interpersonal encounter, sacralization of everyday life, maximal sensory awareness, responsiveness and expression, and related concepts, experiences and activities."

Appendix IV

TRANSPERSONAL PSYCHOLOGY AND THE *AVATAR*

By the time the fourth *chakra* begins to awaken, the mental body has become the predominant force of the individual. This is Piaget's stage of formal operations, with the capacity for deductive reasoning and the manipulation of abstract ideas. The use of symbols, increased depth and complexity of social communications, an enhanced capacity for gratifying one's needs and drives and gaining mastery of the outer world, all lead to great reliance on and respect for this advanced stage of evolution.

With our marvelous minds we can now accomplish through thought experiments that which took great energy to discover by the action of trial and error. But for the fifth *chakra* stage to become fully established, one must work through the challenge of the knot of the fourth *chakra*, which entails giving up our reliance on mind and the security provided by a false sense of a strong independent (and separate) self. This is a major turning point in the evolution of consciousness, one in which there is a marked qualitative change in our orientation to the outer world. To better understand the dynamics and significance of this monumental leap, let's look at the work of Ken Wilber.

In *The Atman Project*, Wilber[1] outlines in brilliant clarity about 20 stages of consciousness, from the level of matter to ultimate union with the divine. His work sheds light on the relationship of lower to higher developmental stages: in particular, the dynamics of transcending the crucial transition point or "knot," of *chakra* 4 in order to awaken and establish *chakra* 5.

In an article[2] published in the Journal of Humanistic Psychology in 1982 he summarizes his work and defines these 10 levels of consciousness: the subconscious sphere—matter-pleuroma, reptile-uroboros and mammal-body; the self-conscious sphere—persona, ego and centaur; and the superconscious, transpersonal or universal sphere—psychic (realm of *siddhi* and psi powers), subtle (home of archetypes and personal deity), causal (the unmanifest void), and ultimate (spirit). These stages describe in detail the general movement from matter to body to mind to soul to spirit.

Wilber's fifth and sixth stages, ego and centaur, correspond to *chakras* 3 and 4 respectively. He grew to an understanding of these two levels by studying the differences between ego and humanistic-existential psychologies. In so doing he combines insights from both psychology and spirituality. Here we see the interrelationship and merging of these two fields—the increased understanding each can bring to the other. Wilber writes:

> The ego psychologies seemed to aim at "making conscious the unconscious," or reuniting the ego with aspects of the psyche that had been split off or dissociated due to past developmental snarls or double-binds ("Where id was, there shall ego be"). Using Jungian terms, I conceptualized this as: The persona (or fraudulent self-image) can be reunited with the shadow (or repressed personal unconscious) so as to allow the emergence of the total ego (or accurate self image, adequate ego strength, and so on). Theoretically, it was almost as simple as: persona + shadow = ego.
>
> The humanistic-existential therapies did not deny this equation; many in fact, made explicit use of it (Perls, for example). But somehow they seemed also to go beyond that equation and talk about the potentials of the total organism, potentials that surpassed any of its parts, whether persona, ego, id, or superego. Rollo May (1969), for instance: "Neither the ego, nor the unconscious, nor the body can be autonomous. Autonomy by its very nature can be located only in the centered self. Logically as well as psychologically we must go behind the ego-id-superego system and endeavor to

understand the 'being' of whom these are expressions." Notice that May does not deny the existence of the ego-id-superego; he simply sees them as expressions of a deeper unity or deeper self, the total being . . . . The total organism encompassed the ego-id-superego, but not vice versa. I therefore began calling this deeper level by the name "centaur" (a mythological term first used by Benoit, 1955, to indicate a total unity of human-mind and animal-body).

If, then, we had to state the general aim of humanistic-existential therapies in one sentence, it might be: They aim at resurrecting and fully actualizing the centauric self. As James Broughton's study disclosed, the most fully developed personalities viewed "both mind and body as experiences of an integrated self," and that integrated self, the centaur, was precisely the paradigm of humanistic-existential therapies (Loevinger, 1977). I would later subdivide these therapies into two classes, noetic and somatic, depending on whether they approached the centaur predominantly through the mind (Rollo May, Binswanger) or through the body (yoga, Rolfing). But the essential point remained: Unite the ego-mind and body-soma so as to resurrect a total identity with the centaur. As Perls (1951) put it, "The aim is to extend the boundary of what you accept as yourself to include all organic activities." The equation here was: ego + body = centaur.

These, of course, were the simplest of generalizations; nonetheless, as generalizations go, they were extremely useful. For example, I could already see the difference between neurotic guilt-anxiety and existential guilt-anxiety; the former was caused by an apprehension of the shadow, the latter, by an apprehension of the general otherness of the world. The former was caused by a split within the subject, the latter, by the prior split between the subject and the object. (And thus, to finish our account with Freud, both views are partially correct: Primary anxiety is existential and given, and it is this primal anxiety that ultimately causes the repression of the shadow — but the repression of the shadow then leads to excess anxiety, surplus anxiety, or neurotic anxiety per se.) Further, these simple generalizations had also given me within the personal sphere alone, three major levels of being or consciousness: the persona level, the ego level, and the centaur/existential level.

From that point, it was a very small step to realize how the mystical traditions fit into the overall scheme. Psychoanalysis aimed at uniting persona and shadow to reveal a whole and healthy ego; going deeper, humanistic therapies aimed at uniting the ego and the body to reveal the total centaur. Just so, the mystic traditions went deeper still and aimed at uniting the centaur and the cosmos to reveal a Supreme Identity, a "cosmic consciousness," as Bucke's rather far-out phrase has it.[3]

Wilber makes an important distinction between ego psychology and the humanistic-existential psychologies in defining what he calls the centaur stage, the union of human-mind and animal-body. But just what is this "body" which, when integrated with the ego, persona and shadow, allows for deeper experience of self? It is not the physical body—nor even the emotional body, as the integration of these elements have always been the aim of traditional medicine and psychology.

It is their appreciation, albeit limited, of the more subtle *prana* energy and/or the 4th *chakra* that differentiates the humanistic-existential therapies from the others. They are aware of the importance of the kinds of body work, such as Rolfing, acupuncture and *yoga*, which bring consciousness in touch with the subtle *prana* energy; and that *prana* affects the opening of man's heart, his deeper human experience—his 4th *chakra* associated with the higher human qualities of compassion, caring, self-sacrifice, selfless service and the yearning to lead a good and just life.

But even the humanistic-existentialist movement's understanding is still quite limited as to the dynamics of transcendence of *chakra* 4. It is precisely here that *yoga*, with its healing and energizing effects on body, emotions, and mind; and its understanding of the origin, evolution and dynamics of *prana* energy—as well as the interrelationship among *prana*, *kundalini*, the *chakras*, and consciousness-raising—it is here that *yoga* can bring a whole new dimension of understanding to Western psychology.

Wilber turns his attention to the understanding of the dynamics of transcendence and adds understanding to the complex problem of the transcendence of *chakra* 4—which he calls the *Apollo* complex:

> . . . the most significant and widespread complex today is not the Oedipus complex—or difficulty transforming from body to mind—but what we might call the *Apollo* complex—a difficulty in transforming from mind to soul, or from personal, mental, egoic realms to transpersonal, subtle, and supraegoic realms. The *Vishnu*

complex, the difficulty in transforming from soul to spirit, occurs on a level so evolved that it afflicts only advanced meditators.

The nature of these higher complexes, such as the *Apollo* and *Vishnu*, was made painfully obvious to me in my own meditation. By the time I had finished writing *No Boundary* (Wilber, 1979), my meditation practice, while not exactly advanced, was no longer in the beginner's phase. The leg pain (from the lotus posture) was manageable, and my awareness was growing in its capacity to maintain an alert yet relaxed, active yet detached stance. But my mind was, as the Buddhists say, that of a monkey: compulsively active, obsessively motive. And there I came face to face with my own *Apollo* complex, the difficulty in transforming from the mental sphere to the subtle sphere. The subtle sphere (or the "soul," as Christian mystics use that term) is the beginning of the transpersonal realms; as such, it is supramental, transegoic, and transverbal. But in order to reach that sphere, one must (as in all transformations) "die" to the lower sphere (in this case, the mental-egoic). The failure to do so or the incapacity to do so is the *Apollo* complex. As the person with an Oedipus complex remains unconsciously attached to the body and its pleasure principal, so the person with an *Apollo* complex remains unconsciously attached to the mind and its reality principle. ("Reality" here means "institutional, rational, verbal reality," which, although conventionally real enough, is nevertheless only an intermediate stage on the path to *Atman*; that is, it is merely a description of actual Reality itself, and thus, if clung to, eventually and ultimately prevents the discovery of that actual Reality.)

The struggle with my own obsessive/compulsive thinking—not particular obsessive thoughts, as per specific neurosis (which is often indicative of an Oedipus-complex holdover), but the very stream of thought itself—was as arduous a task as I would ever handle. It was the most difficult battle I had ever faced; were it 1% more difficult, I would have failed miserably. (An excellent account of such initial battles has been given by Walsh, 1977, 1978). As it was, I was fortunate to make some progress, to be able eventually to rise above the fluctuations of mental contractions and discover, however initially, a realm incomparably more profound, more real, more saturated with being, more open to clarity. This realm was simply that of the subtle, which is disclosed, so to speak, after weathering the *Apollo* complex. In this realm, it is not that thinking necessarily ceases (although it often does, especially at the beginning); it is that, even when thinking arises, it does not detract from this broader background of clarity and awareness (see, for example, John Welwood's (1977) crystal account of this "transpersonal ground"). From the subtle, one no longer "gets lost in thoughts"; rather, thoughts enter consciousness and depart much as clouds traverse the sky: with smoothness, grace, and clarity. Nothing sticks, nothing rubs, nothing grates. Chung Tzu: "The perfect man employs his mind as a mirror. It grasps nothing; it refuses nothing; it receives, but does not keep."[4]

Wilber discusses changes in the experience of mind and what lies beyond mind, as one transcends what he calls the *Apollo* complex. I'd like to add a word of caution here. In this day and age of science and high technology, some spiritually oriented approaches, in an effort to speak in scientific terms, may describe higher spiritual dimensions in terms of consciousness, energy, forces, universal laws and balance, much as physics would discuss an unfeeling cosmos devoid of compassion. Higher spiritual states may be discussed in terms of the quality, type, rhythm and content of thoughts and images experienced during meditation—to the neglect of more subtle and profound aspects such as morality, devotion, God's personal relationship with man and His great eternal love which transcends all laws and forces.

This latter dimension of spirituality cannot be overemphasized. Just as the spiritual practice of meditation leads to an inner experience beyond mind to no thought, expandedness, peace, light and bliss, so do the spiritual practices of morality, devotion and selfless service lead to the equally (if not more) important inner experiences of profound compassion and love. Spontaneous expressions of selflessness and sacrifice toward our fellow human beings bring with them a penetrating feeling of God's omnipresence and His personal relationship with us.

I emphasize this point in order to bring some balance to what may be a Western overemphasis on the scientific, with the danger of displacing God from the picture—and also because man's yearning to merge with God by acquiring His qualities of virtue, truth, righteousness, peace and a selfless giving love which supports all of humanity is the path to transcendence which Sai Baba teaches. God can be experienced in meditative states by a non-attachment to thought—or "here on earth" by and through love and selfless service done in an attitude of non-attachment to the fruits of one's labor. I believe that the insight of *chakra* 4 is that higher states of selfless love, of which this type of service is an expression, not only influence and shape consciousness, but are a necessary precondition in the process of merging with Universal Consciousness.

Wilber calls the two higher transition points *Apollo* and *Vishnu*. I would rather call them *Vishnu* and *Shiva*, respectively, since these are the names *yogis* give to the *granthis* or knots associated with *chakras* 4 and 6. In addition, *Vishnu* is that aspect of the Hindu Godhead (the trinity of *Brahma*, *Vishnu* and *Shiva*) who manifests in human form as the *Avatar* to help mankind reach fourth *chakra* consciousness and beyond. He teaches the path of love and selfless service, and his exemplary life serves as a perfect role model. Sai Baba says that the *Avatar* incarnates from age to age when man's consciousness has fallen and darkness overwhelms the world: *"To grant peace, joy and a sense of fulfillment to seekers who have striven long; to foster dharma (righteousness); to suppress evil and overwhelm the wicked. The descent of God to earth, the incarnation of the formless with form, is the concretization of the yearning of the seekers."*

Incarnations such as those of Christ, Buddha and Krishna have the power to change the course of history, as they elevate human consciousness beyond selfishness to selflessness, beyond duality to divinity.

CHAKRAS 5, 6, AND 7

The expanded consciousness of those who have attained the fourth *chakra* clearly sees that the world of duality leads to suffering and death—to bondage. It also brings direct experience of an inner divine love which transcends duality. Hence arises a heightened yearning to avoid attachment to the duality of the outer world in order to fully merge with divine love. This is the stage of renunciation and detachment, the challenge of the fifth *chakra*.

The fifth *chakra* is located at the level of the larynx and is called the *bishuddsha chakra*, which means purification. It is associated with the third cervical vertebra, the pharyngeal sympathetic plexus, the thyroid gland and the sense of hearing. Symbolized by an oval shape, it is supposedly mauve in color, and its element is ether or space. It has a lotus of 16 petals of a smoky purple hue. The *yogi* able to activate this center is in the process of leaving art, religion, philosophy and even thought behind. He is preparing for a deep inner vision of the divine.

With the activation of *chakra* 5, the spiritual aspirant actively restrains consciousness from flowing to the outer world of duality through the senses, desires and ego. Instead, consciousness is redirected inward and purified (as the name of this center indicates) by the act of renunciation, to heighten the attachment to God, now perceived as an alive, vibrant, internal experience. Thus arises a new appreciation of morality—the control of desires, not imposed by outside forces, but now willingly adopted as a means of transcendence.

> *The Vedas proclaim that immortality (the stage when one is merged in the birthless, deathless, universal entity) is feasible through renunciation and detachment only, and not through rituals, progeny or wealth. When one renounces selfish desires, his love expands into the farthest region of the universe until he becomes aware of cosmic love.*
> (Sathya Sai Baba)

A word of caution. The overzealous aspirant may mistakenly think renunciation means denying the very existence of the body and the outer world all together. Sai Baba teaches that the body and the outer world are divinely created—in fact, divinity itself. Renunciation is not denying the created universe, and having nothing to do with it—but restraining consciousness from relating to creation through the senses, desires and ego, which crave selfish gratification and hence bind us to duality. Rather, consciousness is directed inward to God through meditation, to strengthen the bond with Him—and outward to mankind and creation through selfless service. In this act of renunciation, man's love expands, *"into the farthest region of the universe until he becomes aware of cosmic love,"* giving rise to a new perception of the outer world as the embodiment of God, with every person being divine. Thus creation becomes the vehicle for transcendence.

The sixth and seventh centers, says Leadbeater, stand apart from the rest, coming into action only after a certain amount of spiritual development has taken place. These centers are connected with the pituitary body and the pineal gland respectively. *Chakra* 6, located between the eyebrows, is called *ajna*, meaning command, and is the "third eye" of inner wisdom. Leadbeater states:

> [It] has the appearance of being divided into halves, one chiefly rose-colored, though with a great deal of yellow about it, and the other predominantly a kind of purplish-blue, again closely agreeing with the colors of the special types of vitality that vivify it. Perhaps it is for this reason that this center is mentioned in Indian books as having only two petals, though if we are to count undulations of the same character as those of the previous centers we shall find that each half is subdivided into 48 of these, making 96 in all. This sudden leap from 16 to 96 spokes and again the even more startling variation from 96 to 972 between this and the next *chakra*, show us that we are now dealing with centers of an altogether different order from those which we have hitherto been considering.[6]

When this center is awake, we are aware of our existence as the eternal witness beyond beginning or end, birth or death. We may be in touch with psi phenomena or the *siddhi* powers described by *yogis*, or such profound and awesome experiences of the subtle realm as perceiving archetypal deities, or ourselves as light—boundlessly expansive and blissful. This corresponds to the bliss stage, or *anandamayakosa*, of the *kosas*; but as magnificent and ethereal as it is, it still represents duality, of which the witness stage is the last vestige.

There is still a stage beyond—where witness, that which is witnessed, and the process of witnessing all merge into one: the stage of final union with the universal, the experience of one's divinity. This is *atma*, the level of *chakra* 7 known as the crown or coronal *chakra*, located at the crown of the head and called *sahasarara* by the *yogi*—the lotus of a thousand petals. When the crown *chakra* is fully awakened, one supposedly has the ability to leave the body and experience oneself as pure love and consciousness without limitation—at one with *atma*. Leadbeater describes its appearance to clairvoyants as:

> The most resplendent of all, full of indescribable chromatic effects and vibrating with almost inconceivable rapidity. It seems to contain all sorts of prismatic hues, but on the whole, are predominantly violet. This *chakra* is usually the last to be awakened. In the beginning it is the same size as the others, but as the individual pro-

gresses on the path of spiritual advancement, it increases steadily until it covers almost the whole top of the head.[7]

* * *

The appearance of an *Avatar* has immense meaning. He is striking evidence that the system of psychological and spiritual growth represented by the *chakras* is real and that man's limited consciousness can merge with Universal Consciousness. He is a moving example of how man appears when his 7th *chakra* is fully awakened.

And he has meaning even beyond this. Whereas the system of the *chakras* represents man's *ascent* from limited consciousness to divinity, the *Avatar* represents that most rare occurrence when divinity *descends* into human form. Responding to the prayers of his devotees, He appears from age to age during particularly dark times, not only to prove that mankind is divine, but to teach us the path to transcendence. Beckoning us to awaken, to evolve, to ascend, He shows us the path to eternal freedom, the path from selfishness to selflessness, from duality to unity, from man to divinity.

And the path, the way, the process, the means and the goal—is love. Sai Baba says that love is his form and that consciousness expands by and through the fostering, cultivation, experience and expression of love. Teaching love by love, for love and through acts of pure, unconditional, selfless love, *Avatars* give the faith, strength and inspiration to reach for heaven and to that glorious unitary state beyond.

> Let the different faiths exist. Let them flourish. Let the glory of God be sung in all the languages and a variety of tunes. That should be the ideal. Respect the differences between the faiths, and recognize them as valid so far as they do not extinguish the flame of unity. I have not come to speak on behalf of any particular religion. I have not come on any mission of publicity for any sect or creed or cause. Nor have I come to collect followers for any doctrine. I have come to tell you of this universal unitary faith, this path of love, this duty of love, this obligation to love . . .
>
> The totality of divine energy has come unto humanity as Sathya Sai—to go to each and everyone, to wake up the slumbering divinity of every human being. Even if in your sleepiness or in your weakness for sleep, you growl, grumble or groan; kick, criti-

cize, quarrel or cry, I will not forsake you; I will not let your divinity go to sleep. A mother never forsakes the child she carries or lets the child fall down, even if the child works out its resentment and anger on her. I have come to help, to accompany and to carry you. I can never forsake you. I will never fail in my duty to my children — and I shall be very grateful to each child of mine who helps my task . . .

Wake up, my children: wake up to the dawn of knowledge, wake up to your divine duties, wake up to your divine rights and wake up to your divine reality.

(Sathya Sai Baba)

Notes

1. Author in Transpersonal Psychology, whose dazzling works include, *The Spectrum of Consciousness* (1977), *No Boundary* (1979), *The Atman Project* (1980) and *Up From Eden* (1981).

2. Ken Wilber, "Odyssey: A Personal Inquiry into Humanistic and Transpersonal Psychology" (*Journal of Humanistic Psychology*, Volume 22 #1), pp. 57-90.

3. Ibid., pp. 64-65.

4. Ibid., pp. 79-80.

5. See Chapter 27.

6. Leadbeater's *The Chakras*, p. 10.

7. Ibid., pp. 10-11.

Glossary

abhisheka	Ablution, ritual washing.
advaita	The viewpoint that consciousness can transcend duality—that man can merge with God.
ahimsa	Non-injury, avoidance of violence, harmlessness.
akasa	Ether or space, the first of the five elements evolved from *Brahman*; the subtlest form of matter.
amrita	Nectar of the gods, an ambrosial liquid sometimes materialized by Sai Baba.
ananda	Bliss, joy. Bliss is considered to be the very substance of God (God *is* bliss, not has bliss).
anandaswarupa	Of the very form or nature of bliss; *ananda*.
Anantapur	A town in Andhra Pradesh, South India. The location of the Sri Sathya Sai College of Arts and Science for Women.
Arjuna	The disciple of Lord *Krishna* to whom *Krishna* revealed the truth of human existence just prior to the opening battle of the *Mahabharatha* war. The divine discourse is known as the *Bhagavad-Gita*.
asana	Easy, comfortable sitting pose. *Hatha yoga* posture.
asanthi	Grief, anxiety (absence of peace).
ashram	Hermitage, monastery.
atma	The most subtle aspect of one's being. That which is without change, unmodified, unaffected, timeless.
atma shakti	The force, the power of the *atma*.
Avatar	An incarnation of God.
avatara	The embodied lifetime of the *Avatar*.
avedana	Yearning for the Lord.
Baba	Father.
Bangalore	A city in South India, some fifteen miles from the Sri Sathya Sai College of Arts, Science and Commerce for Men.

315

Bhagavad-Gita	The Hindu "bible." Meaning the "Song of God," this renowned scripture of India is part of the great epic *Mahabharatha*. It contains the spiritual teachings given by Lord *Krishna* to *Arjuna*, and is meant for all mankind.
Bhagavan	Lord. God.
bhajans	Devotional songs.
bhakta, bhakti	A *bhakta* is a devotee, one who has *bhakti*; virtue, self control, faith, devotion.
Bharath	India, the land that has *rathi*, or attachment to *Bha* or *Bhagavan*, the Lord.
Brahma	The creator God of the Hindu trinity, the other two being *Vishnu* and *Shiva*.
Brahman	The immanent principle, said to have three aspects: creation, preservation, destruction. The absolute, the supreme reality.
Brindavan	Place where Sai Baba frequently resides when away from *Prasanthi Nilayam*, his *ashram* and location of his Sri Sathya Sai Arts, Science and Commerce College for Men. Also, the name of a town on the banks of the Jamuna river associated with *Sri Krishna's* childhood.
buddhi	The intellect, intelligence or discriminating faculty.
chakra	Centers or "lotuses" of potential energy arrayed upward in man from the base of the spine to the crown of the head.
darshan	To see a great person and receive his blessing—literally, "to breathe the same air as."
Dasera	Festival celebrating the victory of good over forces resisting progress toward light.
dharma	Righteousness, duty, code of conduct—one of the four ends of human pursuit.
dharmaswarupa	Of the very form or nature of righteousness; *dharma*.
dhyana	Meditation.
Ganesha, Ganapathi	Names for the elephant-headed God, son of *Shiva*. Presiding deity of the first *chakra*.
Ganga	The Ganges.
gopas	The cowherd boys of *Brindavan*, playmates of *Sri Krishna*.
gopis	The milkmaids of *Brindavan*, companions and devotees of *Sri Krishna*.
gunas	The primary qualities of a human being: peaceful (*sathwa*), active (*rajas*) and dull (*thamas*).
guru	Teacher, guide to spiritual liberation.
Hanuman	One of the most devoted of the *bhaktas* of *Rama*, represented as part monkey, part man; mentioned in the *Ramayana*.
hatha yoga	A school of *yoga*; the practice of *asanas* or *yoga* posture for the purpose of physical well-being and for awakening spiritual centers.
Indra	The king of the Gods.
jagath	The objective, transitory, untrue world.
japa, japam	Recitation or repetition of the name of the Lord.
japamala	Religious necklace of 108 beads used in *japa*, the repetition of the name of God with reverence and devotion.

ji	A syllable added to a word to denote respect, e.g., *Swamiji*, *Babaji*.
jivanmukthi	The God-realized person in whom only the divine vision is active. He no longer has any identification whatsoever with his body.
jnana	The *yoga* path in which emphasis is laid on knowledge and discrimination, leading to wisdom, and the awareness of one's identity with the divine. A *jnani* is one who follows this path. The word is also used to denote one who has reached awareness of his divine identity.
jnani	One who has direct knowledge of the highest wisdom.
jyoti	The light and form of a flame.
Kailas	A peak of the Himalayas regarded as the sacred abode of *Shiva*.
Kali	A name of the divine mother; the primal energy.
karma	Action; the law that governs all action and its inevitable consequences on the doer; the law of cause and effect, or moral compensation for acts done in the past.
kosas	The five sheaths of embodiment.
Krishna	An *Avatar* of *Vishnu*. "He who draws you by means of the joy he imparts."
kshema	Preservation of that which one has acquired.
kundalini	Spiritual energy lying dormant in all individuals.
leela (lila)	Divine play or sport, carrying the overtones of joy and spontaneity. The word is used to mean divine miracles. But the whole of creation, being regarded as an inexplicable miracle, is sometimes called the Lord's *leela*.
mahatma	A great soul.
mahima	Superhuman power, miracle.
manas	The mind.
mandir	Prayer hall, temple.
mantra	Sacred words or verse repeated during meditation.
marga	Path, road, way, course.
maya	Ignorance obscuring the vision of God; the primal enticing illusion appearing as duality and called the world; attachment.
moksha	Liberation or final emancipation of the soul from duality and bondage to the world, which is the goal of spiritual practice. *Mukti* has the same meaning.
nagara-sankirtan	Singing *bhajans* in a group while walking slowly through the streets; done in the early hours before dawn.
narada	The ancient *rishi* or seer who wrote the classic of *bhakti yoga*, called *Narada Bhakti Sutras*.
Nilayam	*Prasanthi Nilayam*; abode of eternal peace. Name of Sai Baba's *ashram*.
OM	The primeval sound by which God sustains the cosmos.
paramatma	The *atma* viewed in its universal aspect. God.
Patanjali	The name of the ancient sage who wrote the basic guide to *raja yoga*, known as *Patanjali's Yoga Sutras*.
prakriti	Primordial nature, which in association with *Purusha* (eternal conscious principle) creates the universe.
prana	The vital breath that sustains life in the physical body.

Prasanthi Nilayam	The abode of undisturbed peace. The name of Sai Baba's *ashram*.
prema	Divine love of the most intense kind; universal, unconditional, unblemished love.
premarasa	The flavor of *prema*.
pundit	Scholar.
pura	The physical body.
Purana(s)	Books of Hindu mythology.
Purusha	Eternal conscious principle; soul.
Puttaparthi	The quiet and remote village in southern India where Sai Baba was born (November 23, 1926) and where he now has his *ashram*, *Prasanthi Nilayam*.
Radha	The beloved devotee of *Krishna*.
rajasic	The active, passionate aspect of nature.
Rama	An *Avatar* of God, a divine being. An *Avatar* whose name means, he who pleases; he who fills with *ananda* (bliss).
Ramakrishna Paramahamsa	1836-1886: A great saint of Bengal.
rishi	A sage, one leading a life without desires, with attachments only to the *atma*. A seer of truth.
saadrisya	Acquiring divine nature.
saalokya	Existence in God.
saathi	Calmness of senses, passions, emotions.
sadhaka	A spiritual aspirant engaged in conquering his egoism and greed, the sense of "I" and "mine."
sadhana	Spiritual discipline or practice through activities such as meditation and recitation of holy names.
sadhu	A holy man, generally used with reference to a monk.
Sai	The divine mother of all.
sakhya	One of the five attitudes cherished by the dualistic worshipper toward his chosen ideal: the attitude of one friend to another.
samadhi	Perfect equanimity, devoid of ups and downs, untouched by joy or sorrow—communion with God.
samkhya	One of the six systems of orthodox Hindu philosophy.
samsara	The sensory world which captures consciousness and gives rise to craving, attachment and suffering.
samskara	The tendencies inherent from previous births.
sanathana dharma	The ancient wisdom, the eternal path of righteousness.
Sanathana Sarathi	The eternal charioteer—name of the monthly publication from *Prasanthi Nilayam*.
sankalpa	God's resolve or will.
sankirtan	Reciting or singing with joy.
sanyasi	A Hindu ascetic; one who has adopted the monastic, celibate life.
saris	Traditional ladies attire worn throughout most of India.
Sastra	The scripture that illumines, the moral code.
satchitananda	The supreme state, usually translated as existence, knowledge, bliss.
sathwic	Pure, good, pious; the principle of balance or wisdom.
sathya	Truth—that which is always the same no matter past, present, future or circumstance.

satsang	Being in the society of good, spiritual people.
satwa, rajas, thamas	The three *gunas* or characteristics of embodied beings, translated roughly as peaceful, active and dull.
sevak	One who is dedicated to service.
shakti	The creative divine power; a name of the divine mother; the feminine aspect of God, representing His power and energy.
shanti	Peace, undisturbed peace. A benediction often repeated three times after *Vedantic* prayers.
Shirdi Sai Baba	Indian holy man from whom Sai Baba of Puttaparthi says he was reincarnated.
Shiva	The destroyer God of the Hindu trinity, the other two being *Brahma* and *Vishnu*.
siddha, siddhi	A *siddha* is one who has attained *siddhis* (*yogic powers*).
Sri Aurobindo	1872-1950: His ashram at Pondicherri, in southern India, was turned into a community of spiritual seekers from all over the world, called Auroville. A prolific writer, his works include *The Life Divine*, *Essays on the Gita*, *The Synthesis of Yoga*, *Letters on Yoga*, and many others.
Sri Meher Baba	1894-1969: quarters known as Meherabad. He observed a vow of silence for many years; traveled throughout Europe and America; wrote *Discourses by Meher Baba* and *God Speaks*.
Sri Ramana Maharshi	1879-1950: He was an illumined *rishi* of southern India; taught non-duality through self inquiry—one should constantly ask himself, "Who am I?" His *ashram* was located on a sacred hill called Arunachala.
sudarshana	Holy vision.
swami	Lord, spiritual preceptor.
swarupa	Form, body.
tapa	Religious austerity, sacrifice, asceticism designed to weaken the conviction that man is body.
Telugu	The native tongue of Sri Sathya Sai Baba. The language of Andhra Pradesh.
thamasic	Dull or inert quality.
Treta Yuga	The second of the four *yugas* or cycles or world periods. Hindu mythology divides the duration of the world into four *yugas*; *Sathya*, *Treta*, *Dwapara*, and *Kali*. The first is known as the Golden Age as there is a great preponderance of virtue among men, but with each succeeding *yuga* virtue diminishes and vice increases. In the *Kali yuga* there is a minimum of virtue and a great excess of vice. We are supposedly in the *Kali yuga* now.
upadesa (upadesh)	Spiritual instruction.
Upanishads	A category of Indian scriptures.
vahini	Current, flow, river.
vandana	Reverence toward all life.

veda	Knowledge.
Vedanta	One of the six systems of orthodox Hindu philosophy, formulated by Vyasa.
Vedas	The most sacred scriptures of the Hindu religion, regarded as revelations to great seers and not of human origin. There are four *Vedas*: The *Rig-Veda*, the *Yajur-Veda*, the *Soma-Veda* and the *Arthava-Veda*.
vedic	That which derives from the *Vedas*. (An adjective)
vibuthi	Sacred ash, frequently materialized by Sai Baba.
Vishnu	The preserver God of the Hindu trinity, the other two being *Brahma* and *Shiva*.
Whitefield	A township about thirteen miles from the city of Bangalore.
yaga	Outward-directed activity; sacrifice.
Yasada	Foster mother of *Krishna*.
yoga	Union of the individual soul and the universal soul; also the method by which to realize this union. It is the general term for the several types of devotional practice that are disciplines for controlling the mind and transforming it into an instrument for realizing God.
yogi	A spiritual aspirant who seeks union with God by means of one or more specific mental and physical disciplines which are traditional and which are known by the title of *yoga*.
yugas	The four phases through which life moves to complete a world cycle. (See *Treta Yuga*)